Step by Step Cooking Course

Step by Step Cooking Course
Margaret Wade

Hamlyn
LONDON · NEW YORK · SYDNEY · TORONTO
in association with Phoebus

Contents

Editor **Sarie Forster**
Designer **Roger Hammond**
Editorial assistant **Lesley Toll**

The cover picture shows Spanish Chicken.

Published 1977 by The Hamlyn Publishing Group
Limited
London · New York · Sydney · Toronto
Astronaut House, Feltham, Middlesex, England

ISBN 0 600 31985 7

© 1977 Phoebus Publishing Company/BPC
Publishing Limited, 169 Wardour Street, London
W1A 2JX

Printed in Belgium by H. Proost & Cie p.v.b.a.,
Turnhout

5

6

Introduction

The Step by Step Cooking Course provides a clear and helpful approach to all areas of cooking and covers a wide range of recipes. You will find dishes suitable for all occasions from light snacks and economical family meals to the most festive of celebrations. There are also chapters on appetizers, pasta and rice dishes, vegetables and salads, cooking with eggs and cheese, and cakes and bread. As well as suggestions for new ways with old favourites, like roast pork stuffed with prunes, there are dishes from other countries, such as Jambalaya, a savoury rice dish from the Caribbean, and Kugelhopf, a yeast cake from Austria, which will add new dimensions to your cooking.

This book will show you how, with skilful blending of flavours or the inclusion of an unusual herb or spice, you can transform simple dishes into something quite special.

The step by step photographs, which cover both basic technique and some individual recipes, should ensure success for both the beginner and the more experienced cook.

Pâté de Campagne.

Appetizers

Pâté de Campagne

8 oz (225 g) veal
8 oz (225 g) pork
4 oz (100 g) ham
4 oz (100 g) pigs' liver
3 oz (75 g) pork fat
1 clove garlic
allspice
salt and pepper
½ wineglass brandy
1 bayleaf
clarified butter

1. Set oven at 350°F (180°C) or Mark 4.

2. Assemble all the raw ingredients on a wooden chopping board and cut the meat into pieces.

3. Mince the meat and the pork fat and turn into a mixing bowl.

4. Mix the meats together well and then add the crushed garlic, the allspice and salt and pepper. Pour in the brandy and mix well.

5. Turn the mixture into a terrine, press the meat down well and smooth over the surface. Place a bayleaf on top.

6. Put on the terrine lid and lower the terrine into a roasting tin with a little water in it. Cook in the pre-set oven for 1½ hours, or until the pâté is firm to the touch.

7. Remove from the oven, take off the lid and cover pâté with a sheet of greaseproof paper. Press the pâté under a weight of 2 lb (900 g) until cool. Cover with clarified butter and keep in a cold place until required.

Appetizers

Rabbit Pâté.

Rabbit Pâté

1 lb (450 g) raw rabbit or hare meat
4 oz (100 g) raw lean pork, ham or
 gammon
½ lb (225 g) raw unsalted pork fat
1–2 cloves garlic
1 Spanish onion
6 tbsp (90 ml) dry sherry
1 small egg
salt and pepper
approx 8 thin slices of pork fat for lining tin

To serve
hot buttered toast
few sprigs of parsley
pickled gherkins and onions

Any kind of game may be substituted for
the rabbit or hare suggested in this recipe.
To obtain 1 lb (450 g) meat, you will need
to buy a large animal weighing at least
twice this amount.

1. Set oven at 350°F (180°C) or Mark 4.

2. Cut the meats and pork fat into cubes.
Peel and crush the garlic. Peel the onion
and chop roughly.

3. Mince all these ingredients together,
then put in a bowl.

4. Stir in the sherry and egg with salt and
pepper to taste. Stir well to mix.

5. Line the base and sides of a 2 lb (1kg)
loaf tin or pâté dish with the slices of pork
fat. Spoon in the prepared pâté mixture,
pressing it down well with the back of a
spoon.

6. Cover the pâté with buttered foil and
stand in a roasting tin half filled with hot
water. Bake in pre-set oven for 1–1½ hours
or until the pâté shrinks away from sides of
tin or dish, and the juices run faintly pink
when pâté is pierced in the centre with a
skewer.

7. Remove the pâté from the roasting tin
and leave to cool. Place weights on top of
the foil and chill in the refrigerator overnight. Turn out onto a heatproof plate or
dish. Score the fat in a criss cross pattern
and put under a pre-heated hot grill until
browned.

8. Leave to cool, then arrange on a serving platter. Garnish pâté with sprigs of
parsley and serve with hot buttered toast
and pickled gherkins and onions, if liked.

Fine Liver Pâté

1 lb (450 g) pork liver
milk
½ lb (225 g) raw unsalted pork fat
1–2 cloves garlic
6 tbsp (90 ml) Madeira, port or full bodied
 red wine
2 oz (50 g) fresh brown breadcrumbs
2 eggs
½ tsp (2.50 ml) grated nutmeg
salt and pepper
approx 8 thin slices of pork fat for lining tin

To serve
hot buttered toast

1. Cut the liver into slices, put in a bowl
and cover with milk. Leave for at least 30
minutes.

2. Drain the liver and mince with three
quarters of the pork fat. Put in a bowl. Peel
and crush the garlic and add to the minced
mixture with the Madeira, port or wine,
breadcrumbs, eggs, nutmeg and salt and
pepper to taste. Stir well to mix.

3. Work the mixture in a liquidizer until
fine, or push through a sieve.

4. Set oven at 350°F (180°C) or Mark 4.

5. Line the base and sides of a deep ovenproof dish with the slices of pork fat. Spoon in the prepared pâté mixture, pressing it down well with the back of a spoon.

6. Cover the pâté with buttered foil and stand in a roasting tin half filled with hot water. Bake in pre-set oven for 1–1½ hours or until the pâté shrinks away from the sides of the dish, and the juices run faintly pink when pâté is pierced in the centre with a skewer.

7. Remove from the roasting tin and discard foil. Cut the remaining pork fat into very thin slivers and put in a heavy based pan. Melt over a low heat until fat is runny but not coloured.

8. Pour over the pâté in the dish, leave until cold, and then chill in the refrigerator overnight. Serve from the dish with hot buttered toast.

Fish Roe Pâté

4 oz (100 g) smoked cod roe
½ lb (225 g) soft herring roe
2 slices white bread
water
¼ pt (150 ml) corn oil
juice of 1–2 lemons
cayenne pepper

To finish
few black olives
¼ pt (150 ml) unset aspic

1. Skin the smoked cod roes, slice roughly and place in the top of a steamer. Cover with a lid and steam for 15 minutes. Add herring roe and steam for a further 10 minutes.

2. Meanwhile, remove the crusts from the bread and discard. Soak the bread in a little water for about 5 minutes, then squeeze dry and put in a mortar or bowl.

3. Remove the roe from the steamer, leave to cool a little, then put in mortar. Pound the mixture with a pestle or kitchen mallet until smooth and well mixed. Add the oil a drop at a time, beating vigorously after each addition until the mixture becomes thick. Beat in lemon juice and cayenne pepper to taste.

4. Spoon the pâté into a serving dish, smooth the top and sprinkle with a little cayenne pepper. If liked, the pâté may be decorated with a few strips of pitted black olive and coated in aspic. Chill in the refrigerator until serving time. Serve with hot buttered toast.

Clarified Butter

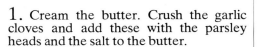

1. Cut up 8 oz (225 g) butter and put in a thick saucepan. Melt it slowly over a very low heat and once melted, continue to cook until foaming well.

2. Skim and strain through a piece of muslin into a basin. The liquid will settle leaving a sediment at the bottom. The clarified butter can then be carefully poured off into another container.

Garlic Butter

4 oz (100 g) butter
2 tbsp (30 ml) fresh parsley heads
2–3 cloves garlic
1 tsp (5 ml) salt

1. Cream the butter. Crush the garlic cloves and add these with the parsley heads and the salt to the butter.

2. Beat the ingredients together and refrigerate in an airtight container for use as required.

Fish Roe Pâté.

Appetizers

Mussels with Cream

3 dozen fresh mussels
juice of 1 lemon
¼ pt (150 ml) single cream
salt and pepper

To finish
finely chopped fresh parsley

1. Scrub mussels thoroughly under cold running water. Discard beards and any mussels that are open.

2. Soak cleaned mussels for an hour in cold water, then drain and place in the top of a steamer. Cover with a lid and steam over high heat for 5–10 minutes until the mussels open.

3. Discard any that are still closed. Scrape mussels from their shells and arrange in a serving dish. Sprinkle over the lemon juice. Season the cream with salt and pepper to taste and pour over the mussels in the dish.

4. Chill in the refrigerator for 2 hours, then sprinkle with parsley just before serving.

Mushrooms in Sour Cream

1 lb (450 g) button mushrooms
juice of ½ lemon
¼ pt (150 ml) soured cream
salt and pepper

To finish
paprika powder

1. Wipe the mushrooms clean with a damp cloth, but do not peel. Slice thinly into a bowl and sprinkle with lemon juice to prevent discoloration.

2. Add the sour cream with salt and pepper to taste and mix gently until the mushrooms are coated in the cream.

3. Transfer to a serving dish and sprinkle with paprika to taste. Chill in the refrigerator and serve as required with hot toast or French bread.

Artichokes with French Dressing

4 globe artichokes
½ lemon
French dressing made with ½ pt
(300 ml) oil

1. Cut the stalks off the artichokes, then remove any tough or damaged outer leaves. Cut off the top peaks of the petals. Wash thoroughly under cold running water and drain. Rub all cut surfaces with lemon.

2. Put artichokes in the top of a steamer or in a pan of boiling salted water, and steam or boil young ones for 25 minutes, older ones for 30–40 minutes, depending on age. The artichokes are ready when an outer leaf can be pulled out easily. Remove from steamer or pan, turn upside down to drain and leave to cool.

3. Remove the choke and discard.

4. Replace the caps upside down in the centre of the artichokes, then arrange on individual serving plates. Pour French dressing into the centre of each artichoke just before serving.

1. Pull the artichokes open gently with the fingers to expose the centres.

5. Using your fingers or a teaspoon, carefully scrape out the hairy choke and discard.

2. Continue until you expose the peaked cap which is slightly paler in colour.

3. Pull out the peaked cap from the centre by twisting slowly.

4. Set the cap aside, as this is edible. The inedible hairy choke is now exposed.

Artichokes with French Dressing.

Appetizers

Stuffed Peppers

4 green peppers
6 eggs
3 tbsp (45 ml) tomato purée
1 tsp (5 ml) paprika powder
3 oz (75 g) chilled butter or margarine
1 small onion
salt and pepper
2 cooked new potatoes
1 cooked carrot
2 oz (50 g) cooked peas

1. Cut the tops off the peppers and re-serve. Scoop out the pith and pips using a grapefruit knife. Wash thoroughly under cold running water, then pat dry with absorbent paper. Set aside.

2. Beat the eggs with the tomato purée and paprika. Grate 1 oz (25 g) of butter or margarine into this mixture.

3. Peel the onion and chop very finely. Melt the remaining butter or margarine in a pan, add the onion and fry gently until soft and golden. Pour in the egg mixture and scramble over high heat, stirring constantly. Season to taste with salt and pepper. Remove from the heat and leave to cool.

4. Dice the potatoes and carrot very finely, then add to the scrambled eggs with the peas. Stir well and mix. Taste for seasoning.

5. Spoon the mixture into the prepared peppers and replace tops. Chill in the refrigerator until serving time.

6. Arrange on serving dish and garnish with lettuce leaves or a macedoine of vegetables. Serve with hot garlic or French bread.

Avocado Vinaigrette

2 avocados
½ lemon
French dressing made with ½ pt
    (300 ml) oil

1. Cut the avocados in half lengthwise, using a silver knife. Remove the stones and rub the exposed flesh with the cut surface of lemon to prevent discoloration.

2. Arrange an avocado half on each individual serving plate. Pour French dressing into avocados and serve as soon as possible.

Variation:
As an alternative, substitute Madeira for the French dressing. Cut the avocados in half as above, then score the flesh in diagonal lines. Arrange on individual plates, pour 1–2 tbsp (15–30 ml) Madeira into each avocado half and leave to steep for 1–2 minutes before serving.

Avocado with Crab

6 tbsp (90 ml) mayonnaise
4 drops of Tabasco sauce
½ tsp (2.50 ml) paprika powder
1 tsp (5 ml) lemon juice
salt and pepper
5 oz (150 g) packet frozen crabmeat,
    thawed
2 avocados
½ lemon

1. Blend 4 tbsp (60 ml) mayonnaise thoroughly with the Tabasco sauce, paprika and lemon juice and season to taste with salt and pepper. Mix the white and dark crabmeat and fold into the mayonnaise.

2. Cut and stone the avocados and rub with lemon as for Avocado Vinaigrette. Spoon the prepared crabmeat mixture into the avocados and, if liked, pipe rosettes around the edge of each avocado half with the remaining mayonnaise. Serve as soon as possible.

Variation:
Shrimps can be substituted for crab.

Stuffed Peppers.

Avocados shown with Crab, French Dressing, Shrimps and Madeira.

Appetizers

Melon and Orange Cocktail.

Melon and Orange Cocktail

1 large honeydew melon
4 large oranges
2 tsp (10 ml) medium or dry sherry
½ tsp (2.50 ml) ground ginger

For sweet orange sauce
juice of 4 oranges
1 tbsp (15 ml) soft brown sugar
½–1 tsp (2.50–5 ml) ground cinnamon

1. Cut a slice off the base of the melon so that it will stand upright. Cut melon into a basket shape with a handle by removing 2 sections from the top, leaving a thin strip of skin in the centre to form a handle. Take out the flesh with a melon scoop or

sharp knife, discarding all seeds. Snip the edges of the melon with scissors to make a zigzag pattern. Set aside.

2. Skin the oranges and divide into segments. Remove all pith and pips. Put in a bowl with the melon flesh, sprinkle with the sherry and ginger and leave to marinate for approximately 15 minutes, stirring occasionally.

3. Meanwhile, make the sauce. Put the orange juice and sugar in a pan and heat gently until the sugar has dissolved. Increase the heat and boil rapidly for 1–2 minutes, then remove from the heat and leave to cool. Fill melon baskets with fruit and serve sauce separately.

Béchamel Sauce

1 pt (600 ml) milk
1 stick of celery
1 onion
bayleaf
2 oz (50 g) butter or margarine
2 oz (50 g) plain flour
salt and pepper
nutmeg (optional)

1. Heat the milk with the celery, onion, and bayleaf for a few minutes. Take off the heat and leave in the pan for 30 minutes, then strain.

2. Melt the butter or margarine in a pan. Stir in the flour with a wooden spoon and cook gently for 1–2 minutes until the mixture forms a soft ball. Stir constantly.

3. Remove pan from the heat and gradually stir in the hot milk, beating vigorously all the time to obtain a smooth sauce. When all the milk is incorporated, return pan to heat and bring to the boil, stirring constantly. Simmer and stir for 3–4 minutes, adding seasoning and nutmeg if required.

4. Remove from the heat and use immediately, or cover sauce with a piece of dampened greaseproof paper and leave until required. Reheat gently before serving.

Mornay Sauce

2 oz (50 g) butter or margarine
2 oz (50 g) plain flour
dry mustard
1 pt (600 ml) hot milk
3 oz (75 g) grated cheese

1. Melt the butter or margarine in a pan. Stir in the flour and a pinch of dry mustard with a wooden spoon and cook gently for 1–2 minutes until the mixture forms a soft ball. Stir constantly.

2. Remove the pan from the heat and gradually stir in the hot milk, beating vigorously all the time to obtain a smooth sauce. When all the milk is incorporated, return the pan to the heat and bring to the boil, stirring continuously. Simmer and stir for 3–4 minutes, then stir in the grated cheese with seasoning.

Cucumber Tubs

1 large cucumber
salt
2 tbsp (30 ml) mayonnaise
¼ tsp (1 ml) cayenne pepper
4 oz (100 g) shelled prawns or shrimps

To finish
4–5 fried bread croûtes
4–5 strips of tomato
1 large bunch of parsley

1. Cut both ends off the cucumber and discard, then cut cucumber into 4 or 5 equal portions. Cut a very thin slice off each one and set aside.

2. Make cuts from top to bottom of each portion using a canelle knife. Hollow out the insides with a grapefruit knife. Sprinkle with salt, leave to drain in a colander or sieve for 30 minutes, then wipe the insides dry with absorbent paper.

3. Blend the mayonnaise with cayenne pepper. Chop the prawns or shrimps roughly, setting aside 4–5 whole ones for decoration. Fold chopped prawns or shrimps into mayonnaise.

4. Arrange croûtes on a serving dish or platter. Place on cucumber portion on each, then carefully spoon in the mayonnaise mixture. Garnish the top of each portion with reserved cucumber slices and whole prawns or shrimps and decorate with strips of tomato.

5. Surround the cucumber tubs with sprigs of parsley, then chill in the refrigerator before serving.

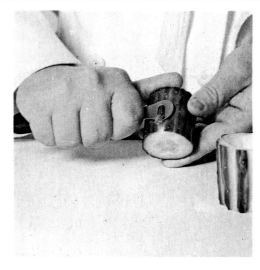

1. Cut cucumber into 4 or 5 chunks. Using a canelle knife, cut vertical strips of peel from chunks of cucumber.

2. Scoop out a hollow from the top of each cucumber chunk.

Cucumber Tubs.

Vol au Vents or Bouchées

These little cases for individual servings are a good party way of using up small quantities of leftover cooked meat or fish, bound with a white sauce or, sometimes, a hollandaise or mayonnaise sauce. 1 lb (450 g) puff pastry will yield 12–16 vol au vents or double this amount of bouchées. Bouchées incidentally, or 'mouthfuls', are simply tiny vol au vents.

1. Set oven at 425°F (220°C) or Mark 7.

2. Remove the pastry from the refrigerator and roll out into a rectangle ¾ inch (2 cm) thick.

3. With a pastry cutter approximately 3 inches (7 cm) in diameter, stamp out bases and transfer to a dampened baking sheet.

4. With a 2 inch (5 cm) diameter pastry cutter, cut each round until almost but not quite through.

5. Brush with beaten egg and bake in the pre-set oven for 15–20 minutes, or until golden brown and cooked.

6. When cooked and cooled, remove top neatly with a teaspoon, leaving a cavity to be filled.

Kidney and Mushroom Filling

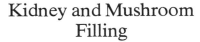

4 lambs' kidneys
6 oz (150 g) button mushrooms
1 oz (25 g) butter
1 oz (25 g) plain flour
1–2 tbsp (15–30 ml) dry sherry
¼ pt (150 ml) stock
3–4 fl oz (90–120 ml) double cream
salt and pepper

1. Skin and blanch the kidneys and leave in a pan of hot water for 15 minutes. Wash and finely slice mushrooms.

2. Melt butter in a pan over a gentle heat, remove kidneys from pan and pat dry with absorbent paper. Slice finely. Sauté in the butter for 2–3 minutes, then add the flour and stir until blended. Add the sherry, and, gradually, the stock, stirring all the time. Finally add the mushrooms and stir in the cream.

3. Taste for seasoning and continue to simmer gently for 3–4 minutes over a gentle heat. Do not allow kidneys to overcook.

4. Fill vol au vent cases with mixture, replace tops and heat through in the oven for a few minutes. Serve hot.

1. Dip pastry cutters in boiling water each time you use them.

2. Using the large cutters, cut out circles and place them on a dampened baking sheet.

Vol au Vents with Kidney and Mushroom Filling.

Chicken and Mushroom Filling

4 oz (100 g) cooked chicken
2 oz (50 g) button mushrooms
½ oz (15 g) butter
½ oz (15 g) plain flour
3 fl oz (75 ml) dry white wine
1–2 fl oz (25–50 ml) milk
1–2 fl oz (25–50 ml) single cream
salt and pepper

For garnish
1 cooked carrot
1 tbsp (15 ml) cooked peas
1 tbsp (15 ml) cooked green beans
1 or 2 stuffed green olives
aspic

3. Using the smaller cutters, press three quarters of the way through the pastry circles.

4. When the vol au vents are cooked, the lids will have contracted and be easy to lift off.

1. Chop the chicken meat, finely dice mushrooms and shred the carrot. Dice the green beans, slice the olives and prepare the aspic.

2. Melt the butter in a pan and add the flour when melted. Stir to a straw coloured roux, (this should take about 1 minute) then add the wine. Blend well, stirring vigorously, then add the milk and bring to the boil. Using a balloon whisk, whisk up sauce until smooth, then add the cream and continue whisking. Add the mushrooms, cook for a few minutes before adding the chicken and seasoning to taste.

3. Allow to cool before filling the cases and garnishing each one with a sprinkling of diced vegetables, topped with a slice of stuffed olive. The topping can be kept in place with a little aspic. Otherwise replace the lid as usual and omit the garnish.

Seafood Filling

8 oz (225 g) prawns or shrimps
½ oz (15 g) butter
½ oz (15 g) plain flour
3 fl oz (90 ml) dry white wine
1–2 fl oz (25–50 ml) milk
3 fl oz (75 ml) single cream
salt and pepper

For garnish
parsley, watercress

1. Make the white sauce as for the Chicken and Mushroom Filling.

2. Add the prawns or shrimps and season to taste.

3. Allow to cool before filling the cases and garnish.

Appetizers

Peperoni Croûtes

8 oz (225 g) onions
1 lb (450 g) red and green peppers
3½ fl oz (100 ml) cooking oil
1 tsp (5 ml) powdered ginger
1 lb (450 g) tomatoes
6 oz (150 g) soft brown sugar
4 oz (100 g) raisins or sultanas
1 tsp (5ml) mixed spice
1 clove garlic crushed with a little salt
½ pt (300 ml) wine vinegar
1 tsp (5 ml) dried tarragon
bread croûtes

1. Peel and finely chop the onions. Halve the peppers, remove the core and the seeds, and chop the flesh into dice.

2. Heat oil in a pan and add the peppers and onions. Fry gently over a low heat, until onions are transparent. Place lid on pan and continue to cook for 7–8 minutes.

3. Add rest of ingredients, stir gently until mixed, and cook for a further 10 minutes until thoroughly cooked and mushy. Remove the lid and cook for a further 10 minutes.

4. Prepare the croûtes. Cut rounds from 3 or 4 slices of bread with a 3 inch (7 cm) diameter plain cutter. Fry rounds in a little oil or butter until golden brown and crisp and drain on absorbent paper.

5. Pile mixture on top of croûtes and serve hot or chilled.

Peperoni Croûtes.

PEELING PIMIENTOS

1. Halve the pimientos and remove pith and seeds. Place under a very hot grill.

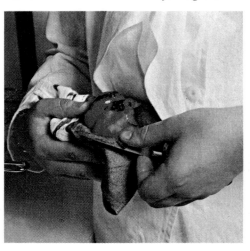

2. When the skin has blackened and cracked you can peel it away.

Austrian Cream Cheese

4 oz (100 g) cream cheese
4 oz (100 g) unsalted butter
1 tsp (5 ml) paprika pepper
caraway seeds
5 capers
1 anchovy fillet
1 tsp (5 ml) Dijon mustard
salt and pepper

1. Put the butter in a warm place to cream; chop a sprinkling of caraway seeds; drain and chop capers finely. Soak anchovy fillet in a little milk to remove excess saltiness, then drain and chop.

2. Beat warmed butter until light and fluffy, then beat in the cream cheese by degrees. When mixture is smooth, add paprika, caraway seeds, capers, anchovy fillets and mustard and continue beating. Check seasoning.

3. Shape into a rectangle or square and chill before serving on triangles of brown toast, dark rye bread or pumpernickel.

Note: This is an Austrian version of the classic Hungarian recipe. Chopped chives, or garlic or finely chopped onion are alternatives to add as variations. Liptauer cheese is also good spread quickly over warmed water biscuits.

Salmon Asparagus Rolls

¼ lb (100 g) smoked salmon cut into slices
1 small can asparagus tips, or fresh asparagus if available

For garnish
thick mayonnaise
lemon wedges

1. Drain asparagus tips and pat dry on absorbent paper, or cook and drain if fresh. Roll each tip in a slice of smoked salmon and place the rolls on a serving dish.

2. Pipe rosettes of mayonnaise on each roll to garnish. Surround with lemon wedges.

Variation:
Serve the salmon asparagus rolls with the mayonnaise in a bowl, so that guests may dip in their rolls.

Bouchées à la Grecque.

Bouchées à la Grecque

5 oz (125 g) butter beans
8 slices white bread from a sandwich loaf
1 onion
2 cloves garlic
ground coriander
1 tsp (5 ml) bicarbonate of soda
salt and pepper
parsley to garnish

1. Soak butter beans overnight. Remove the crusts from the slices of bread and soak the bread for a few minutes. Peel the onion and the garlic.

2. Pass the soaked beans through a mincer or mouli sieve, with the onion and garlic. Pound in a pestle and mortar with the soaked bread, or use a liquidizer, to achieve a smooth dough. Pound in, or add, a pinch of ground coriander and the bicarbonate of soda, season and chill the mixture for 2 hours.

3. Roll into small balls and deep fry until golden and crisp. Drain on absorbent paper and serve immediately on cocktail sticks. Sprinkle with chopped parsley if wished.

Tomato Sauce with Herbs

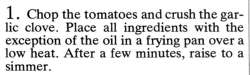

1 lb (450 g) ripe tomatoes
1 clove garlic
1 crushed peppercorn
1 oz (25 g) chives
2 sprigs thyme
2 sprigs tarragon
1 level tsp (5 ml) salt
4 tbsp (60 ml) cold water
2 tbsp (30 ml) oil

1. Chop the tomatoes and crush the garlic clove. Place all ingredients with the exception of the oil in a frying pan over a low heat. After a few minutes, raise to a simmer.

2. When tender, rub the mixture through a sieve returning it to the pan. Add the oil and simmer for about 3 minutes. Chill before serving.

Appetizers

Sardine Salad

3 cans sardines in oil
1–2 tsp (5–10 ml) wine vinegar
pepper
6 hard boiled eggs
few sprigs of fresh parsley
3 lemons
French dressing made with ½ pt
    (300 ml) oil

1. Drain 6 sardines, remove the tails and bones and mash the sardines with the wine vinegar and pepper to taste. Arrange near the centre of an oval serving platter.

2. Drain the remaining sardines and arrange in a fan shape on the platter. Separate the whites and yolks of the eggs and chop finely, keeping whites and yolks separate.

3. Arrange the whites and yolks in separate sections on the platter around the sardines. Put a border of parsley heads along the outside edge of the whole sardines. Cut the lemons into decorative slices, using a canelle knife and use to garnish the dish, adding thin strips of lemon peel around the edge.

4. Serve with French dressing served separately.

Mayonnaise

Sardine Salad.

Basic Recipe

1 egg yolk
¼ tsp (1 ml) dry English
    mustard
salt and pepper
¼ pt (150 ml) olive or corn oil
1 tbsp (15 ml) lemon juice or wine vinegar

It is essential to keep mixing bowl and utensils cool when making mayonnaise, and all ingredients should be at room temperature. Be careful to add the oil very slowly at first, or the mayonnaise will curdle.

1. Put the egg yolk, mustard and salt and pepper to taste in a bowl. Beat with a wooden spoon, electric or rotary beater until well mixed. Add the oil a drop at a time, beating well all the time until the mayonnaise begins to thicken.

2. Beat in the oil faster when the mayonnaise thickens, then add the lemon juice or wine vinegar. Beat until well mixed and taste for seasoning. Cover and store in a cool place until required.

Note: if mayonnaise curdles, start again with a fresh egg yolk. Beat the curdled mayonnaise into the egg yolk a drop at a time until the mixture becomes thick and smooth then add the remaining oil.

Lemon Mayonnaise

Basic Recipe

2 egg yolks
½ tsp (2.50 ml) ready prepared
    French mustard
salt
½ tsp (2.50 ml) crushed black peppercorns
½ pt (300 ml) olive or corn oil
juice of 1 lemon

To finish
1 lemon
1 tbsp (15 ml) fresh single cream

Orange juice and segments can be substituted for the lemon in this recipe. See the basic Mayonnaise recipe for rules on making and how to rescue mayonnaise that has curdled.

1. Put the egg yolks, mustard, salt and pepper in a bowl. Beat with a wooden spoon, electric or rotary beater until well mixed. Add the oil a drop at a time, beating well all the time until the mayonnaise begins to thicken.

2. When half the oil is incorporated, beat in half the lemon juice. Continue adding the oil in a steady stream, then beat in the remaining lemon juice. Taste for seasoning, then cover and store in a cool place until required.

3. Cut the peel, pith and skin away from the lemon by cutting from the top and working in a spiral down to the bottom, using a sawing motion. Cut the lemon into segments, then chop into small pieces. Discard all pips, pith and central core.

4. Stir lemon pieces into the mayonnaise with the cream just before serving.

MAKING MELBA TOAST

1. Cut off the crusts of thin slices of bread and toast lightly. Using a sharp knife, cut through the middle to make 2 slices.

2. Lightly toast the untoasted sides and serve hot immediately.

French Dressing

Basic Recipe

½ tsp (2.50 ml) salt
½ tsp (2.50 ml) crushed black
  peppercorns
½ tsp (2.50 ml) ready prepared French
  mustard
¼ pt (150 ml) olive or corn oil
4 tbsp (60 ml) vinegar

1. Put the salt, pepper and mustard in a salad bowl with a little oil. Beat with a wooden spoon or fork until thick. Add the remaining oil gradually, beating it in alternately with the wine vinegar.

2. Taste for seasoning and add more salt if too oily. Beat again to combine before tossing salad vegetables.

3. The dressing can also be made quickly by putting all ingredients in a screw top jar and shaking vigorously until well mixed. It can be stored in the jar for a few months.

Variation:
For a classic vinaigrette add 2 tsp (10 ml) finely chopped herbs, shallot or onion to the dressing just before serving.

Roquefort Dressing

Basic Recipe

3 tbsp (45 ml) vinegar
¼ pt (150 ml) olive oil
salt
black pepper
French mustard
sugar
3 oz (75 g) Roquefort cheese
lemon juice

1. Pour the vinegar in a small bowl and add the oil, a spoonful at a time, beating with a fork. Add the salt, pepper, mustard and sugar to taste. Beat well.

2. Put the cheese in another bowl and mash to a paste with a fork. Add the oil and vinegar dressing and beat well until blended. Flavour with a little lemon juice and check seasoning.

Melba Toast.

Appetizers

Cheese Soufflés in Pastry

2 oz (50 g) butter or margarine
8 oz (225 g) quantity puff pastry
1 egg
1½ oz (40 g) plain flour
7½ fl oz (225 ml) hot milk
2 oz (50 g) grated Parmesan cheese
ground nutmeg
ground mace
salt and pepper
4 egg whites

1. Set oven at 425°F (220°C) or Mark 7.

2. Soften ½ oz (15 g) butter or margarine and use to brush the insides of 4 individual soufflé dishes.

3. Roll out the dough on a floured board and cut into 4 squares large enough to fit inside the soufflé dishes. Put the squares in the dishes, pressing them down in the middle so that the 4 corners protrude above the rim of each dish. Beat the whole egg and use to brush the dough. Stand the soufflé dishes on a baking sheet and set aside.

4. Melt the remaining butter or margarine in a large pan. Stir in the flour with a wooden spoon and cook gently for 1–2 minutes until the mixture forms a soft ball, stirring constantly.

5. Remove the pan from heat and gradually stir in the hot milk, beating vigorously all the time to obtain a smooth sauce. When all the milk is incorporated, return pan to the heat and bring to the boil, stirring constantly.

6. Lower the heat and add a pinch of each of the seasonings. Simmer gently until the sauce thickens, stirring constantly. Remove the pan from the heat and stir in the cheese.

7. Beat the egg whites until stiff. Fold into the sauce until evenly distributed. Divide soufflé mixture between prepared dishes. Bake in the pre-set oven on the shelf above centre for 10–15 minutes or until well risen and golden brown. Serve immediately.

Caviare Stuffed Tomatoes

12 small tomatoes
½ pt (300 ml) double cream
1 small jar or can caviare or lumpfish roe
2 tsp (10 ml) lemon juice
browned almonds to garnish
salt
freshly ground black pepper

1. Place the tomatoes in very hot water for a few moments to split the skin and make it easy to remove. Peel the tomatoes and whip the cream thoroughly.

2. Slice the tops off all the tomatoes from the flower end. Remove and discard seeds, and turn each tomato upside down to drain.

3. Drain and stir the caviare or lumpfish roe into the whipped cream and then, very carefully, add the lemon juice to flavour the cream. Season to taste with salt and black pepper.

4. Place tomatoes upright on a serving dish and, with a forcing bag and plain pipe – or use a small teaspoon – fill each tomato case. Replace tops and garnish with flaked browned almonds, if liked.

Note: Lumpfish roe is often known as poor man's caviare. It is quite delicious, and much cheaper than caviare itself!

Cheese Soufflé in Pastry.

Soufflé Tomatoes.

Soufflé Tomatoes

10–12 large tomatoes
1½ oz (40 g) butter or margarine
1½ oz (40 g) plain flour
7½ fl oz (225 ml) hot milk
2 oz (50 g) mature Cheddar cheese
1 tsp (5 ml) anchovy essence
pepper
4 egg whites

To finish
1–2 tbsp (15–30 ml) snipped chives

1. Set oven at 400°F (200°C) or Mark 6.

2. Cut the tops off the tomatoes, scoop out all flesh, seeds and central cores and reserve for use in casseroles, soups, stock, etc. Put the tomato cases on a baking sheet and set aside.

3. Melt the butter or margarine in a large pan. Stir in the flour with a wooden spoon and cook gently for 1–2 minutes until the mixture forms a soft ball, stirring constantly.

4. Remove pan from heat and gradually stir in the hot milk, beating vigorously all the time to obtain a smooth sauce. When all the milk is incorporated, return pan to the heat and bring to the boil, stirring constantly.

5. Lower the heat and simmer gently. Grate the cheese and add to the pan with the anchovy essence and pepper to taste. Stir constantly until the cheese melts and the sauce is thick and smooth. Remove pan from heat.

6. Beat the egg whites until stiff. Fold into the sauce until evenly distributed. Spoon into prepared tomato cases. Bake in the pre-set oven on shelf above centre for 15 minutes until well risen and golden brown. Transfer to a warmed serving dish, sprinkle with snipped chives and serve immediately.

Butter Bean Soup.

Soups

Butter Bean Soup

½ lb (225 g) dried butter beans
1 large onion
1 clove garlic
4 oz (100 g) firm white cabbage
1 large can tomatoes
2 oz (50 g) pork or goose dripping
3 pt (1½ l) well flavoured stock
½ tsp (2.50 ml) dried oregano
salt and pepper

To finish
4 tbsp (60 ml) finely chopped fresh parsley

1. Put the butter beans in a bowl, cover with cold water and leave to soak overnight.

2. The next day, peel the onion and slice into fine rings. Peel and crush the garlic. Chop the cabbage finely. Purée the canned tomatoes in a liquidizer or work through a sieve.

3. Melt the dripping in a large pan. Add the onion, garlic and cabbage. Cover pan with a lid and simmer gently for 5 minutes, shaking the pan occasionally.

4. Drain the butter beans and add to the pan with the tomatoes, stock, oregano and salt and pepper to taste. Stir well to mix.

5. Bring to the boil, stirring constantly. Lower the heat and cover the pan. Simmer very gently for 1½–2 hours until the beans are tender, stirring in a little more stock or water if level becomes low during cooking.

6. Remove soup from the heat. Skim off any fat on the surface of soup. Taste for seasoning. Pour into warmed soup bowls, sprinkle each with 1 tbsp (15 ml) parsley and serve hot.

Soups

Cream of Cauliflower Soup

1 cauliflower
1 small onion
2 large potatoes
2 oz (50 g) butter or margarine
1 pt (600 ml) milk
1¼ pt (750 ml) well flavoured chicken stock
¼ tsp (1 ml) ground mace
salt and pepper
¼ pt (150 ml) single cream

To serve
toasted croûtons

1. Divide cauliflower into flowerets, then chop roughly. Peel the onion and chop finely. Peel the potatoes and cut into small dice.

2. Melt the butter or margarine in a large pan. Add the prepared vegetables. Cover the pan with a lid and simmer gently for 5 minutes, shaking the pan occasionally.

3. Stir in the milk gradually, then add the stock, mace and salt and pepper to taste. Bring to the boil, then lower the heat and cover the pan with a lid. Simmer gently for 25–30 minutes, or until the cauliflower and the potatoes are tender, stirring occasionally.

4. Remove the pan from the heat and leave to cool slightly. Purée until smooth in a liquidizer or work through a sieve.

5. Return the soup to the rinsed out pan and stir in the cream. Reheat gently, but do not allow to boil. Remove the pan from the heat and taste the soup for seasoning. Pour into warmed soup bowls and serve hot with toasted croûtons.

Watercress and Potato Soup

1 small onion
2 bunches watercress
¾ lb (350 g) old potatoes
2 oz (50 g) butter or margarine
1 pt (600 ml) milk
1 pt (600 ml) well flavoured chicken stock
salt and pepper

To serve
salted almonds

1. Peel the onion and chop finely. Chop the watercress finely, reserving a few whole leaves for the garnish. Peel the potatoes and cut into dice.

2. Melt the butter or margarine in a pan. Add the onion and watercress. Cover the pan with a lid and simmer gently for 5 minutes, shaking the pan occasionally.

3. Stir in the milk, stock and salt and pepper to taste, then add the potatoes. Bring to the boil, stirring constantly. Lower the heat and cover the pan with a lid. Simmer gently for about 20 minutes, or until the potatoes are tender, stirring occasionally.

4. Remove pan from the heat and leave to cool slightly. Purée soup until smooth in a liquidizer or work through a sieve.

5. Return the soup to the rinsed out pan and reheat gently. Taste for seasoning and add more milk if the soup is too thick. Pour into warmed soup bowls and garnish with reserved watercress leaves. Serve hot with a dish of salted almonds served separately, if liked.

Country Beef and Vegetable Soup

1 lb (450 g) stewing beef
2 tbsp (30 ml) plain flour
salt and pepper
1 large onion
2 large carrots
4 stalks celery
2 leeks
2 oz (50 g) beef dripping or lard
4 pt (2½ l) water
bouquet garni
2 large potatoes

Make this soup the day before it is required, as it must be chilled overnight in order to take off the fat.

1. Cut the stewing beef into very thin strips, then coat in the flour seasoned with salt and pepper. Peel the onion and carrots and chop finely with the celery and leeks.

2. Melt the dripping or lard in a large pan. Add the beef and fry briskly until browned on all sides, stirring occasionally. Remove from the pan with a slotted spoon and set aside.

3. Add the prepared vegetables to the pan and cover with a lid. Simmer gently for 5 minutes, shaking the pan occasionally.

4. Return the beef to the pan. Stir in the water and bring to the boil. Lower the heat, add the bouquet garni and cover the pan with a lid. Simmer very gently for about 2 hours or until the beef is tender. Skim and stir occasionally during cooking and top up with more water if the level becomes rather low.

5. Peel the potatoes and cut into dice. Add to the pan and cook for a further 20 minutes or until tender.

6. Remove pan from the heat. Discard the bouquet garni and taste soup for seasoning. Leave until cold, then chill in the refrigerator overnight.

7. The next day, remove the fat that has risen to the surface of soup. Reheat the soup until bubbling, then taste for seasoning. Pour into warmed soup bowls and serve hot with French bread.

Artichoke Soup

1 lb (450 g) Jerusalem artichokes
juice of 1 lemon
salt
1 clove garlic
1 oz (25 g) butter or margarine
1 oz (25 g) plain flour
1 pt (600 ml) hot milk
1 pt (600 ml) well flavoured chicken stock
½ tsp (2.50 ml) ground mace
pepper
3 oz (75 g) grated Parmesan cheese

1. Peel the artichokes and sprinkle immediately with lemon juice to prevent discoloration. Cut into dice and boil in salted water for about 30 minutes or until tender.

2. Meanwhile, peel and crush the garlic. Melt the butter or margarine in a pan. Add the garlic and fry gently for 1–2 minutes. Stir in the flour and cook gently for a further 1–2 minutes, stirring constantly.

3. Remove pan from the heat and gradually stir in the hot milk, beating vigorously after each addition.

4. When all the milk is incorporated, return pan to the heat. Stir in the chicken

Artichoke Soup.

stock, mace and salt and pepper to taste.

5. Bring to the boil, stirring constantly, then lower the heat and simmer for a few minutes. Drain the artichokes when tender and stir into the sauce.

6. Remove the pan from the heat and leave to cool slightly. Purée soup until smooth in a liquidizer or work through a fine sieve.

7. Return the soup to rinsed out pan. Stir in 1 oz (25 g) Parmesan and reheat soup until cheese melts, stirring occasionally. Taste for seasoning and add more milk if the soup is too thick.

8. Pour into warmed soup bowls and serve hot with remaining Parmesan served separately.

Soups

Crab Soup

1 packet frozen crab meat
2 oz (50 g) butter or margarine
2 oz (50 g) plain flour
1 pt (600 ml) fish stock
½ pt (300 ml) dry white wine or cider
cayenne pepper
salt
½ pt (300 ml) creamy milk or single cream

1. Unwrap the frozen crab and leave to thaw.

2. Melt the butter or margarine in a large pan. Stir in the flour and cook gently for 1–2 minutes, stirring constantly.

3. Remove pan from the heat and gradually stir in the fish stock. Stir in the wine or cider with cayenne pepper and salt to taste.

4. Bring to the boil, stirring constantly, then lower the heat and simmer gently until the soup thickens. Beat in the thawed crab until evenly distributed. Stir in the milk or cream and heat through. (Do not allow to boil if using cream.)

5. Remove the pan from the heat and taste soup for seasoning. Pour into warmed soup bowls and serve hot with a sprinkling of cayenne pepper on each serving.

Croûtons

Basic Recipe

Cut some slices from a stale white loaf and chop them into dice. Then shallow fry them in equal quantities of butter and olive oil until golden brown. Leave to drain on absorbent paper.

Croûtes (a larger version of croûtons): dip the stale bread pieces in a mixture of beaten egg and milk before frying as above.

Crab Soup.

Minestrone

3 oz (75 g) dried haricot beans
1 large onion
few stalks celery
1 clove garlic
2 carrots
2 courgettes
2 potatoes
2 tbsp (30 ml) olive or vegetable oil
1 large can tomatoes
2 pt (1 l) chicken stock
1 bouquet garni
salt and pepper
4 oz (100 g) frozen green beans
4 oz (100 g) frozen peas

To serve
grated Parmesan cheese
bread sticks
croûtons

1. Put the haricot beans in a bowl and cover with cold water. Leave to soak overnight.

2. The next day, peel the onion and chop finely. Chop the celery. Peel and crush the garlic. Peel and grate the carrots. Slice the courgettes finely. Peel the potatoes and cut into dice. Drain the haricot beans.

3. Heat the oil in a large pan. Add the onion, celery and garlic and fry gently for about 5 minutes until lightly coloured. Add the remaining prepared vegetables, the haricot beans, canned tomatoes and stock. Stir well and bring to the boil.

4. Lower the heat, add the bouquet garni and salt and pepper to taste. Cover the pan with a lid and simmer gently for $1\frac{1}{2}$–2 hours until the haricot beans are tender and all the other vegetables are soft and broken down.

5. Discard bouquet garni. Add the frozen beans and peas and cook for a further 5 minutes or until tender.

6. Taste for seasoning. Pour into warmed soup bowls and serve hot with grated Parmesan cheese, potato sticks and croûtons handed separately.

Egg and Brandy Soup

1½ lb (675 g) Spanish onions
½ lb (225 g) ripe tomatoes
1½ oz (40 g) butter or margarine
2 tbsp (30 ml) olive or corn oil
2 tbsp (30 ml) plain flour
2 pt (1 l) well flavoured beef stock
1 pt (600 ml) full bodied red wine
salt and pepper
2 egg yolks
6 tbsp (90 ml) brandy

To serve
grated Parmesan cheese

1. Peel the onions and slice very thinly. Skin the tomatoes and chop roughly.

2. Heat the butter or margarine and oil in a large pan. Add the onions and tomatoes and cover pan with a lid. Cook gently for 5 minutes, shaking the pan occasionally.

3. Stir in the flour and cook for a further 2 minutes, stirring constantly. Stir in the red wine gradually, then add the stock. Season to taste with salt and pepper.

4. Bring to the boil, then lower the heat and cover the pan with a lid. Simmer gently for 20–25 minutes or until the onions are soft and broken down.

5. Remove pan from the heat and leave to cool slightly. Purée until smooth in a liquidizer or work through a sieve.

6. Return the soup to the rinsed out pan and reheat gently. Meanwhile, put the egg yolks and brandy in a bowl, or in the serving tureen, and whip together. Pour a little of the hot soup over the egg and brandy mixture. Whip to combine, then stir gradually into the soup.

7. Taste soup for seasoning. Serve in warmed soup bowls, with grated Parmesan cheese handed separately.

1. Fry the onions gently in oil and butter until very soft.

2. Add the tomatoes and cook until soft.

6. Pour into a large saucepan.

7. Add remaining stock and stir until well blended.

8. Whip the eggs and brandy together in the serving tureen. Gradually pour in the soup, still whipping.

3. Stir in the flour and seasoning.

4. Increase the heat, add the wine and stir until it is absorbed.

5. Add some stock and stir well.

Egg and Brandy Soup.

33

Soups

Stock
Basic Recipe

2¼ lb (1 kg) raw beef bones or
*   veal or chicken bones*
1 large onion studded with cloves
bouquet garni
4–5 pt (2½–3 l) cold water

1. Place bones, onion and bouquet garni in a large pan, cover with the cold water and bring slowly to the boil.

2. Skim the surface, refresh with a cup of cold water and return to the boil. Leave to simmer gently for about 2 hours.

3. For a stronger stock, continue to simmer with the pan half covered to allow the liquid to reduce. The more it reduces the stronger the stock will be.

4. When the stock has cooled, skim the fat off the surface before using.

Stockpot Soup with Noodles

1 large onion
2 stalks celery
¾ lb (350 g) carrots
1 oz (25 g) butter or margarine
2½ pt (1¼ l) well flavoured beef stock
salt and pepper
2 oz (50 g) small noodles

1. Peel the onion and chop finely. Chop the celery. Peel and grate the carrots.

2. Melt the butter or margarine in a large pan. Add the onion and celery and fry gently for about 5 minutes until lightly coloured. Add the carrots. Cover pan with a lid and cook gently for a further 5 minutes, shaking the pan occasionally.

3. Stir in the stock and season to taste with salt and pepper. Bring to the boil, stirring occasionally. Lower the heat and cover pan with a lid. Simmer for about 20–30 minutes or until the carrots are tender.

4. Remove pan from the heat and leave to cool slightly. Purée until fairly smooth in a liquidizer or work through a sieve. If the soup is too thick, add a little stock or water.

5. Return soup to rinsed out pan, add

noodles and simmer until tender. Taste for seasoning. Pour into warmed soup bowls and serve hot with pretzels or crusty French bread.

Note: It is essential to use homemade stock for this soup, or it will lack flavour and texture.

Sweetcorn Soup

1 onion
1 oz (25 g) butter or margarine
1 tbsp (15 ml) plain flour
¾ pt (450 ml) hot milk
¾ pt (450 ml) well flavoured chicken stock
1 large can creamed sweetcorn
½ tsp (2.50 ml) celery salt
pepper
2 fl oz (60 ml) single cream

1. Peel the onion and chop finely. Melt the butter or margarine in a pan. Add the onion and fry gently for about 5 minutes until lightly coloured.

2. Stir in the flour and cook gently for 1–2 minutes, stirring constantly. Remove pan from the heat and gradually stir in the hot milk, beating vigorously after each addition.

3. When all the milk is incorporated, return the pan to the heat. Stir in the remaining ingredients, except the cream. Bring to the boil, stirring constantly.

4. Lower the heat, stir in the cream and heat through. Taste for seasoning. Pour into warmed soup bowls and serve hot with bread sticks or crusty French bread and butter.

Vichyssoise

1½ lb (675 g) leeks
1½ lb (675 g) potatoes
2 oz (50 g) butter or margarine
1 pt (600 ml) well flavoured clear chicken
*   stock*
1 pt (600 ml) milk
salt and white pepper

To finish
¼ pt (150 ml) fresh single cream
snipped chives

1. Slice the leeks finely. Peel the

potatoes and cut into small dice.

2. Melt the butter or margarine in a large pan. Add the prepared vegetables. Cover pan and simmer for 5 minutes.

3. Stir in the stock, milk and salt and pepper to taste. Bring to the boil. Lower the heat and cover the pan. Simmer gently for 20–25 minutes until the vegetables are tender, stirring occasionally.

4. Remove the pan from the heat and leave to cool slightly. Purée soup until very smooth in a liquidizer or work several times through a fine sieve.

5. Stir cream into puréed soup and chill in the refrigerator for at least 3 hours. Pour into chilled soup bowls and sprinkle with snipped chives just before serving.

French Countrystyle Soup

½ lb (225 g) dried haricot beans
4 medium carrots
2 large onions
1 small head of celery
6 oz (175 g) firm white cabbage
1 lb (450 g) boned belly pork
bouquet garni
¼–½ tsp (1 ml) powdered turmeric
salt and pepper

1. Put the haricot beans in a bowl, cover with water and leave to soak overnight.

2. Peel the carrots and onions and chop very finely with the celery and cabbage.

3. Cut the belly pork into very small dice and fry briskly over high heat until crisp and browned on all sides. Remove from pan with a slotted spoon.

4. Set oven at 300°F (160°C) or Mark 2. Drain the haricot beans and put in a large casserole dish. Add the prepared vegetables, fried pork, bouquet garni, and turmeric and salt and pepper to taste. Cover with cold water and stir well to mix. Cover the casserole with a lid and cook in pre-set oven for 4–5 hours until all the ingredients are soft and broken down and the soup is very thick.

5. Discard bouquet garni. Taste for seasoning. Serve hot with hunks of crusty French bread.

French Countrystyle Soup.

Soups

Spinach Soup

1 lb (450 g) fresh spinach leaves
4 oz (100 g) butter or margarine
salt
1 pt (600 ml) well flavoured chicken stock
½ tsp (2.50 ml) grated nutmeg
pepper
4 egg yolks
¼ pt (150 ml) double cream

To finish
4 tbsp (60 ml) single cream

1. Put the spinach in a large pan with 3 oz (75 g) butter or margarine and salt to taste. Cover pan with a lid and cook gently for 8–10 minutes until the spinach is tender, stirring occasionally.

2. Remove pan from the heat and leave to cool slightly. Purée in liquidizer or work through a sieve, adding a little chicken stock if the spinach is too dry to work.

3. Heat spinach, stock, nutmeg and pepper to taste in the top of a double saucepan or in a large heatproof bowl standing over a pan of gently bubbling water. Stir to combine spinach and stock.

4. Whisk together the egg yolks and cream in a separate bowl. Pour in a little of the hot spinach mixture and stir well to combine.

5. Stir this mixture slowly into the spinach and stock. Add the remaining butter or margarine and heat through until the soup thickens, stirring constantly with a wooden spoon.

6. Taste for seasoning. Pour into warmed soup bowls, swirl each serving with a spoonful of cream and serve immediately.

Pea and Ham Soup

½ lb (225 g) dried split peas
2 pt (1 l) well flavoured ham stock
few stalks celery
few sprigs parsley
approx 4 oz (100 g) cooked ham
pepper
a little milk

To garnish
fried bread croûtons

Make the stock for this hearty winter soup with a ham shank, then you can strip the bone of meat and use it in the soup.

1. Put the split peas in a bowl, cover with cold water and leave to soak overnight.

2. The next day, chop the celery and parsley roughly. Cut the ham into dice. Drain the split peas.

3. Put all the ingredients in a large pan and bring to the boil. Lower the heat, cover pan with a lid and simmer gently for 1½–2 hours until the peas are tender, stirring occasionally.

4. Remove pan from the heat and leave to cool slightly. Purée soup until fairly smooth in a liquidizer or work through a sieve.

5. Return the soup to the rinsed out pan and add enough milk to make a pouring consistency. Reheat gently, then taste for seasoning. Pour into warmed soup bowls and serve hot with fried bread croûtons.

Spinach Soup.

Pot au Feu

2 lb (1 kg) leg of beef, with the bones
water
1 tsp (5 ml) salt
1 small head of celery
1 lb (450 g) carrots
½ lb (225 g) swede or turnip
2 large onions
few whole cloves
6 black peppercorns
bouquet garni

1. Slice the beef and chop the bones. Remove excess fat and discard. Put beef and bones in a large pan, cover with water and add the salt. Bring slowly to the boil, then lower the heat. Simmer gently for 1 hour, skimming regularly to remove all scum that comes to the surface.

2. Meanwhile, chop the celery roughly. Peel the carrots and chop if large, or leave whole if small. Peel the swede or turnip and cut into dice. Peel the onions and chop 1 finely. Press cloves into remaining whole onion. Crush the peppercorns.

3. Add the prepared vegetables to the pan with the crushed peppercorns and bouquet garni. Bring to the boil, then lower the heat and cover pan with a lid. Simmer very gently for a further 3 hours or until all ingredients are tender. Skim and stir occasionally during cooking.

4. Remove pan from the heat and taste soup for seasoning. Discard the clove studded onion. Leave until cold, then chill in the refrigerator overnight.

5. The next day, remove the fat that has risen to the surface of soup. Reheat the soup, then strain through a fine wire sieve. Return broth to rinsed pan, taste for seasoning and reheat gently.

6. Select pieces of meat and vegetables from the sieve. Put a few pieces in the bottom of each individual warmed soup bowl and pour over the hot broth. Put any remaining meat and vegetables in a warmed serving bowl. Serve crusty French bread separately.

Pot au Feu.

Soups

French Onion Soup.

French Onion Soup

1½ lb (675 g) Spanish onions
1–2 cloves garlic
1½ oz (40 g) butter or margarine
2 tbsp (30 ml) olive or corn oil
1 heaped tbsp (15 ml) plain flour
2 pt (1 l) well flavoured beef stock
½ pt (300 ml) dry white wine
salt and pepper

To finish
4 slices of French bread
butter or margarine for spreading
4 slices of Gruyère or Emmenthal cheese

1. Peel the onions and slice very thinly. Peel and crush the garlic.

2. Heat the butter or margarine and oil in a large pan. Add the onions and garlic and fry very gently for 10–15 minutes until golden, stirring occasionally.

3. Stir in the flour and cook for a further 1–2 minutes, stirring constantly.

4. Stir in the stock gradually, then add the white wine. Season to taste with salt and pepper.

5. Bring to the boil, then lower the heat and cover pan with a lid. Simmer gently for 20–25 minutes or until the onions are soft and broken down.

6. During the last 10 minutes of cooking time, spread the French bread with butter or margarine and top each slice with a slice of cheese.

7. Put under a pre-heated hot grill until the cheese bubbles and begins to brown.

8. Remove soup from the heat. Taste for seasoning. Pour into warmed soup bowls, float a slice of toasted cheese in each bowl and serve immediately.

Potage Bonne Femme

¼ lb (225 g) carrots
½ lb (225 g) leeks
2 large potatoes
2 oz (50 g) butter or margarine
2 pt (1 l) well flavoured chicken stock
salt and pepper
a little milk

1. Peel and grate the carrots. Slice the leeks finely. Peel the potatoes and cut into small dice.

2. Melt the butter or margarine in a large pan. Add the prepared vegetables. Cover pan with a lid and simmer gently for 5 minutes, shaking the pan occasionally.

3. Stir in the stock and add salt and pepper to taste. Bring to the boil. Lower the heat and cover pan with a lid. Simmer gently for 20–30 minutes until the vegetables are tender, stirring occasionally.

4. Remove pan from the heat and leave to cool slightly. Purée soup until smooth in a liquidizer or work through a sieve.

5. Return the soup to the rinsed out pan. Add enough milk to make a pouring consistency. Reheat gently, then taste for seasoning.

6. Pour into warmed soup bowls and serve hot with granary bread.

Potage Bonne Femme.

Red Mullet with Tomatoes.

Fish and shellfish

Red Mullet with Tomatoes

4 small red mullet
6 large ripe tomatoes
1 tsp (5 ml) dried thyme
2 tsp (10 ml) chopped parsley
coriander seeds
1 small bayleaf
saffron
salt and pepper
3 tbsp (45 ml) red wine
3 tbsp (45 ml) olive oil
juice of 1 small lemon

For garnish
anchovies
freshly chopped tarragon

1. Set oven at 400°F (200°C) or Mark 6.

2. Scald and skin the tomatoes. Chop them up finely and remove the seeds. Tip into a bowl and mix in the thyme, parsley, a few coriander seeds, bayleaf, a pinch of saffron and seasoning.

3. Pour the olive oil into an ovenproof dish. Arrange the mullet in it, add the wine and then the tomato mixture. Cover and bake in the centre of the pre-set oven for about 15 minutes.

4. Lift out the fish, arrange on a heated dish and pour the tomato pulp around them. Sprinkle over the lemon juice. Garnish if liked with anchovies and chopped tarragon.

FILLETING A PLAICE OR SOLE

1. Using a sharp knife, remove the head of the fish in one clean movement.

2. Remove the tail tip at the point only halfway down the fish's tail.

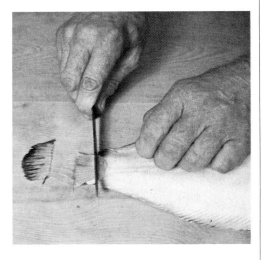

3. Scrape off the edge of the skin on the rest of the tail area.

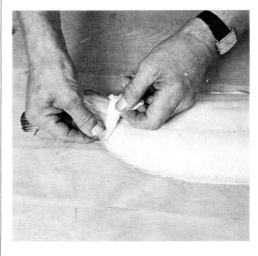

4. Having loosened the tail skin, ease it away with one hand underneath and the other hand pulling the skin free.

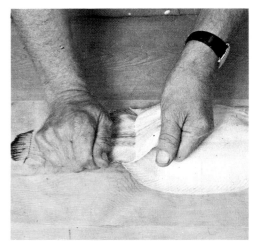

5. When you can get a grip on the tail, hold it firmly and pull the skin steadily away with the other hand.

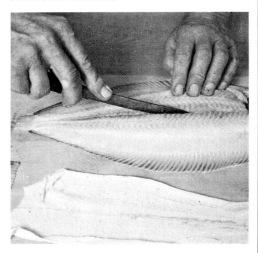

6. Run the tip of the knife down the fish's spine from head to tail.

7. Insert the knife and hold it parallel to the fish, flat against the bone. Slowly pare the fillet away.

8. Slip the knife under the free part of the fillet. Cut the remainder away from the fin bones.

9. Having removed one fillet, repeat the process until the whole fish is filleted.

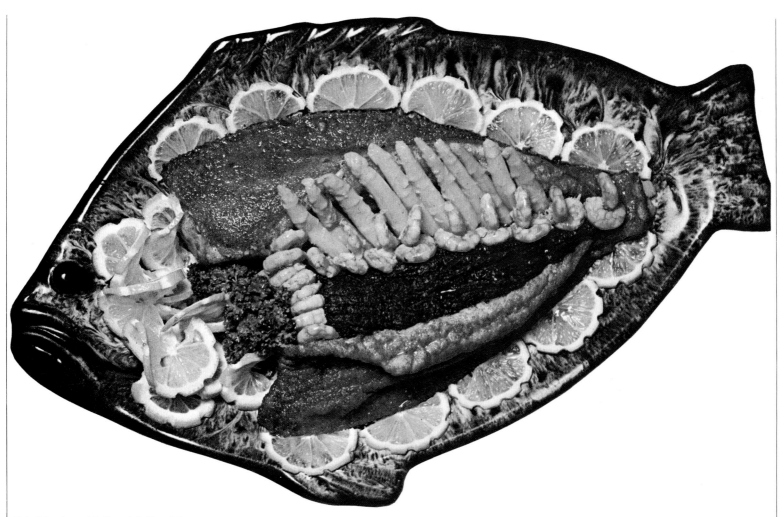

Fried Plaice with Special Garnish.

Fried Plaice with Special Garnish

1 large plaice weighing about 1 lb (450 g)
seasoned flour
1 beaten egg
fine breadcrumbs
oil for deep frying

For garnish
1 small packet frozen spinach
½ pt (300 ml) shrimps
1 can asparagus tips
1 lemon
sprigs of parsley

1. First prepare the ingredients for the garnish. Warm the chopped spinach in a pan. Shell the shrimps and drain the asparagus tips. Slice the lemon up thinly.

2. Take a small, sharp knife and make an incision on one side of the fish down each side of the backbone. Then, using the knife, ease the flesh away from the backbone on each side to form 2 flaps. Slices of raw potato can be placed between backbone and flesh to prevent these flaps sealing up again during cooking.

3. Dip the fish in a little flour, then in the beaten egg and breadcrumbs. Place carefully in the deep fryer and fry until golden brown. Drain on absorbent paper and remove potato slices.

4. Arrange the fish on a warmed serving dish. Tip the warmed spinach down one side with the flap turned back, and the asparagus tips along the other side, with the shrimps down the middle. Garnish the dish with the thinly sliced lemon and sprigs of parsley before serving.

Fish and shellfish

Sole and Shrimp Tartlets

1 lb (450 g) quantity savoury shortcrust
pastry
6 oz (175 g) fillet of sole
¼ pt (150 ml) shrimps
1 egg
1 egg yolk
4 tbsp (60 ml) single cream
¼ pt (150 ml) milk
1 oz (25 g) freshly grated Parmesan cheese
salt and pepper
12 thin slices Emmenthal cheese

1. Set oven at 400°F (200°C) or Mark 6.

2. Roll out the pastry quite thinly and line into 12 tartlet moulds.

3. Remove any skin from the sole, and shell the shrimps. Cut the sole into narrow strips and arrange in the bottom of the moulds with the shrimps on top.

4. Tip the eggs, cream, milk, Parmesan cheese and seasoning into a bowl together and beat with a hand whisk. Divide the mixture between the tarts and top each one with a slice of Emmenthal.

5. Bake in the pre-set oven on the shelf above centre for 5 minutes. Then turn the oven down to 300°F (150°C) or Mark 2 and continue to bake for about 20 minutes, or until the tarts have browned and the filling has risen a little.

Sole Paprika

8 fillets of sole
1 small onion or shallot
½ oz (15 g) butter
2 tsp (10 ml) olive oil
1 tsp (5 ml) paprika
2 tomatoes
7 fl oz (200 ml) fish stock
4 fl oz (100 ml) dry white wine
¼ pt (150 ml) cream
salt and pepper

To finish
lemon juice
salt and pepper
½ oz (12 g) butter
crescents of puff pastry

1. Peel and chop the onion into small dice. Heat the butter and oil in a pan and cook the onion until soft and transparent taking care not to let it brown. Sprinkle in the paprika.

2. Scald and skin the tomatoes, roughly chop and add to the pan. Allow the mixture to simmer for a while. Then add the fish stock and the wine, followed by the cream and seasoning.

3. When the contents of the pan have thoroughly blended, pass through a sieve and back into the pan. Now add the folded fish fillets and poach them in the sauce for about 15 minutes.

4. When they are cooked lift out very carefully and arrange on a warmed serving dish.

5. Now finish off the sauce by adding a few drops of lemon juice, salt and pepper to taste and the butter. Reduce the sauce a little if necessary.

6. Pour the sauce over the sole fillets and decorate with crescents of puff pastry if wished.

Sole and Shrimp Tartlets garnished with pastry spoons.

Sole Paprika.

Skate in Black Butter

1–2 wings of skate weighing about 2 lb
 (900 g)
court bouillon to cover
salt and pepper
2 tsp (10 ml) freshly chopped parsley
2 oz (50 g) butter
2 tsp (10 ml) wine vinegar
1 tbsp (15 ml) capers

1. Cover the skate pieces well with the court bouillon. Bring to the boil and then allow to simmer for about 15 minutes or until tender. Drain fish on absorbent paper, transfer to a heated serving dish. Season with salt and pepper and the chopped parsley, and keep warm.

2. Melt butter in a pan and cook until it turns golden brown. Then add the vinegar and capers and quickly pour over the fish. Serve bordered with piped creamed potatoes if liked.

Jolly Roger Parcel

6 fillets of plaice or sole
12 mussels with their shells
12 prawns with their shells
4 tbsp (60 ml) dry white wine
4 tbsp (60 ml) single cream
1 tbsp (15 ml) chopped parsley
2 oz (50 g) shelled shrimps
salt and pepper
oil

1. Set oven at 350°F (180°C) or Mark 4.

2. Line a small deep baking tin with foil and brush the base with a little oil.

3. Roll up each fillet and stand upright on foil base. Shell prawns but leave on heads and tails and put 2 in the middle of each roll. Clean mussels thoroughly and arrange between rolls.

4. Moisten each roll with the wine and cream. Sprinkle with parsley and shrimps. Season. Fold up the foil to cover the rolls and bake in the pre-set oven for 20–25 minutes.

Fish and shellfish

Fried Dabs with Herb Sauce.

Fried Dabs with Herb Sauce

4 dabs or any small flat fish
a little plain flour
1 beaten egg
fine breadcrumbs
oil for deep frying

For herb sauce
¼ pt (150 ml) double cream
1 tsp (5 ml) chopped fennel leaves
1 tsp (5 ml) chopped chives
bouquet garni
salt and pepper
1 tsp (5 ml) grated lemon rind

For garnish
2 hard boiled eggs
1 tbsp (15 ml) freshly chopped parsley .

1. Dip the dabs in flour, then the beaten egg and breadcrumbs. Deep fry until crisp and golden. Drain on absorbent paper and keep warm.

2. Tip cream into a heavy based saucepan. Add the chopped fennel, chives, bouquet garni and seasoning. Bring to the boil and simmer until sufficiently thickened. Remove the herb bag and stir in the lemon rind. Pour into a bowl ready to serve.

3. Finely chop the hard boiled eggs. Arrange the dabs on a serving dish, and sprinkle with chopped egg and parsley. Serve with French bread and butter if liked.

Halibut Steaks with Prawn Sauce

6 halibut steaks
½ pt (300 ml) prawns
½ pt (300 ml) double cream
salt and pepper

For garnish
1 lb (450 g) potatoes
1 large egg yolk
½ oz (12 g) butter
salt and pepper
freshly chopped parsley

1. Peel the potatoes, place them in a pan of cold, salted water and bring to the boil. Simmer until tender. Drain immediately and return to the heat to dry off any excess moisture. Rub the potatoes through a sieve and then beat in the egg yolk, butter and seasoning.

2. Season the halibut steaks and cook them in a buttered steamer for 10–12 minutes. Take out, remove the skin and keep the steaks warm.

3. Peel the prawns. Reserve about half for decoration and chop the rest up finely. Tip the cream into a heavy based saucepan. Bring to the boil and add the skin from the fish and the prawn shells only. Season with salt and pepper and simmer until the sauce has thickened sufficiently.

4. Pipe a border of creamed potato round the heated serving dish. Arrange the fish steaks in the centre. Strain the sauce, stir in the chopped prawns and pour over. Decorate with the reserved prawns and chopped parsley. Alternatively serve on individual platters.

Court Bouillon

1 carrot
1 onion
1 sprig thyme
½ bayleaf
2 peppercorns
3 tbsp (45 ml) wine vinegar
2 pt (generous 1 l) cold water

1. Peel and slice carrot and onion thinly.

2. Place all the ingredients in a saucepan, bring to the boil and simmer for 15–20 minutes. Strain before using.

Halibut Steaks with Prawn Sauce.

Fish and shellfish

Cod and Mussel Casserole.

Cod and Mussel Casserole

2 lb (900 g) cod fillet
3 pt (1.75 l) mussels
seasoned flour
2 oz (50 g) butter
2 fl oz (50 ml) oil
4 shallots or small onions
½ lb (225 g) tomatoes
2 lb (900 g) potatoes
4 oz (100 g) Cheddar cheese
1 large clove garlic
½ pt (300 ml) dry white wine
3 pt (1.75 l) fish stock
saffron
salt and black pepper

1. First prepare the mussels. Wash and scrub them well scraping away any weed. Discard any which are open. Rinse them under running water, then soak in a bowl of fresh water.

2. Set oven at 325°F (160°C) or Mark 3.

3. Remove any skin from the cod and cut into rectangular chunks. Dip in seasoned flour and fry in the oil and butter until lightly browned.

4. Peel and finely slice the shallots. Scald and skin the tomatoes, remove seeds and chop the flesh. Peel the potatoes and slice fairly thinly. Cut the cheese into fine slithers.

5. Now layer these ingredients into a large casserole dish. Begin with the shallots, then cod pieces, tomatoes, cheese and finally the potatoes. Repeat this once, finishing with the potatoes on top.

6. Crush the garlic with a little salt and mix it in with the wine, stock, a pinch of saffron and seasoning. Add this to the casserole and cover.

7. Cook in the centre of the pre-set oven for about 45 minutes. At this point add the mussels making sure they are well covered with the liquid. Cook for a further 7 minutes and serve piping hot.

Cod in Spicy Tomato Sauce.

Cod in Spicy Tomato Sauce

2 lb (900 g) cod
6 tomatoes
1 shallot or small onion
1 tsp (5 ml) dried oregano or thyme
1 tsp (5 ml) dried basil
1 tsp (5 ml) chopped chives
½ pt (300 ml) fish stock or equal quantities
*   of fish stock and white wine*
1 tbsp (15 ml) olive oil
salt and pepper

1. Wrap the cod in foil and steam it over a pan of boiling water for about 20–30 minutes until tender. Strain off the juices and reserve. Place the cod in a dish and keep warm in the oven.

2. Scald, skin and chop up the tomatoes. Peel and grate the shallot.

3. Place the tomatoes, onion, herbs and chosen liquid in a pan and cook slowly until the tomatoes have turned to pulp.

4. Adjust the seasoning to taste, add the olive oil and reserved juices from the fish. Continue to cook until the sauce is thick and well reduced. Then pour over the cod and serve with plainly boiled carrots and potatoes.

Turbot with Shrimp Sauce.

50

Turbot with Shrimp Sauce

1 small turbot 2½–3 lb (1¼–1½ kg)
butter
salt and pepper
1 pt (600 ml) mornay sauce
4 oz (100 g) shelled shrimps
2 tsp (10 ml) tomato purée
knob of butter

For garnish
2 hard boiled eggs
sprigs of parsley

1. Set oven at 350°F (180°C) or Mark 4.

2. Place the turbot on a buttered sheet of foil, dot with butter and season with salt and pepper. Seal loosely, put on a baking sheet and cook in the pre-set oven for 25–35 minutes.

3. Meanwhile prepare the sauce. Make up the mornay sauce and chop the shrimps. Stir the shrimps and tomato purée into the sauce and finish with a knob of butter.

4. Arrange the cooked fish on a warmed dish. Slice up the hard boiled eggs and use to garnish the fish with the sprigs of parsley. If liked, one of the eggs can be finely chopped and sprinkled onto the fish. Pour the shrimp sauce around or serve separately.

Fish Croquettes

1 lb fresh cod
½ pt (300 ml) thick white sauce made with:
   1½ oz (40 g) butter
   1½ oz (40 g) flour
   ½ pt (300 ml) milk
1 egg yolk
salt and pepper
plain flour
2 beaten eggs
fine breadcrumbs
oil for deep frying

For garnish
wedges of lemon
chopped parsley

1. Place the cod on a buttered dish over a pan of boiling water, season and cover. When cooked, allow to cool a little, then remove any bits of skin and flake fish from the bone.

Fish Croquettes with Butter Sauce.

2. Now prepare the sauce. Melt the butter in a pan over low heat and stir in the flour. Add the milk gradually, stirring all the time. Bring sauce to the boil and allow to simmer for 3–5 minutes.

3. Take off the heat and beat in the egg yolk. Then add the flaked cod and season with salt and pepper. Tip the mixture into a shallow dish and chill in the refrigerator.

4. Once the mixture has chilled, divide into portions – about 1½ oz (40 g) each – and roll into fat sausage shapes. Dip in the flour, beaten egg and breadcrumbs and then chill again.

5. Cook the croquettes in the deep fryer, a few at a time, until crisp and golden brown. Drain well on absorbent paper, then pile onto a heated serving dish and garnish with lemon and chopped parsley. If liked, serve with sauté potatoes and butter sauce.

Butter Sauce

4 oz (100 g) butter
1 shallot or small onion
1½ tbsp (22 ml) wine vinegar
salt and black pepper
3 tsp (15 ml) boiling water

1. Peel and chop up the shallot very finely. Place in a small pan, add the vinegar and seasoning. Cook until shallot is soft and virtually all the liquid has been absorbed. Pass the mixture through a sieve.

2. Cream the butter until soft. Then start to whip it with an electric or hand beater, adding the shallot purée drop by drop.

3. Now add the first teaspoonful of boiling water. Whip and repeat for the second and third. The mixture should be fluffy and almost white. Pile into a bowl and serve with Fish Croquettes.

Fish and shellfish

Rock Salmon in White Wine Sauce.

Rock Salmon in White Wine Sauce

2 lb (900 g) rock salmon
2 oz (50 g) butter
¼ pt (150 ml) dry white wine
1 tbsp (15 ml) freshly chopped parsley
¼ pt (150 ml) cream
salt and pepper

For potato border
2 lb (900 g) potatoes
3 egg yolks
1½ lb (40 g) butter
salt and pepper

1. First remove backbone from fish. Divide the fish lengthwise, exposing the bone on one half and leaving the other half boneless. Lift the bone in one hand and, with the other, use a sharp knife to pare away the flesh from the bone. Cut the 2 fillets into even size pieces about 4 inches in length.

2. Now prepare potato border. Peel and cut into even size pieces. Place in a pan of cold, salted water, bring to the boil and cook until tender. Drain at once, return to pan and leave over heat for a minute to dry off any excess moisture. Pass through a sieve into a bowl and beat in egg yolks, two-thirds of the butter and seasoning.

3. Turn on the grill. Tip the potato mixture into a piping bag and pipe a thick border round an oval ovenproof dish. Melt the remaining butter, brush over the potato and leave to brown under the grill.

4. Meanwhile melt butter in a pan and brown the fish pieces lightly in it. Lift them out and pour in the wine. When this has heated return fish to the pan and simmer gently for about 5 minutes, turning once.

5. Now add the chopped parsley and cream. Season to taste. Take out the fish fillets and arrange on the potato-bordered dish. When sauce has reduced to a creamy consistency pour over and serve.

Baked Stuffed Mackerel

6 filleted mackerel

For stuffing
2 rashers back bacon
5 oz (150 g) fresh white breadcrumbs
2 tbsp (30 ml) chopped chives
2 tbsp (30 ml) freshly chopped parsley
grated rind and juice of 1 lemon
salt and pepper

For lemon sauce
2 lemons
2 cloves garlic
2 tsp (10 ml) dried tarragon
1 tbsp (15 ml) freshly chopped parsley
salt and pepper
½ pt (300 ml) olive oil
1 tbsp (15 ml) wine vinegar

For garnish
thin slices of lemon
sprigs of parsley

1. Set oven at 375°F (190°C) or Mark 5.

2. Cut the rind off the bacon and chop the bacon into thin strips. Then fry until lightly browned.

3. Mix the breadcrumbs, bacon, herbs and seasoning together in a bowl. Then add the rind and juice of the lemon.

4. Place a little of the stuffing mixture in each mackerel, then wrap the fish individually in foil, place on a baking sheet and bake in the pre-set oven on the shelf above centre for 20–25 minutes.

5. Meanwhile prepare the sauce. Peel the lemons, divide into segments and remove all the pips and pith. Crush the garlic with the herbs and seasoning. Then begin to add the olive oil slowly, beating it in drop by drop with intermittent drops of vinegar. Once thoroughly blended, add lemon segments and heat sauce gently.

6. Remove the mackerel from the foil, arrange on a warmed serving dish and pour the sauce over. Serve garnished with thin slices of lemon and sprigs of parsley.

Baked Stuffed Mackerel.

Fish Stock

Basic Recipe

1¼ lb (700 g) fish trimmings
(heads, tails, backbones, skin)
¼ small onion or shallot
1 wedge lemon
2 parsley stalks
1 sprig fennel (optional)
3 peppercorns
salt
cold water, or equal quantities of water and white wine, to cover

1. Place the fish trimmings, onion, lemon, herbs and seasoning in a pan. Add enough liquid just to cover and bring to a fast boil.

2. Now skim the surface and refresh with a cup of cold water.

3. Bring back to the boil and continue to cook briskly for a further 10 minutes. Strain before using.

Mackerel with Gooseberry Sauce

6 mackerel
1 lb (450 g) raw gooseberries
oil
salt and pepper
fennel or parsley sprigs

For sauce
½ oz (12 g) butter or margarine
½ oz (12 g) plain flour
½ pt (300 ml) plus 2 tbsp (10 ml) water
1 tsp (5 ml) sugar
green vegetable colouring (optional)

1. Set oven at 350°F (180°C) or Mark 4.

2. Remove the heads and tails of the mackerel and discard. Clean each mackerel thoroughly, inside and outside. Top and tail the gooseberries.

3. Stuff each mackerel cavity with an equal quantity of gooseberries and place the fish, split sides upwards, in a lightly greased ovenproof dish.

4. Brush the fish lightly with oil, cover with foil, and bake in the pre-set oven for 20–25 minutes, or until the fish are cooked.

5. Meanwhile make the gooseberry sauce. Cook the gooseberries with 2 tablespoonfuls (10 ml) of water in a pan over a gentle heat. When soft, rub them through a sieve.

6. In another pan, melt the butter or margarine, stir in the sifted flour, then gradually add ½ pt (300 ml) boiling water. Add the sieved gooseberries, the sugar and vegetable colouring to enhance the colour of the sauce if desired. Bring the sauce to the boil, pour into a sauce boat and keep warm.

7. Take the cooked mackerel from the oven, and season with salt and pepper. Sprinkle a little chopped fennel or parsley over. Serve the sauce separately.

Fish and shellfish

Baked Herrings with Lemon and Caper Sauce

6 filleted herrings
1 small shallot
2 bayleaves
a few peppercorns
salt
sprigs of parsley
¼ pt (150 ml) wine vinegar
¼ pt (150 ml) water
melted butter

For stuffing
3 oz (75 g) soft breadcrumbs
1 tbsp (15 ml) chopped chives
1 tbsp (15 ml) chopped parsley
1 soft herring roe
salt and pepper
1 egg

To finish
1 tbsp (15 ml) capers
1 lemon
chopped parsley

1. Peel and slice the shallot finely. Arrange the herrings in a shallow dish and intersperse with the shallot, bayleaves, peppercorns and parsley sprigs. Season with salt and pour over the vinegar and water. Marinate for 24 hours.

2. Set oven at 375°F (190°C) or Mark 5.

3. Strain off the marinade and reserve. Mix the herbs, roe and seasoning into the breadcrumbs. Beat the egg and work into the mixture.

4. Fill some stuffing mixture into each herring. Place them on a baking sheet, brush with melted butter and bake in the pre-set oven for about 12 minutes.

5. Now prepare the sauce. Make sure that the capers are well drained and pressed. Peel the lemon, divide into segments and remove all the pith and pips. Pour the strained marinade into a pan and bring to the boil. Remove from heat and add capers, lemon segments and chopped parsley.

6. Arrange the baked herrings on a warmed serving dish, pour the sauce over and serve.

Baked Herrings in Lemon and Caper Sauce.

Whitebait

whitebait
plain flour
oil for deep frying

To serve
slices of lemon
brown bread and butter

1. Sift the flour. Take a few whitebait at a time, toss them in the flour and then shake in a sieve to remove any surplus.

2. Arrange the fish in the bottom of the frying basket so that they do not overlap. Now plunge them into the oil and cook until crisp and golden brown – about 1–2 minutes.

3. Turn onto absorbent paper and keep warm while you cook the rest as above.

4. Serve with thick slices of lemon and thinly cut brown bread and butter.

3. Immerse the frying basket containing the fish in the hot oil for 1 minute.

1. Take a handful of whitebait and turn in flour. Put in a sieve and shake off the surplus flour.

4. Drain on a piece of absorbent paper and keep warm whilst frying rest of fish.

2. Cook only a few fish at a time otherwise they will stick together. Heat the oil in a deep fat frying pan to 390°F (200°C) keeping the basket out of the oil.

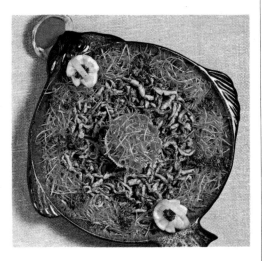

5. Serve whitebait with cut lemon for squeezing over and matchstick potatoes.

Fish and shellfish

Salmon Cutlets in Red Wine Sauce.

Salmon Cutlets in Red Wine Sauce

2 lb (900 g) salmon
1 oz (25 g) butter
½ pt (300 ml) French red wine
¼ pt (150 ml) strong fish stock
¼ pt (150 ml) double cream
salt and pepper

For garnish
8 oz (225 g) petits pois
6 mushrooms
½ lb (225 g) creamed potatoes
sprigs of fennel

1. Divide the salmon into 6 cutlets. Wash and dry them. Butter a flameproof dish, place the cutlets in it and cover with the red wine. Poach gently until cooked. Then drain them on absorbent paper, arrange on a serving dish and keep warm.

2. Add the fish stock to the dish with the wine and allow to bubble until liquid has reduced by a third. Add the cream and continue to simmer. Season to taste.

3. Take a small, sharp knife and cut swirls in the caps of the mushrooms. Then poach these mushrooms in a little oil or butter.

4. Strain the sauce and pour over the salmon cutlets. Garnish the dish with rosettes of creamed potato, turned mushrooms, petits pois and sprigs of fennel.

Soused Herrings

6 fresh herrings
2 onions
2 tsp (10 ml) black peppercorns
5 small bayleaves
6 thin strips lemon rind
5 fl oz (150 ml) wine vinegar
5 fl oz (150 ml) water
salt and pepper

1. First fillet and clean the herrings. Cut off the heads and tails and slit the fish down the underside. Flatten out and then, starting from the top, pull the back bone out gently. Now slit down the back as well and wash under the cold tap, discarding the entrails.

2. Roll up the herring fillets with tail end innermost and secure with a cocktail stick.

3. Peel and slice the onions into thin rings. Take a large screw top glass jar and arrange the herrings in it interspersed with the onion, lemon rind, bayleaves and peppercorns.

4. Heat the vinegar, water and seasoning together in a pan. Pour into the jar, seal tightly and keep in the refrigerator for at least 48 hours.

1. Cut off the heads and tails, then carefully split each herring down the underside from top to tail.

2. Open up the herrings so that all the bones are clearly visible.

3. Pull out the spine with one hand, gently pushing from behind with a finger or thumb.

4. Cut the herrings in half and wash thoroughly under running water to clean.

5. Roll each cleaned and wiped fillet, tucking in the tail piece, and impale with a cocktail stick to secure.

A jar of Soused Herrings with pickles.

Variations:

Soused Herring Salad. Drain the herrings and chop up into neat pieces. Mix with a diced apple, a little grated onion, diced, cooked potato, and chopped hard boiled egg. Blend with soured cream and season to taste. Chill, then serve on a bed of lettuce.

Baked Herring Rolls. Drain and unroll some soused herrings. Make a paste of equal amounts of breadcrumbs and butter, some chopped parsley, lemon juice, seasoning and as little hot water as possible. Spread this paste on the herrings, roll them up again and fasten as before. Place in a greased baking dish, cover with foil and bake in the oven, pre-set at 350°F (180°C) or Mark 4, for 15 minutes.

Lobster Mornay

2 small lobsters
court bouillon
½ pt (300 ml) béchamel sauce
2 oz (50 g) freshly grated Parmesan cheese
salt and pepper
2 level tbsp (30 ml) double cream
1 oz (25 g) melted butter
½ oz (12 g) fine breadcrumbs

For garnish
watercress
freshly chopped parsley

1. Place lobsters in a pan with lukewarm court bouillon. Cover and bring slowly to the boil. Then simmer for about 15 minutes until they turn bright pink in colour. Take out and allow to cool.

2. When cold, place lobsters on a wooden board with the tails tucked underneath. Take a very sharp knife and divide them straight through the middle lengthwise. Remove the poisonous pouches from each side, then the coral and the lobster meat. Crack the claws and remove the flesh from these too.

3. Make up the béchamel sauce. Stir in the coral and half the Parmesan cheese. Season as necessary, then whip up the cream and add this to the sauce as well.

4. Tip a little sauce into each shell and cover with the lobster meat. Then pour over remaining sauce. Sprinkle with the rest of the cheese, the melted butter and finally the breadcrumbs.

5. Brown the lobsters under the grill or in a hot oven. Serve garnished with watercress and chopped parsley.

1. Tuck the lobster tail underneath its body. Insert a sharp knife into the centre back of the body and cut through towards the tail end.

2. Cut through the top half towards the head in exactly the same manner.

3. Discard the grey-green poisonous pouch and the dark threadlike intestine.

4. Remove body flesh in one piece using a skewer, then scrape out all the remaining meat from the body and claws.

Lobster Mornay.

58

DRESSING A CRAB

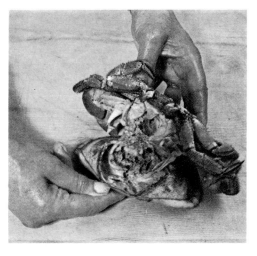

1. Break off the large claws of the crab then the small ones, and set aside.

2. Hold the shell as above and grip the body with the other hand. Pull back until the body comes away from the shell.

3. These grey bits are poisonous and must be discarded.

Dressed Crab.

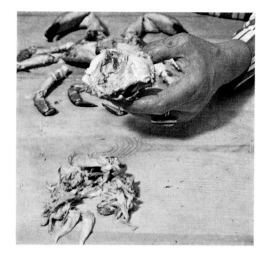

4. Take out the poisonous pouch: do this by pressing from underneath against the body and it comes away in one piece.

5. Using a skewer, get out all the flesh from the cleaned crab body. Set aside.

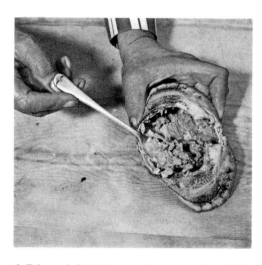

6. Discard the thin membrane on the shell, then remove all the meat.

7. Arrange the claws around the empty shell, then fill one side with brown meat and the other with white meat. Decorate with chopped egg yolk, chopped egg white and chopped parsley.

Coquilles St Jacques

6 scallops with their shells
1½ oz (37 g) plus ½ oz (12 g) butter or
*   margarine*
1½ oz (37 g) plain flour
¾ pt (450 ml) milk
1 tbsp (15 ml) chopped parsley
1 oz (25 g) Parmesan cheese
salt and pepper
creamed potato
1 tbsp (15 ml) breadcrumbs
1 tbsp (15 ml) Gruyère cheese

1. Set the oven at 375°F (190°C) or Mark 5.

2. Cut each scallop from the shell, wash well and remove any black bits. Roughly chop each scallop.

3. Melt 1½ oz (37 g) butter or margarine in a small pan. Stir in the flour to form a roux. Gradually add the milk, beating well. Stir in the parsley, the grated Parmesan and the seasoning.

4. Put a large spoonful of this mixture on each shell. Add chopped scallop and cover with more sauce.

5. Fill a piping bag, fitted with a rosette nozzle, with creamed potato and pipe around each scallop shell. Scatter the tops with the breadcrumbs, then the grated Gruyère cheese, and lastly a few tiny pieces of butter.

6. Place the shells on a baking sheet and bake in the pre-set oven for 15 minutes or until the potato piping is golden brown.

Boiled Shrimps

2 pts (1 l) shrimps
½ pt (300 ml) water
salt
1 sprig parsley
1 clove
1 tsp (5 ml) vinegar

1. Wash the shrimps, remove the shells and the black thread.

2. Bring the water to the boil with a pinch of salt, the parsley, clove and vinegar. Add the shrimps and cover the pan. Simmer for 5–10 minutes or until tender. Cool in the cooking water and drain.

Roast Sirloin of Beef.

Meat

Roast Sirloin of Beef

1. Set oven at 425°F (220°C) or Mark 7.

2. Make sure that you have removed the joint from the refrigerator at least 30 minutes before you plan to put it in the oven.

3. Wipe the meat and spread lightly with a little dripping. Put some extra dripping in the bottom of the roasting pan and place in centre of the pre-set oven.

4. After 15 minutes reduce the oven temperature to 375°F (190°C) or Mark 5 and roast at this temperature for the remainder of the cooking time, basting frequently. For a rare roast allow 15 minutes per lb (450 g) plus an extra 15 minutes. For a well done joint allow 20 minutes per lb (450 g) plus the extra 15 minutes.

5. When the joint is cooked, place on a serving dish and leave to stand in a warming drawer for 10–15 minutes before beginning to carve it. This makes the job of carving much easier.

6. To make the gravy tip the fat off from the roasting tin, leaving the juices and sediment from the meat. Add 2 tsp (10 ml) flour, allow to colour, then pour in about $\frac{3}{4}$ pt (450 ml) stock or vegetable water. Bring to the boil and simmer until sufficiently reduced. Season to taste and strain into a gravy boat.

Boeuf en Croûte

3 lb (1.5 kg) fillet of beef
1 lb (450 g) quantity puff pastry
4 oz (100 g) mushrooms
butter
salt
black pepper
2 tsp (10 ml) dried mixed herbs
beaten egg

1. Set oven at 400°F (200°C) or Mark 6.

2. Trim and tie up the fillet. Melt a little butter in a pan, sprinkle the joint with salt and black pepper and seal it in the hot butter. Then roast in the pre-set oven for 15–20 minutes. Take out and allow to cool.

3. Wash and slice the mushrooms very finely. Sauté them in butter for a few minutes, then add the mixed herbs. Draw off heat and allow to cool.

4. Set the pastry on a lightly floured surface and roll out to a piece large enough to fold lengthwise over the fillet.

5. Lay the pastry over the roasting dish. Remove string from the cooled fillet and place meat on the pastry. Pour over the mushroom mixture, then fold over the pastry to cover. Trim and press edges well together. Turn so that the joins are on the underneath. Make a few slits in the top pastry to allow steam to escape. Brush the pastry all over with beaten egg. Roll out any pastry trimmings and cut out medallions or crescents for decoration.

6. Bake in the pre-set oven for 30–40 minutes or until pastry is well browned.

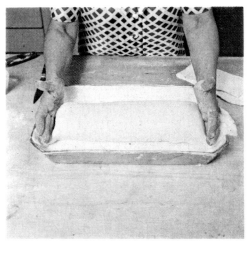

1. After wrapping pastry around the fillet, seal the edges by brushing with cold water and pressing together.

2. Trim the ends neatly with a knife.

3. Brush the pastry case generously with beaten egg.

4. Decorate with pastry trimmings.

LARDING

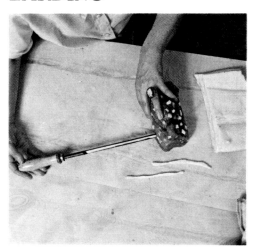

1. Some very lean cuts of meat such as fillet of beef or veal have a tendency to dry out when they are roasted. In order to prevent this the meat can be larded – a method by which you actually insert fat into the meat.
Take a piece of raw, unsalted pork fat, which should ideally be cold and firm. Cut off very narrow, long strips and slot these, one by one, into a larding needle.

Boeuf en Croûte.

Variations:
For an even more extravagant version of Boeuf en Croûte, try rubbing the beef fillet with brandy before seasoning and browning in butter.
Alternatively, omit the mushrooms and mixed herbs, and spread a generous amount of pâté de foie gras or chicken liver pâté over the top and sides of the beef before wrapping in pastry.
The layer of mushrooms or pâté between the meat and the pastry helps to keep the fillet juicy and moist.
This dish is also delicious using a fillet of veal instead of beef.

2. Push the needle through the joint. Then withdraw it again, leaving the fat threaded through the meat. Do this at roughly $\frac{1}{2}$ inch (1.5 cm) intervals starting at the bottom of the joint and working up to the top, and at 2 inch (5 cm) intervals along it.

3. Snip the long ends off with scissors. The joint is now ready for roasting.

PREPARING TOURNEDOS FOR GRILLING

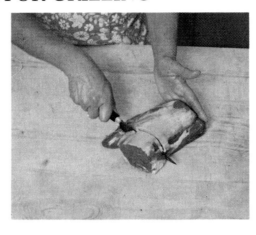

1. You will need a sharp knife, scissors, plenty of string and a thin slice of raw, unsalted pork fat.

2. Place the beef fillet on a chopping board and, using a very sharp knife, cut into slices about 1½ inches (4 cm) thick.

3. Trim away any fat or sinuous matter and shape steaks into rounds. Then take a piece of pork fat and cut into strips 1½ inches (4 cm) wide.

4. Wrap a strip of fat around each steak.

5. Trim the fat off neatly so that the ends just meet around the middle.

6. With fine string tie around the middle. Make a double knot and cut the string. Place under a hot grill in the highest position for a minute on each side. Continue to grill on a lower level for 3½ minutes on each side for rare steaks, 4½ minutes for medium steaks, and 5 minutes for well done steaks.

Tournedos.

Steak Paprika.

Maître d'Hôtel Butter

Basic Recipe ☆

4 oz (100 g) unsalted butter
1 tbsp (15 ml) finely chopped
   parsley
juice of ½ lemon
salt and pepper

1. Soften the butter on a plate. Then add the chopped parsley, strained lemon juice and seasoning. Blend in well.

2. Form into a roll, chill in the refrigerator and serve in pats.

Steak Paprika

6 sirloin steaks
butter
4 oz (100 g) flat mushrooms
1 onion
6 fl oz (180 ml) dry white wine
13 fl oz (400 ml) béchamel sauce
paprika
salt and pepper

1. Chop the mushrooms into very tiny pieces.

2. Finely chop the onion and fry in a little butter until soft. Pour in the wine and béchamel sauce, stirring. Add the mushrooms and enough paprika to colour the sauce. Leave to simmer whilst preparing the steaks.

3. Season the steaks and fry them in butter.

4. Season the sauce. Arrange steaks in a serving dish and pour sauce over.

Steak Diane

3 well beaten steaks
oil and butter for frying
2 tbsp (30 ml) brandy
2 shallots or small onions
1 tbsp (15 ml) freshly chopped parsley
8 fl oz (225 ml) jellied stock
1 tbsp (15 ml) tomato purée
salt and pepper
Worcestershire sauce

1. Peel and finely chop the shallots. Heat some butter and oil in a large frying pan and carefully put in the steaks.

2. Brown them lightly on each side, then add the brandy. Set alight and allow the flames to burn out.

3. Now add the shallots followed by the parsley and, when slightly softened, spoon in the jellied stock. At this point remove the steaks to a heated dish and keep warm.

4. Bring the stock to the boil and cook until well reduced. Stir in the tomato purée and season with salt and pepper and a few drops of Worcestershire sauce. Pour the sauce over the steaks and serve immediately. If liked, garnish with some French fried potatoes and chopped parsley.

1. For clarity a single steak is shown being cooked but you can cook as many as your pan will allow. To lift up each steak after beating, use the prongs of a fork, rolling the steak round it.

2. Carefully unroll the steak into a pan of hot oil and butter.

6. Stir in jellied stock. Remove the steak from the pan and keep warm.

7. Bring the sauce to the boil and cook until well reduced. Season and pour the sauce over the steak.

3. Seal the steak on both sides then reduce the heat and continue cooking.

4. Over a high heat, pour in the brandy and ignite. When the flames subside, add the onions and cook gently.

5. Sprinkle chopped parsley over.

Steak Diane.

Meat

Marsala Steaks

6 rump steaks
2 shallots or 1 onion
6 oz (175 g) button mushrooms
butter and oil for frying
1 tbsp (30 ml) plain flour
1 fl oz (25 ml) Marsala
¾ pt (450 ml) stock
salt and pepper

For garnish
lemon slices
sprigs of parsley

1. Peel and finely chop the shallots. Wash and slice the mushrooms.

2. Heat enough butter and oil to cover the base of a large pan. Seal the steaks in the hot fat, then lower the heat and cook to your own taste. Lift out carefully, place on a heated serving dish, season and keep warm.

3. Add the chopped shallot to the pan and cook gently until soft and transparent. Tip in the flour and stir until well blended.

4. Now gradually pour in the stock and Marsala, stirring continually. Allow to bubble up well. Add the chopped mushrooms and continue to cook for a further 3–4 minutes. Season to taste.

5. Pour the sauce over the steaks and garnish with lemon slices and sprigs of parsley before serving.

Rump Steaks à la Maison

2 thick rump steaks
butter for frying
2 tbsp (30 ml) well flavoured stock
salt and pepper

For garnish
2 tomatoes
watercress
sauté potatoes
4 oz (100 g) unsalted butter
4 tbsp (60 ml) freshly chopped chives
salt and pepper

1. Trim the steaks of all excess fat and gristle. Melt the butter in a pan, increase the heat and add the steaks. Seal them quickly on each side before turning down the heat to continue cooking.

2. Cook steaks gently for 2½ minutes on each side for rare meat, or for 3 minutes for medium done. Then place them on a heated serving dish, season and keep warm.

3. Add stock to the pan, blend in well with meat juices and bring to the boil. Then pour over the cooked steaks.

4. Serve garnished with lightly grilled tomatoes, watercress, a few sauté potatoes and chive butter. For the chive butter, soften the butter on a plate, mix in the chopped chives and season with salt and pepper. Divide into 4 pats and serve 2 on each steak.

Beef Stroganoff

½ lb (225 g) fillet steak
2 onions
8 oz (225 g) mushrooms
2 tbsp (30 ml) oil
1 oz (25 g) butter
2 tbsp (30 ml) sherry
¼ pt (150 ml) soured cream
grated nutmeg
salt and pepper

1. Cut the steak into very thin strips with a sharp knife. Chop the onions finely.

2. Heat the oil and butter in a pan and fry the onions gently until soft but not brown.

3. Increase the heat and add steak to the pan. Fry briskly until lightly browned all over. Slice the mushrooms and add to the pan with the sherry. Stir for 2–3 minutes or until the mushrooms are cooked.

4. Stir in the soured cream, a pinch of nutmeg and seasoning. Heat through, but do not allow to boil. Serve with boiled rice.

Marsala Steaks.

Rump Steaks à la Maison.

Meat

Beef Beaujolais

3–4 lb (1.5–1.75 kg) topside or similar
   joint of beef
oil
12 small onions or shallots
bouquet garni
½ pt (300 ml) water
salt and pepper

1. Set oven at 350°F (180°C) or Mark 4.

2. Brown the beef all over in a flame-proof casserole, using the minimum of oil.

3. Place the peeled but whole onions round the meat, pour on the wine and tuck in the bouquet garni. Cover and place in the pre-set oven for 30 minutes.

4. Reduce the heat to 275°F (135°C) or Mark ½ and continue cooking until the onions are tender. If necessary add up to ¼ pt (150 ml) water.

5. When the meat is done – test with a skewer – lift out onto a serving dish. Arrange the onions around the joint and keep warm.

6. Make a gravy by adding the remaining water to the cooking pot, season to taste, and take out the bouquet garni. Stir over a high heat to reduce a little, then pour over the meat and onions.

Beef Espagnole

6 small rump steaks
salt and pepper
butter for frying

For mirepoix
2 carrots
2 onions
½ lb (225 g) celery
1 oz (25 g) butter
1 fl oz (25 ml) oil
2 sprigs thyme
2 crushed bayleaves
2 tbsp (30 ml) sherry

For espagnole sauce
1 oz (25 g) butter
1 oz (25 g) plain flour
2 pt (generous 1 l) stock
2 tomatoes
half the given quantity of mirepoix

1. First prepare the mirepoix. Peel and grate the carrots and onions. Wash, trim and chop the celery very finely. Heat the oil and butter in a heavy based pan. Add the prepared vegetables, herbs and sherry, and simmer gently until soft.

2. Now prepare the sauce. Melt the butter in a pan, blend in the flour and allow to cook through. Then add the stock, a little at a time, beating well after each addition.

3. Scald, skin and chop up the tomatoes. Add these to the sauce, followed, after a few minutes, by half the mirepoix. Allow the sauce to simmer until reduced by half.

4. Set oven at 350°F (180°C) or Mark 4.

5. Place the steaks on a board and beat until well flattened. Season and brown lightly in butter.

6. Strain off any excess liquid from the remaining mirepoix and spread a little of the mixture over each steak. Roll up and secure with cocktail sticks.

7. Place the meat rolls in an ovenproof dish. Strain the finished sauce over them, cover and cook in the pre-set oven for 30–35 minutes or until tender.

8. Serve with red cabbage and baked potatoes in their jackets if liked.

Beef Espagnole with Red Cabbage and Baked Pota

Boiled Beef with Vegetables.

Boiled Beef with Vegetables

*4–5 lb (1.75–2.25 kg) salted silverside of
   beef*
6 onions
8 carrots
2 lb (900 g) potatoes

1. Place the meat in a large pan, cover with cold water and bring slowly to the boil. Remove any scum which may come to the surface. Cover and simmer gently for 2–2½ hours.

2. Meanwhile, prepare the vegetables. Peel the onions and leave whole. Peel the carrots and half or quarter them if necessary. Peel the potatoes.

3. An hour before the end of cooking, add the onions and carrots and then, half an hour later, the potatoes.

4. Place the silverside on a warmed serving dish, and surround with the vegetables. Strain off some of the liquor and serve separately in a sauce boat.

Stuffed Beef

1 breast of beef

For stuffing
3 rashers bacon
6 oz (175 g) breadcrumbs
2 oz (50 g) suet
1 tsp (5 ml) oregano
1 egg
salt and pepper

1. Set oven at 350°F (180°C) or Mark 4.

2. Chop the bacon finely, and put in a bowl with the breadcrumbs, suet and oregano. Mix well, then beat in the egg. Season to taste.

3. Remove excess fat from the beef. Pack the stuffing tightly into the cavity thus formed. Tie up with string and place in a roasting tin.

4. Roast in the pre-set oven for 1¼–1½ hours.

Roast Stuffed Veal

1 small boned and rolled shoulder of veal
2 oz (50 g) butter
salt and pepper

For stuffing
3 oz (75 g) fresh breadcrumbs
1 onion
butter for frying
1 tbsp (15 ml) freshly chopped parsley
1 tsp (5 ml) dried mixed herbs
juice of ½ lemon
salt and pepper
1 beaten egg

1. Set oven at 400°F (200°C) or Mark 6.

2. Prepare the stuffing. Peel and chop the onion finely. Sauté in a little butter until soft and transparent.

3. Place the breadcrumbs in a bowl. Add the onion, herbs, seasoning, lemon juice and a little beaten egg to bind. Mix together well.

4. Unroll the veal and spread with the stuffing. Roll up again and tie securely. Spread the joint with the butter, season and wrap in foil. Place in a baking tin and roast in the pre-set oven.

5. When the joint has cooked for 25 minutes for each lb (450 g), fold back the foil, baste the joint thoroughly and roast uncovered for another 20–25 minutes until it is cooked and well browned. Serve with baked parsnips and white cabbage if liked.

Roast Stuffed Veal.

Meat

Garnished Scallopine.

Wiener Schnitzel.

Wiener Schnitzel

4 thin veal escalopes
seasoned flour
fine breadcrumbs
beaten egg
1½ oz (40 g) butter
1½ fl oz (40 ml) oil

For garnish
2 hard boiled eggs
4 anchovy fillets
slices of lemon
sprigs of parsley

1. Roll the escalopes in seasoned flour, then brush with beaten egg and cover well with breadcrumbs.

2. Peel the hard boiled eggs and separate the whites from the yolks. Then chop each very finely and reserve. Divide the anchovy fillets in half lengthwise. Set aside for garnish.

3. Heat the butter and oil together in a frying pan. Lay the crumbed escalopes in carefully and fry over moderate heat for about 10 minutes depending on thickness, turning once only.

4. Arrange the escalopes on a heated serving dish and garnish with the chopped egg white and yolk. Add the strips of anchovy and decorate with slices of lemon and parsley. If liked serve with garden peas or French beans.

Garnished Scallopine

4 veal escalopes
seasoned flour
butter for frying

For mirepoix
½ lb (225 g) celery
¾ lb (350 g) carrots
4 oz (100 g) lean ham
3 oz (75 g) butter
1 bayleaf
2 sprigs thyme
salt and pepper

For garnish
croûtons
black olives
freshly chopped parsley
cream cheese
watercress

1. First prepare the mirepoix. Wash and trim the celery and chop up into small dice. Peel and grate the carrot. Chop the ham finely. Melt the butter in a heavy based pan. Add the celery, carrot and herbs and allow to cook gently for about 5 minutes. Then add the ham and seasoning. Continue to cook until quite soft.

2. Divide each escalope in half and beat out well until you have 8 small escalopes. Pass each one through seasoned flour. Melt butter in a pan and fry the scallopine for about 4 minutes, turning once.

3. Arrange the cooked scallopine in a serving dish and pile a little of the mirepoix onto each one.

4. Garnish by placing a croûton in the centre of each escalope, topped with a black olive and sprinkled with freshly chopped parsley. If liked the olives can be stuffed with a little cream cheese. Decorate the dish with sprigs of watercress.

PREPARING VEAL ESCALOPES

The slice of veal fillet used for Wiener Schnitzel is correctly called an escalope, but is also known variously as a scallop, scallopine or collop. It must be sliced as thin as possible; no amount of beating will help a slice that is too thick – it will merely revert to size while being cooked. Butchers do not often prepare this cut so it is a good idea to learn how to do it yourself.

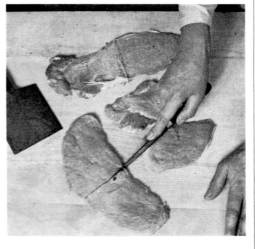

1. Place the escalopes on a board. Trim off any excess fat and, with a very sharp knife, divide each escalope in half.

2. Have a bowl of cold water handy in which to dip your meat beater. This prevents the meat from tearing. Alternatively, lay the escalopes between greaseproof paper before beating.

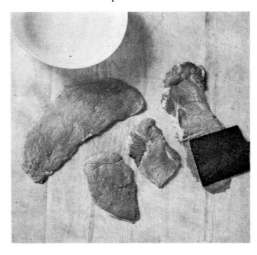

3. Beat out each half escalope into small individual escalopes.

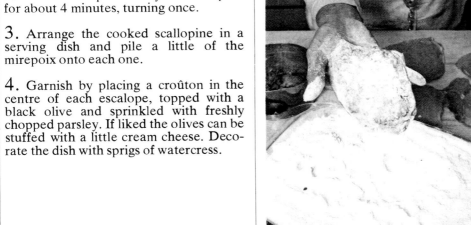

4. Dip in flour before preparing as wished.

Baked Escalopes with Cream Sauce

4 veal escalopes
oil
1 onion
¼ lb (225 g) mushrooms
salt and pepper
dry white wine
2 egg yolks
7 fl oz (200 ml) single cream

1. Set oven at 375°F (190°C) or Mark 5.

2. Tear off 4 generous size strips of foil, brush the centre of each piece with oil and lay one escalope on each.

3. Peel and grate the onion. Wash and slice the mushrooms finely, including the stalks. Then cover each escalope with a layer of onion followed by a layer of chopped mushroom. Season with salt and pepper.

4. Sprinkle a little white wine over each escalope – just sufficient to moisten the mushrooms. Pinch the foil together at the top to make loose parcels, taking care to turn up the corners to prevent liquor escaping during baking.

5. Place the foil parcels on a baking tray and bake in the pre-set oven for 45 minutes or until cooked.

6. Meanwhile prepare liaison for the sauce. Beat the 2 egg yolks together with 1 fl oz (25 ml) of the cream.

7. When the escalopes are cooked, strain off the excess liquor from each one into a small pan and arrange them in a heated serving dish. Add the cream to the pan, bring to the boil and simmer for about 5 minutes. Add a little of this sauce to the liaison, blend in well, then return to the pan and reheat, stirring continuously, but do not allow to reboil. Check for seasoning. Now pour this rich creamy sauce around the escalopes in their dish and serve, if liked, with Dauphine potatoes sprinkled with chopped parsley.

1. Place an escalope in each piece of foil. Sprinkle with grated onion, and salt and pepper to taste.

2. Sprinkle on some of the chopped mushrooms.

3. Flick a little white wine over the veal to moisten it before wrapping up the foil parcels and baking.

Baked Escalopes with Cream Sauce.

Bocconcini

3 veal escalopes
3 slices of cooked ham
dried sage
Gruyère cheese
2 oz (50 g) butter
2 fl oz (50 ml) dry white wine
4 fl oz (100 ml) well flavoured stock
1 tbsp (15 ml) tomato purée
salt and pepper

1. Divide each escalope in half and beat out well. Divide the cooked ham as well and place a piece of ham on each small escalope. Add a pinch of sage and a finger of Gruyère cheese. Roll up each one and secure with a cocktail stick.

2. Melt the butter in a heavy based pan, add the veal rolls and allow them to brown on all sides. Now add the wine, stock, tomato purée and seasoning. Cover and cook for about 30 minutes.

3. Remove the veal rolls to a heated dish, boil up the sauce until sufficiently reduced and pour over.

Veal with Chestnut Sauce

6 veal cutlets
1 tbsp (15 ml) oil
1 tbsp (15 ml) dry white wine
¼ clove crushed garlic
chopped parsley
salt and pepper
butter
parsley or lemon for garnish
1 can chestnut purée
brown stock

1. Make a marinade with the oil and wine and add the garlic, seasoning and a little chopped parsley. Put in the veal cutlets and leave for several hours.

2. Set oven at 350°F (180°C) or Mark 4.

3. Remove the cutlets from the marinade and place them in an ovenproof dish without draining. Put a little butter on the top of each one, cover with foil and cook in the pre-set oven for about 45 minutes.

4. To make the chestnut sauce: heat a can of chestnut purée with enough brown stock to give a smooth consistency. Stir thoroughly and pour over the cutlets.

Escalopes with Mushrooms.

Escalopes with Mushrooms

4 veal escalopes
1 oz (25 g) butter
1 fl oz (25 ml) oil
seasoned flour
1 shallot or small onion
¾ pt (450 ml) stock
8 oz (225 g) mushrooms
4 fl oz (100 ml) dry white wine
salt and black pepper

For garnish
3 oz (75 g) diced carrot
1 lb (450 g) creamed potatoes

1. Divide each escalope in half and beat each piece well so that you have 8 small escalopes. Dip them in seasoned flour.

2. Peel and grate the shallot. Wash and slice the mushrooms finely with their stalks. Heat the oil and butter in a frying pan and add the shallot. Allow to cook for about a minute before adding the escalopes. Brown them lightly on both sides, then lower the heat and add the stock. Leave to simmer for about 5 minutes.

3. Place the mushrooms in a small pan, season with black pepper and add the wine. Cover and simmer gently until soft.

4. Now add mushrooms and their juice to the frying pan with the escalopes. After 2 minutes remove the veal to a warmed dish and boil the sauce briskly until sufficiently reduced. Pour round the veal, sprinkle with steamed diced carrot and pipe on rosettes of creamed potatoes.

Sauté of Veal

1 lb (450 g) top leg of veal
2 small onions
6 oz (175 g) mushrooms
2 oz (50 g) butter
2 fl oz (50 ml) olive oil
seasoned flour
¾ pt (450 ml) white stock
¼ pt (150 ml) single cream
salt and pepper
1 tbsp (15 ml) freshly chopped parsley

1. Peel and slice the onions finely. Wash and slice the mushrooms with their stalks.

2. Cut the meat into narrow strips and toss in seasoned flour. Shake in a sieve to remove any excess flour.

3. Heat the butter and oil together in a frying pan. Add the onions and cook gently until soft and transparent. Then add the mushrooms and cook for 3–4 minutes.

4. Now add the floured veal pieces to the pan. Once browned, tip in a little of the given stock and blend in well. Add the rest of the stock and bring to the boil.

5 Pour in the cream, a little at a time, stirring continuously. Season with salt and pepper and then add the parsley.

6. Tip into a warmed dish and serve with broad beans and croûtons.

1. Cover the strips of veal with seasoned flour, place in a sieve and shake off the surplus flour.

2. Add veal to the vegetables in the pan and cook, stirring continuously.

3. When the veal is browned, add the wine or stock over a fierce heat.

4. When the sauce has thickened pour in the cream, working it in well.

5. Season with salt and pepper.

6. Stir in the chopped parsley.

Easter Lamb.

Easter Lamb

1 saddle of lamb
1 clove garlic
salt
2 oz (50 g) butter

For garnish
6 lambs kidneys
6 rashers back bacon
2 lb (900 g) spring greens
1 white cabbage

1. Set oven at 375°F (190°C) or Mark 5.

2. Crush the garlic clove with a little salt. Cream the butter and add the garlic.

3. Spread the saddle of lamb with the garlic butter and wrap in foil. Roast in the pre-set oven for 1¼–1½ hours. Fold back the foil and cook for another 30 minutes.

4. Halve the kidneys, remove skin and core. Halve the bacon rashers and wrap half a kidney in each piece of bacon. Sec-ure them with toothpicks and bake in the oven for the last 20 minutes of roasting time.

5. Wash and shred the spring greens and white cabbage and steam in separate containers until tender.

6. Arrange the cooked cabbage on a warmed serving dish, place the saddle of lamb on it and garnish with the bacon and kidney rolls.

Meat

Carré d'Agneau

*1 best end of neck weighing about 2 lb
  (900 g)*
dripping for roasting
3½ oz (90 g) butter
2 tbsp (30 ml) freshly chopped parsley
1 clove garlic
salt
black pepper
fresh breadcrumbs

1. Set oven at 375°F (190°C) or Mark 5.

2. Skin the joint if your butcher has not already done so. Then make a deep incision across the joint about 2½ inches (6 cm) from the ends of the cutlet bones. Peel away the fat and meat, then cut down between the bones and remove the meat which joins them. Scrape away any clinging pieces so that the bones are quite clean.

3. Wrap the bones with foil to protect them from charring. Melt a very small amount of dripping in the roasting tin. Season the joint and roast in the pre-set oven for about 45 minutes.

4. Meanwhile prepare the crumb crust. Melt the butter in a pan and crush the garlic with a little salt. Remove the butter from the heat, add the chopped parsley, the crushed garlic and pepper to season. Then start to add the breadcrumbs and blend well together until the mixture forms a smooth paste.

5. Remove joint from the oven and increase the oven temperature to 425°F (220°C) or Mark 7. Once the lamb has cooled sufficiently to handle, spread the paste evenly over the fat side of the joint. Return it to the oven to brown for 10–15 minutes.

6. If you are serving this dish for a special occasion top the bones with cutlet frills and serve with colourful vegetable accompaniments.

Carré d'Agneau with Vegetables.

BONING A LEG OF LAMB

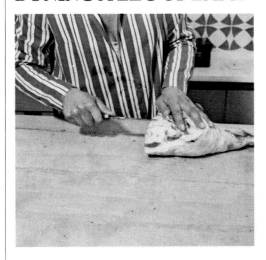

1. Lay the leg of lamb upside down with the broad end facing you. Insert a sharp knife into the joint and ease it round the edge of the bone.

2. Pare away the flesh from the bone until it begins to emerge.

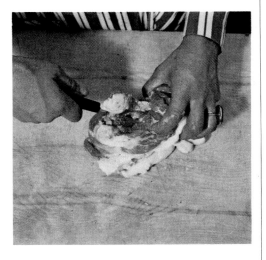

3. Continue to work the knife round the bone, freeing it from gristle.

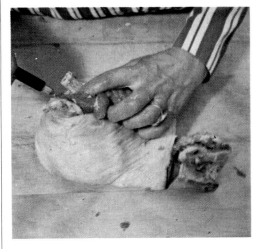

4. Now turn the joint round the other way and approach the bone from this end with the same paring movement, until the flesh comes easily away from it.

5. Turn the joint round again. Hold the broad end bone with the left hand and begin to scrape with the knife down towards the tip end.

6. As the bone becomes looser, continue to roll the flesh back from it until you can pull the bone free.

7. Reshape the joint. The bone on the left has been removed whole; the bones on the right show the same bone after it has been cut in half for easier removal.

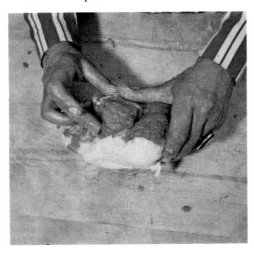

8. Stuff the meat with chosen stuffing and sew up both ends with thread.

9. The finished joint ready for roasting. Remove the thread before serving.

Guard of Honour

2 best end of neck joints of equal size
dripping for roasting
salt and pepper

1. Set oven at 375°F (190°C) or Mark 5.

2. Place one of the joints on a chopping board with the fat side up. Skin the meat if your butcher has not already done so. Then, with a very sharp knife, cut straight across the joint right through to the cutlet bones at the point where the meatiest part of the cutlets ends. Peel away the meat and fat from the bones.

3. Now turn the joint upside down and cut down between the bones to remove the meat which joins them. Scrape any remaining fat or meat from the bones leaving them quite clean. Season the meat.

4. Repeat this process with the second best end of neck. Then place the 2 joints facing one another so that the cutlet bones interlace. Cover the bones with foil to prevent them turning black while roasting.

5. Melt a little dripping in the roasting pan, place the joint in it and roast in the pre-set oven for about an hour depending on the size of the joints. Decorate with cutlet frills and serve with sweetcorn and flageolets if liked.

1. Make an incision through to the bone and pare away the flesh and fat.

2. Cut the meat back from the bones so that the bones are exposed.

3. Scrape the bones really clean.

4. Prepare the second joint as before. Stand the 2 joints face to face and push together so that the bones interlace.

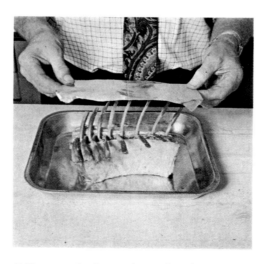

5. Prevent the bones from charring by covering them with a sheet of foil.

Guard of Honour with Sweetcorn and Flageolet Beans.

Meat

Mutton Soubise

1 shoulder of mutton
stock
4 onions
1 carrot
2 parsley stalks
bouquet garni
onion cream sauce

1. Wipe the meat and trim off the excess fat. Place the joint on a trivet in a large saucepan.

2. Pour on enough boiling stock to cover. Peel and quarter the onions, slice the carrot into rounds.

3. Add the vegetables to the pan with the herbs. Cover and simmer until the meat is tender – the exact time will depend on the size of the joint.

4. Take out the cooked shoulder of mutton and place on a serving dish. Cover with plenty of hot onion cream sauce.

Onion Cream Sauce

Basic Recipe

8 oz (225 g) onions
milk to cover
3 fl oz (100 ml) double cream
salt and pepper

1. Peel and slice the onions finely. Place them in a pan and add enough milk to cover well. Cover and cook until soft.

2. Strain off the milk and reserve. Pass the onions through a nylon sieve.

3. Return the milk to pan and cook gently until reduced to about 4 tbsp (60 ml). Then add the sieved onions and double cream. Season with salt and pepper.

WINGED VICTORY

1. Remove the skin from a saddle of lamb.

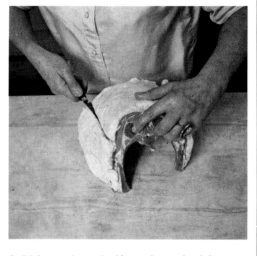

2. Using a sharp knife make an incision from left to right through to the bones on both sides of the joint.

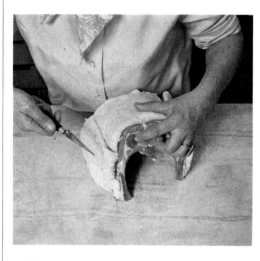

3. Note exact position of the incision.

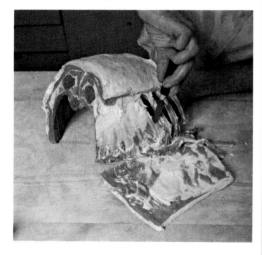

4. Pare away the meat from the bone below the incision line so that the bones are bare on both sides.

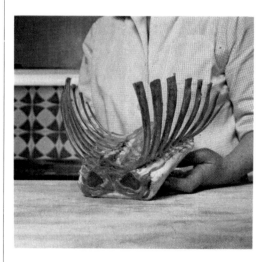

5. This is the prepared joint ready for roasting as for Guard of Honour.

French Roast Lamb

1 small leg of lamb weighing about 3 lb
   (1.5 kg)
1 aubergine
6 tomatoes
2 courgettes
1 green pepper
½ lb (225 g) mushrooms
2 onions
salt and pepper
2 cloves garlic
3 oz (75 g) butter
2 tbsp (30 ml) freshly chopped parsley

For garnish
1 lb (450 g) French beans
4 tomatoes

1. Set oven at 350°F (180°C) or Mark 4.

2. Prepare the vegetables. Wash and slice the aubergine and chop up the tomatoes. Top and tail the courgettes and cut into rounds. Remove core and pips from the pepper and chop into dice. Wash and slice the mushrooms. Peel and slice the onions.

3. Peel and chop up the garlic cloves and crush them in a pestle and mortar with a little salt. Cream the butter, add the crushed garlic and chopped parsley and blend well together.

4. Line the baking tin with foil. Score the fat surface of the leg of lamb with a sharp knife and chop off the knuckle bone. Spread the joint with the garlic butter.

5. Lay the prepared vegetables in the bottom of the baking tin and season well with salt and pepper. You can also add the knuckle bone if wished. Then place the joint on top of the vegetables and cover with a piece of foil.

6. Bake on the centre shelf of the pre-set oven for about 1 hour and 30 minutes. Remove the foil from the top of the joint for the last 30 minutes of cooking time to allow it to brown well.

7. Serve the cooked joint with the baked vegetables and garnish with French beans and grilled tomatoes.

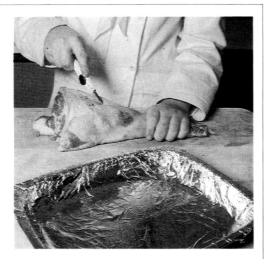

1. Score the lamb skin lightly.

2. Cut off the knuckle bone. Spread the joint generously with garlic butter.

3. Arrange the prepared vegetables in a foil lined baking tin and lay the leg of lamb on top of the vegetables.

Lamb Baked in Puff Pastry

1 small to medium size leg of lamb
dripping for roasting
2 lb (900 g) puff pastry
beaten egg

For stuffing
8 oz (225 g) pork sausage meat
1 onion
oil for frying
1 tbsp (15 ml) freshly chopped parsley
1 tbsp (15 ml) dried mixed herbs
1 clove garlic
salt and pepper

1. Set oven at 400°F (200°C) or Mark 6.

2. Bone out the joint.

3. Prepare the stuffing. Peel and chop the onion finely. Heat a little oil in a pan and cook onion gently until soft and transparent. Place sausage meat in a bowl, add the herbs, cooked onion and the garlic, crushed. Season with salt and pepper and mix together well.

4. Stuff the lamb with this mixture and sew up ready for roasting. Place in a roasting pan with some dripping and roast in the pre-set oven for 20 minutes per lb (450 g). Remove joint from the oven and cool joint quickly.

5. Meanwhile roll out the puff pastry into 2 sections, one long and narrow and the other square.

6. Brush the cooled lamb joint with cold water and encase the broad end with the square piece of pastry. Cut the other section into long strips measuring about 1½ inches (4 cm) across and wrap them round the joint gradually working up to the narrow end. Make sure that each piece is sealed well to the last by brushing with beaten egg.

7. Brush the joint all over with beaten egg, place on a clean baking sheet and continue to bake in the moderately hot oven until pastry is crisp and brown – about 30 minutes.

Noisettes of Lamb

*2 lb (900 g) best end of neck
  or loin of lamb
2 tsp (10 ml) chopped mixed herbs
salt and pepper*

1. Using a very sharp knife cut the bone from the meat. Sprinkle the underside of the meat with herbs and season with salt and pepper. Then roll the joint up very tightly and use skewers to hold it together.

2. Tie string around the joint at 1 inch intervals. Now slice into noisettes.

3. To cook, roast in the oven for 15–20 minutes at 375°F (190°C) or Mark 5, or else fry in butter for 6–7 minutes.

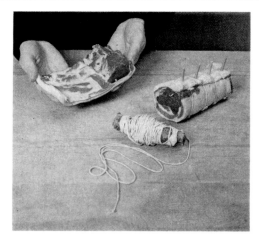

1. You can make noisettes with either best end of neck or a loin of lamb. Whichever joint you use the technique is basically the same. Skin the joint, trim any surplus fat and remove all the bones if the butcher has not already done so.

2. Roll the joint up tightly and use short wooden skewers to hold it in place.

3. Tie up with string in sections of about 1½ inches (4 cm).

Noisettes of Lamb.

Lamb Cutlets à la Nivernaise

6 lamb cutlets
salt and pepper
plain flour
beaten egg
breadcrumbs
1½ lb (675 g) carrots

1. Remove the meat and fat from each cutlet bone, scraping each bone clean. Season cutlets, then dip each one first in flour, then in beaten egg, and lastly in breadcrumbs.

2. Deep fry the cutlets in hot oil until golden brown. Drain well, arrange on a serving dish, put cutlets frills on and keep warm.

3. Peel and slice carrots into rounds. Steam until tender. Place a carrot slice on each cutlet and purée the remaining carrots. Season the purée and pipe it round the cutlets. Serve with French beans and sauté potatoes.

Sweet and Sour Kebabs

2 lb (450 g) boned lamb, cut from the leg
large can pineapple chunks
2 tbsp (30 ml) lemon juice
2 tbsp (30 ml) soy sauce
1 clove garlic
12 black olives

1. Strain the pineapple chunks and place in a bowl. Add the soy sauce, lemon juice and the crushed clove of garlic.

2. Cube the meat and marinate overnight in the pineapple mixture.

3. Drain the meat. Thread pieces of lamb onto kebab skewers alternately with stoned black olives and drained pineapple chunks.

4. Turn on the grill to its highest setting. Lay the full kebab skewers in the grill pan. Baste with marinade and keep turning the skewers, basting well, until the meat is cooked.

Lamb Chops with Garnish.

Lamb Chops with Garnish

2 lamb chump chops
1 lb (450 g) new potatoes
2 large tomatoes
1 oz (25 g) butter
1 fl oz (25 ml) oil
2 tsp (10 ml) freshly chopped parsley
  or chives
watercress

1. Wash and scrape the new potatoes. Boil in lightly salted water until just tender.

2. Heat the oil and butter in a frying pan. Seal the chops over strong heat, then reduce the heat and cook for another 6–7 minutes. Place the chops on a heated serving dish and keep warm.

3. Cut the tomatoes in half and fry in the meat juices. Drain the potatoes and toss in a little butter.

4. Arrange the tomatoes and potatoes on the dish with the chops and garnish with watercress.

Roast Stuffed Blade of Pork

1 blade of pork weighing
 2½–3lb (1.25–1.5 kg)

For stuffing
4 oz (100 g) breadcrumbs
2 small onions
2 oz (50 g) bacon
2 oz (50 g) sultanas
1 tbsp (15 ml) chopped chives or parsley
2 tsp (10 ml) mild paprika
salt and pepper
beaten egg

1. Set oven at 350°F (180°C) or Mark 4.

2. Now bone out the joint. Pull away the skin. Then take a very sharp pointed knife and gradually work the meat away from the flat bone in the joint. Do this on both sides of the bone until you can remove the whole bone.

3. Now prepare the stuffing. Peel and chop the onion into small dice. Chop the bacon and fry lightly. Add the onion and cook gently until soft and transparent. Place the crumbs in a bowl, add the onion, bacon, herbs and seasoning. Mix together well, then add enough beaten egg to bind.

4. Sew up one side of the joint, add the stuffing from the other side and then sew it together as well. Season the meat. Add a small amount of water to the roasting pan and roast the joint in the centre of the pre-set oven for about 2 hours basting from time to time.

1. Remove skin on the top of the joint.

2. Using a sharp knife, pare away flesh from the flat blade bone.

3. Continue the paring movement until the bone is exposed down to the ridge.

Roast Stuffed Blade of Pork with Savoury Crust.

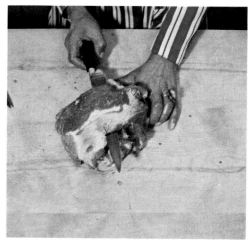

Pork Geneva

1½ lb (675 g) seedless white grapes
2½ lb (1¼ kg) boned rolled loin of pork
½ tsp (3 ml) salt
½ tsp (3 ml) black pepper
½ tsp (3 ml) ground coriander
½ clove garlic
1 finely chopped shallot
8 crushed juniper berries
½ tbsp (8 ml) plus ½ tsp (3 ml)
　　Worcestershire sauce
1 oz (25 g) butter or margarine
3 fl oz (75 ml) plus ½ tbsp (8 ml) dry
　　white wine
1 fl oz (25 ml) gin
½ tbsp (8 ml) cornflour
cayenne pepper

To garnish
1 oz (25 g) butter
1 lb (450 g) seedless white grapes

1. Extract the juice from the grapes and discard the pulp. Trim the pork of excess fat. Place in a shallow dish and rub with salt and pepper. Pour over the grape juice. Add the coriander, berries, garlic, half the shallot and ½ tbsp (8 ml) of the Worcestershire sauce. Leave to marinate for 8 hours.

2. Remove the pork from the marinade and set aside, reserving the marinade. Melt the butter over a moderate heat in a large casserole and add the remaining half shallot. Cook for a few minutes until soft but not brown. Then cook the pork in the casserole for a few minutes, turning occasionally. When lightly browned, add the juniper berries, wine, a pinch of cayenne pepper, the rest of the Worcestershire sauce and about half of the marinade. Bring liquid to the boil then cover; reduce the heat to low and cook until well done. To test: pierce meat with a knife point. The juices which run out should be clear.

3. To make the garnish. Melt the butter in a pan over a low heat. Add the grapes and cook until lightly browned. Remove from the heat and keep warm.

4. Warm the gin; pour over the pork and set alight. When the flames have died down, transfer to a serving dish and arrange the grapes around it. Dissolve the cornflour in ½ tbsp white wine and stir into the casserole liquid. Increase the heat slightly and cook for 10 minutes stirring frequently. Serve sauce separately.

4. With the flesh away from the ridge, put the knife right through and sever. Take out the bone and reshape joint.

Variation:
For a blade of pork topped with a savoury crust, blend 8 oz (225 g) fresh breadcrumbs with enough melted garlic butter to bind thoroughly. Remove the rind from the roasted joint. Pile the mixture on top of the pork and increase the oven temperature to the highest setting. Return the joint to the oven on a high shelf and brown the crust.

Meat

Sweet and Sour Spare Ribs

2 lb (450 g) pork spare ribs
3 tbsp (45 ml) soy sauce
salt
2 tsp (10 ml) brown sugar
3 tbsp (45 ml) sherry
2 tbsp (30 ml) pineapple pulp
2 tbsp (30 ml) wine vinegar
1 tbsp (15 ml) arrowroot

1. Cut the meat into individual ribs and place in a pan with ½ pt (300 ml) water, the soy sauce and a pinch of salt.

2. Bring to the boil, cover and simmer for about an hour, stirring occasionally.

3. Stir in the sugar and increase the heat. Add the sherry, pineapple pulp and vinegar. Keep stirring as the mixture bubbles vigorously.

4. Blend the arrowroot in a little water and stir into the sauce. Stir well until the liquid is reduced and clear.

Apple Sauce

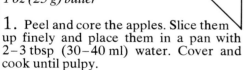

1 lb (450 g) cooking apples
1 tbsp (15 ml) sugar
1 oz (25 g) butter

1. Peel and core the apples. Slice them up finely and place them in a pan with 2–3 tbsp (30–40 ml) water. Cover and cook until pulpy.

2. Beat with a wooden spoon, add the sugar and butter and serve hot.

Roast Pork with Crackling

1 loin or leg of pork
cooking salt
2 lb (900 g) potatoes
1 large can celery hearts
freshly chopped parsley
1 tbsp (15 ml) plain flour
¾ pt (450 ml) stock

1. Set oven at 350°F (180°C) or Mark 4.

2. Place the joint on a board and choose the sharpest knife you can find. The secret of good crackling is very thorough scoring. The rind of the pork should be scored at ¼ inch (1 cm) intervals, the knife cutting deep into the soft fat underneath.

3. Once you have scored the joint, rub cooking salt into it. Then place on a baking tin with no additional fat and roast in the pre-set oven on the middle shelf. Cook for 25 minutes per lb (450 g) and 25 minutes over.

4. Peel the potatoes and cut into even size pieces. Place them in a pan of cold salted water and bring to the boil. Drain and dry thoroughly. Place them in the fat around the meat 45 minutes before the end of the roasting time. Turn them over halfway through their cooking time.

5. About 30 minutes before the end of the cooking time take joint out of the oven, baste thoroughly and raise the temperature to 450°F (230°C) or Mark 8. Return joint to oven and baste again 15 minutes later.

6. Tip the celery into a pan and heat in its own juice. Dish the pork up on a warmed serving dish, surround with the roast potatoes and the celery and sprinkle with chopped parsley.

7. To make the gravy, tip off all but about 1 tbsp (15 ml) of fat from the roasting tin. Add the flour and blend in well. Then tip in the stock and allow to bubble up well before serving in a sauce boat.

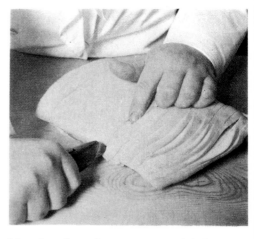

Most butchers do not score pork joints to produce the best crackling. Usually their scoring is too wide and not deep enough. For really crispy crackling, the rind should be scored at ¼ inch (1 cm) intervals and the cuts should be deep. Joints from the hind quarters of the pig give the best crackling.

Roast Pork with Crackling.

Pork Stuffed with Prunes

1 boned and rolled loin of pork weighing
4 lb (1.75 kg)
18 prunes
strained tea
1 tbsp (15 ml) plain flour
½ pt (300 ml) stock
2 tbsp (30 ml) sherry
salt and pepper
sprigs of parsley

1. Leave the prunes to soak in strained, freshly brewed tea overnight. Stone them just before using.

2. Set oven at 375°F (190°C) or Mark 5.

3. Use a larding needle or a skewer to make a cavity in the rolled joint. With a long knife or similar implement push the soaked prunes into the joint. Reserve remaining prunes and tea marinade. Cover the bottom of the roasting tin with a small amount of water and place the joint in it. Roast in the centre of the pre-set oven for about 2 hours basting occasionally.

4. Poach the reserved prunes in their marinade until tender.

5. Place the cooked joint on a serving dish and keep warm. Add the flour to the meat juices in the roasting tin and blend in well. Then add the stock stirring well and followed by the sherry. Bring to the boil and season with salt and pepper. Pour into a sauce boat to serve.

6. Garnish the joint with the poached prunes and sprigs of parsley. Serve with apple sauce, roast potatoes and sautéed mushrooms.

1. Push a larding needle through the rolled boned joint. Pull it out with the meat it contains in the groove.

2. Using a sharp knife make this cavity large enough for you to stuff with prunes.

Pork Stuffed with Prunes.

Meat

Pork Chops with Tortellini

2 lean loin pork chops
olive oil
½ lb (225 g) tortellini
2 oz (50 g) butter
1 tsp (5 ml) ground rosemary
2 tsp (10 ml) dried sage
salt and black pepper
sprigs of parsley

1. Trim off any rind on the chops. This can be grilled separately and used for garnish. Brush the chops with olive oil and grill slowly on both sides for 15–20 minutes, making sure that the meat is cooked through without burning the outsides. Season to taste and keep the chops warm until ready to serve.

2. Tip pasta into a large pan of boiling salted water. Bring back to the boil and cook for 12–15 minutes. Strain and return to pan with the butter. Then sprinkle in the dried herbs and season with salt and pepper.

3. Have ready a warmed serving dish. Tip the pasta onto this and lay the pork chops on top. Garnish with sprigs of parsley.

Note: Tortellini is a stuffed variety of pasta. If you are unable to obtain it the dish can be made just as well with tagliatelli (noodles). Tagliatelli will require only 10–12 minutes cooking.

Pork Fillets Baked in Puff Pastry

2 small pork fillets
¾ lb (350 g) puff pastry
beaten egg

For marinade
¼ pt (150 ml) dry cider
2 tbsp (30 ml) olive oil
1 shallot or small onion
4 oz (100 g) mushrooms
1 sprig thyme
1 stick celery
4 peppercorns
2 parsley stalks
salt and pepper

1. The pork fillets should be marinated overnight. To prepare the marinade, peel and chop the shallot very finely. Wash and slice the mushrooms including the stalks. Wash and chop up the celery. Lay the fillets in an ovenproof dish, pour over the cider and oil and add the shallot, mushrooms, celery, herbs and seasoning.

2. Set oven at 350°F (180°C) or Mark 4.

3. Divide the pastry in half and roll into 2 pieces large enough to fold generously over each pork fillet.

4. Remove fillets from marinade and drain well. Then lay each one on a piece of pastry. Remove the mushrooms from the marinade, squeeze out any excess liquid and place some on top of each fillet.

5. Fold the pastry over the fillets and brush the edges with water to secure them well. Tuck joined edges underneath. Brush pastry with beaten egg, place on a baking tray and cook on the shelf above centre for 30 minutes. If pastry gets too brown, cover with foil.

6. Meanwhile remove celery, parsley, thyme and peppercorns from the marinade leaving just the shallot in the liquid. Tip this into a pan and simmer gently until shallot is cooked. Serve separately with the pork.

Pork Chops with Tortellini.

Pork Fillets Baked in Puff Pastry.

Meat

Kidney and Liver Sauté.

Kidney and Liver Sauté

6 lambs' kidneys
¼ lb (100 g) lambs liver
1 large onion
1½ oz (35 g) butter
1¼ fl oz (35 ml) oil
¼ pt (150 ml) stock
1 tbsp (15 ml) tomato purée
salt and pepper

For garnish
¾ lb (350 g) carrots
1 lb creamed potatoes for piping
croûtons
1 oz (25 g) freshly grated Parmesan cheese

1. Peel and chop the carrots into rounds and simmer in slightly salted water until tender. Prepare the creamed potato for piping.

2. Peel and chop the onion very finely. Heat the butter and oil in a pan, add the onion and cook until soft and transparent.

3. Halve the kidneys, remove skin and core, and cut liver into thin strips. Wash well and dry. Add kidneys to the pan followed by the stock. Then add the liver and simmer gently for a few minutes. Add the tomato purée and season with salt and pepper.

4. Have ready a warmed serving dish. Tip the kidney and liver mixture into the centre. Surround with the cooked carrots and then pipe creamed potato round the edge. Garnish with croûtons and sprinkle the finished dish with Parmesan cheese.

Liver Créole

1¼ lb (675 g) calves' liver
4 bananas
3 tbsp (45 ml) fresh breadcrumbs
4 rashers bacon
oil
butter
1 tbsp (15 ml) plain flour
7 fl oz (200 ml) stock
salt and pepper to taste

1. Turn on the grill to a moderate heat.

2. Halve the bananas lengthwise and brush in a little butter. Coat in bread-crumbs and brown under the grill. Keep warm.

3. Remove the rind from the bacon, roll up the rashers and cook under the grill. Keep warm.

4. Heat a little oil and butter in a frying pan and fry the liver for about 3 minutes on each side. Arrange on a serving dish and keep warm.

5. Add the flour to the frying pan and blend with the pan juices. Gradually stir in the stock and seasoning. Simmer 1–2 minutes.

6. Strain the sauce over the liver and garnish with bacon rolls and bananas. Serve with boiled rice.

Kidneys and Mushrooms in Wine Sauce

8 lambs' kidneys
2 oz (50 g) butter
1 onion
6 oz (175 g) mushrooms
1 tbsp (15 ml) plain flour
7 fl oz (200 ml) white wine
¼ pt (150 ml) stock
salt and pepper
3 tbsp (45 ml) double cream

1. Skin, halve and core the kidneys. Peel and chop the onion finely. Wash and slice the mushrooms.

2. Melt the butter in a pan, add the kidneys and sauté for about 5 minutes. Take them out and set aside.

3. Now add chopped onion and mushrooms to the pan. After 3 or 4 minutes, blend in the flour. Then pour in the wine and stock and bring to the boil. Return the kidneys to the pan and simmer for 10–12 minutes. Finally add the cream and season with salt and pepper.

4. Serve with plainly boiled rice and runner beans.

Kidneys in Puff Pastry.

Kidneys in Puff Pastry

6 pigs' kidneys
6 rashers streaky bacon
1 lb puff pastry
English mustard
dried tarragon
beaten egg

For garnish
3 tomatoes
flaked almonds
watercress

1. Set oven at 375°F (190°C) or Mark 5.

2. Slit the kidneys down one side, remove skin and core. De-rind the bacon, fold rashers in half and slip one into each kidney.

3. Roll out the pastry and cut into 6 rectangular pieces – about 6 inches by 8 inches. Spread some made English mustard in the centre of each and lay a stuffed kidney on top. Spread the kidney with a little more mustard and add a pinch of dried tarragon. Fold over the pastry and brush the edges with cold water before sealing. Tuck the edges underneath.

4. Brush the pastry with beaten egg, place on a baking tray and bake in the pre-set oven on the shelf above the middle for about 40 minutes.

5. Serve garnished with flaked almonds, browned under the grill, watercress and grilled tomatoes.

Roast Stuffed Capon.

Poultry and game

Roast Stuffed Capon

1 capon
butter
salt and pepper

For stuffing
4 oz (100 g) butter
4 oz (100 g) fresh white breadcrumbs
grated rind of 1 lemon
4 tbsp (60 ml) freshly chopped parsley
marjoram
salt and pepper

1. Set oven at 375°F (190°C) or Mark 5.

2. Prepare the stuffing. Melt butter in a saucepan. Place breadcrumbs, lemon rind chopped parsley and a pinch of marjoram in a bowl. Pour over the melted butter and season with salt and pepper. Mix together well and spoon into the carcass. Skewer the tail end closed and tie the legs firmly in position.

3. Spread the capon with some of the butter and season with salt and pepper. Put the remaining butter in the roasting tin and place the bird in it.

4. Cover with a buttered paper and roast in the pre-set oven for 20 minutes per lb (450 g) plus 20 minutes. Towards the end of cooking time remove the paper and baste the bird well to brown.

5. Serve with bread sauce and artichoke bottoms filled with peas.

Poultry and game

Spanish Chicken

6 chicken breasts
2 oz (50 g) plain flour
1 tsp (5 ml) salt
½ tsp (2 ml) black pepper
2 fl oz (50 ml) olive oil
2 cloves garlic
1 onion
1 pimiento
1 green pepper
10 fl oz (300 ml) chicken stock
2 tbsp (10 ml) butter
8 oz (225 g) mushrooms
6 tomatoes
10 stuffed green olives
10 stoned black olives

1. Set oven at 325°F (160°C) or Mark 3.

2. Mix the flour, salt and pepper and coat the chicken in this seasoned flour. Heat the oil in a large pan and brown the chicken all over then transfer to a casserole.

3. Crush the garlic. Slice the onion, pimiento and green pepper, and fry these for 5 minutes then transfer to the casserole.

4. Pour hot stock over the chicken and vegetables. Cover the casserole and cook in the pre-set oven for 1–1¼ hours or until the chicken is tender.

5. Slice the mushrooms and tomatoes. Halve the stuffed olives. Fry the mushrooms and tomatoes in butter for 5 minutes and add to the casserole with both types of olive. Return to the oven for a further 10 minutes.

CUTTING A CHICKEN INTO PIECES

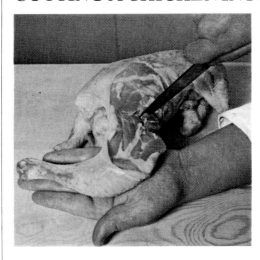

1. Skin the chicken and cut off the legs.

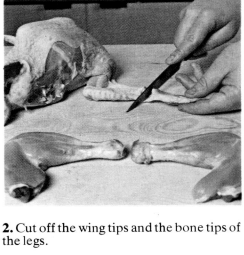

2. Cut off the wing tips and the bone tips of the legs.

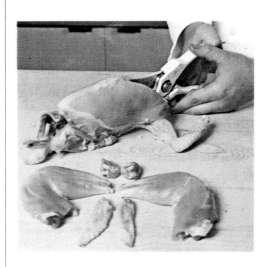

3. Cut right through the centre of the bird from head to tail.

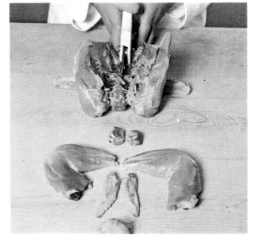

4. Remove the parson's nose and finish separating the 2 halves of the bird.

5. Cut the wing from the breast.

TRUSSING POULTRY

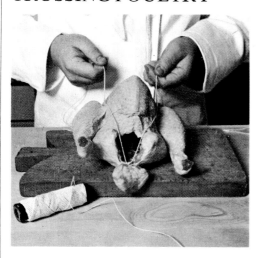

1. Tie string over the parson's nose leaving 2 long ends of string.

2. Wind string around the wings so that the wings are held against the body.

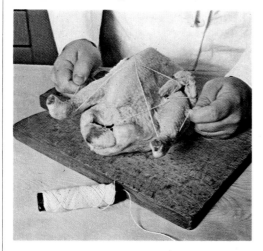

3. Cross the string over the breast then under and over the legs to pull them tight against the body.

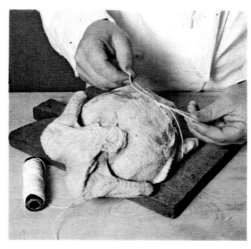

4. Turn the bird over and tie the string in a bow. When the bird is roasted, just pull the string to undo the bow.

If you wish to stuff poultry, do so before you truss it. Wash the inside well, retaining the giblets for gravy. Do not stuff the bird until just before you roast it, although you can make the stuffing in advance and keep in the refrigerator until needed. Spoon the stuffing generously into the bird and sew the opening together with thread and secure it with skewers.

Roast Poussins with Cream Sauce

3 double poussins
12 pistachio nuts
3 oz (75 g) ground almonds
2 oz (50 g) smooth pâté
1 tbsp (15 ml) dry sherry
2 tbsp (30 ml) double cream
salt and black pepper
butter

For the sauce
½ pt (300 ml) stock
2 sprigs thyme
pared rind from 1 orange
1 fl oz (25 ml) sherry
4 oz (100 g) canned or frozen petits pois
5 fl oz (125 ml) double cream
salt and pepper

Double poussins are baby chickens 6–10 weeks old. They are larger than ordinary poussins and one should be sufficient to serve 2 people.

1. Set oven at 400°F (200°C) or Mark 6.

2. Shell and halve the pistachio nuts. Place them in a bowl with the ground almonds, pâté, sherry and cream and season with black pepper. Blend the ingredients together well with a wooden spoon and place some of the mixture inside each of the birds. Allow frozen peas to thaw.

3. Spread the poussins with butter and season with salt and pepper. Place them in a roasting tin and cover well with foil.

4. Roast in the pre-set oven on the shelf above centre for about half an hour.

5. Meanwhile prepare the sauce. Pour the stock into a pan, add the thyme and the orange rind and simmer until reduced by half.

6. Pass the peas through a sieve and add them to the flavoured stock together with the sherry. Simmer for a few minutes, then add the cream and simmer again. Season to taste with salt and pepper and remove the thyme and the orange rind.

7. Arrange the roast poussins on a warmed serving dish and pour the sauce around them. Serve with new potatoes and French beans.

Poultry and game

Swiss Chicken

3½ lb (1.5 kg) roasting chicken
3 oz (75 g) butter
salt and pepper

For the sauce
2 tsp (10 ml) potato flour
¼ pt (150 ml) dry white wine
4 oz (100 g) Gruyère cheese
1 clove garlic
2 egg yolks
¼ (150 ml) single cream

croûtons to serve

1. Set oven at 350°F (180°C) or Mark 4.

2. Brush the chicken with melted butter and season with salt and pepper. Cover loosely with foil and roast in the pre-set oven for 45 minutes. Keep warm on a serving dish.

3. Blend the potato flour with a little of the wine to make a smooth paste. Pour the wine into a heavy based pan with the grated Gruyère cheese and the crushed garlic. Place over a very low heat and cook until blended, stirring occasionally.

4. Beat the egg yolks with the cream. Add the potato flour paste to the cheese mixture. Stir vigorously to prevent separation. When thick and creamy, stir in the egg and cream mixture. Season.

5. Pour the sauce over the chicken and surround with croûtons to serve.

Chicken Provençale

3–3½ lb (1.5 kg) roasting chicken
butter
salt and pepper
4 fl oz (100 ml) olive oil
1 shallot or small onion
4 pimientos
½ tsp (2 ml) thyme or oregano
½ tsp (2 ml) basil
½ tsp (2 ml) chervil
12 black olives

For garnish
paprika pepper
watercress

1. Set oven at 375°F (190°C) or Mark 5.

2. Line the roasting tin with foil. Spread the chicken with butter and season with salt and pepper. Place it in the lined tin and cover with another piece of foil taking care not to wrap the chicken too tightly.

3. Roast the chicken in the pre-set oven for about an hour. Cooked in this way it should require no basting and emerge at the end of the cooking time beautifully browned.

4. While the chicken is roasting prepare the pimiento garnish. Peel and chop the shallot finely. Cut the pimientos in half and remove the seeds and core. Then cut them in half again. Cut the olives in half and remove the stones.

5. Heat the olive oil in a pan and add the chopped shallot and herbs. Cook gently until shallot is soft and transparent, then add the pimientos. When these are tender add the olives.

6. Dish the chicken up on a warmed serving dish and sprinkle with paprika. Spoon the pimiento mixture around it.

Chicken Provençale.

1. Line a baking tin with foil. Place the chicken in it. Season and brush the chicken with melted butter. Cover the bird with more foil and seal the edges.

2. The cooked chicken will be golden brown without any basting.

Spatchcock Chicken.

Spatchcock Chicken

4 poussins
black pepper
lemon juice
3 oz (75 g) butter

For garnish
watercress
wedges of lemon

1. Cut through the backs of the birds with a pair of scissors. Cut away the back-bone lay the poussins flat on a chopping board and beat well to flatten them.

2. Melt half of the given butter. Season the birds with black pepper, squeeze a little lemon juice over and brush with the melted butter. Then leave for 30 minutes before cooking.

3. Turn on the grill and melt the rest of the butter. Place the poussins under the grill, skin side uppermost, and grill slowly until a good golden brown. Brush with the melted butter when necessary. Turn over and grill on the other side. Allow about 7 minutes per side.

4. Arrange the cooked poussins on a warmed serving dish and pour over juices from the pan. Garnish with wedges of lemon and watercress. Allow one poussin per person.

Chicken Kiev

2 3¼ lb (1.5 kg) roasting chickens
4 oz (100 g) butter
salt and black pepper
seasoned flour
beaten egg
dried white breadcrumbs
oil for deep frying

1. Chop off the leg tips and first 2 wing joints from the chickens. Pinch the skin all over and then remove. Pull back each leg and cut away at the point where it joins the body of the chicken.

2. Now begin to cut away the breasts. Start by removing the wishbone. Then gently pare the flesh away from the breast bone gradually working right down to the wing. When you have cut around it sufficiently just pull the whole breast away from the carcass.

3. Lay it on a board with the inside facing up to you. You will see a delicate long piece of flesh loosely attached to the rest of the breast. Pull this away gently and reserve. This piece is called the 'filet'. With a very sharp knife make 2 horizontal slits in the thicker end of the breast taking great care not to cut right through the flesh. This will form a pocket to hold the wrapped butter.

4. Now dip the 'filet' in cold water and, using a meat batter, work it into a flat rectangular shape.

5. Place a 1 oz (25 g) knob of well chilled butter in the centre of the 'filet', season with salt and pepper and wrap up into a small parcel. Now tuck this into the pocket which you have made in the chicken breast. Re-shape with the fingertips so that butter is well sealed inside. Repeat this process with all 4 breast pieces. Then turn them in seasoned flour and dip in the beaten egg. Roll in breadcrumbs, pressing these on well. They are now ready for deep frying.

6. Place in the hot fat and cook for 6–7 minutes until crisp and golden brown. Drain on absorbent paper and serve garnished with parsley, potato crisps and corn on the cob if liked.

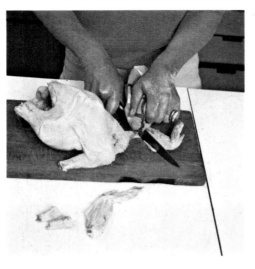

1. Remove the leg bone tips and the first 2 joints of the wing tips.

2. Pinch the skin on the breast and legs to loosen it, then pull the skin off.

6. Cut through the place where the wing bone meets the carcass.

7. Pare away the remaining wing bone piece with the filet attached and pull it out. Detach the filet and set aside.

11. Place a cube of butter in the centre of the filet and season.

12. Wrap the butter in the filet so that the butter is quite hidden.

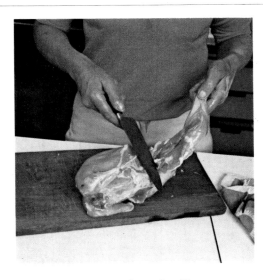

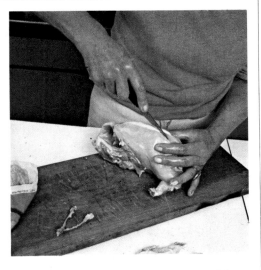

3. Pull the leg out as far as it will go until you see the bone where it joins the carcass. Cut right through this bone.

4. Hold the wishbone and scrape the flesh away right up to the tip. Remove the wishbone.

5. Cut along the breast bone on one side to pare away the breast.

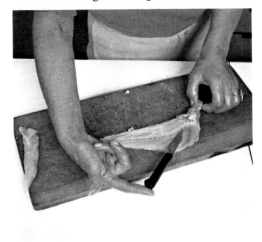

8. Lay the breast on a board and make an indentation down the centre from the bone tip to within 1 inch (2.5 cm) of the other end. Do not cut through.

9. Carefully cut through the fat flesh to make a wide, deep pocket on each side of the central indentation.

10. Dip the filet in cold water and beat into a wide flat piece of meat.

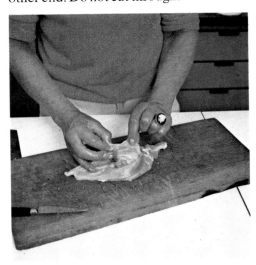

13. Place the butter parcel inside one of the pockets in the breast. Push it right in. Bring the second pocket over the first and press it down.

14. Shape the chicken piece so that one end is fat and the other tapers.

15. This is how the chicken portion should look before cooking.

Poultry and game

Chicken Marengo.

Chicken Marengo

1 3 lb (1.5 kg) roasting chicken
2¼ oz (65 g) butter
2¼ fl oz (65 ml) oil
¼ lb (100 g) button mushrooms
1 tbsp (15 ml) brandy
¼ pt (150 ml) white wine
7 fl oz (200 ml) white stock
8 crayfish (optional)
2 tbsp (30 ml) tomato purée

For garnish
8 heart shaped croûtes
4 fried eggs
chopped parsley

1. Cut the chicken into joints or get your butcher to do it for you. Heat the butter and oil in a pan and lay in the chicken joints skin side down. Cook slowly until golden brown on both sides. Remove and keep warm.

2. Add the mushrooms, washed but left whole. Cook until tender, then remove and keep warm.

3. Return the chicken joints to pan and increase the heat. Now add the brandy and set it alight. Shake the pan and allow it to burn for about half a minute. Lower the heat and add the wine and the stock.

4. Wash and clean the crayfish, if using, and add to the pan. Allow to simmer for about 10 minutes, then take them out and keep warm with the mushrooms.

5. Continue to cook the chicken until tender, then arrange the joints on a warmed serving dish and surround with the mushrooms and crayfish.

6. Bubble up the liquid in the pan, spoon in the tomato purée and stir in well. Once the sauce has thickened sufficiently, pour it over the chicken. Sprinkle with chopped parsley and garnish with heart shaped croûtes and a fried egg for each person.

Chicken with Orange Flavoured Sauce

1 boiling fowl weighing about 4 lb (1.75 kg)
3 onions
2 pt (1 l) white stock
bouquet garni
salt and pepper
½ lb (225 g) mushrooms
¼ pt (150 ml) white wine
¼ pt (150 ml) single cream
grated rind of ½ orange

For garnish
1½ lb (700 g) creamed potatoes
2 tbsp (30 ml) flaked almonds

1. Place the bird in a large pan. Peel and quarter the onions and add to pan. Season with salt and pepper and pour over the stock to cover. Tuck in the bouquet garni cover the pan and simmer very gently on top of the stove for about 1½–2 hours or until tender. Skim the fat off.

2. Wash and roughly chop the mushrooms. Brown and flaked almonds under the grill. When the chicken is cooked remove from pan leaving cooking liquid to cool for a little. Skin the chicken and cut away the flesh in large pieces. Pile them on to a heated dish and keep warm.

3. Skim the fat off the top of the cooking liquor and then pour about half of it into another pan with the onions. Boil up rapidly until reduced to ½ pt (300 ml).

4. Add the wine and cream and boil again to reduce further. Finally add the grated orange rind. Pour the sauce over the chicken, pipe a border of creamed potato round the edge of the dish and sprinkle with the flaked almonds.

Chicken with Orange Flavoured Sauce.

Poultry and game

Chicken Sauté with Mushrooms.

Chicken Sauté with Mushrooms

4 lb (1.75 kg) roasting chicken
2 oz (50 g) butter
2 oz (50 g) oil
18 small shallots or onions
2 leeks
4 small tomatoes
1 clove garlic
6 fl oz (180 ml) white wine
6 fl oz (180 ml) white stock
salt and pepper
6–8 flat mushrooms of equal size
butter
¼ pt (150 ml) double cream

1. Cut the chicken up into joints or get your butcher to do it for you. Skin the joints, if liked. Heat the butter and oil in a pan and cook the chicken joints gently until golden brown on both sides. Then place them in a flameproof casserole.

2. Peel the shallots but leave them whole. Wash and chop the leeks, discarding the green part. Scald and skin the tomatoes, chop roughly and remove the seeds. Peel and crush the garlic clove with a little salt.

3. Add the shallots and leeks to the pan and cook gently for a few minutes. Then put them in the casserole with the chicken together with the tomatoes and garlic. Pour over the wine and stock and season with salt and pepper. Cover and cook gently on top of the stove for about 45 minutes.

4. Peel and remove stalks from the mushrooms. Cook them in a small pan with some butter.

5. When the chicken is tender lift out with a draining spoon, together with the leeks and onions, and arrange on a warmed serving dish. Pour the cream into the cooking liquor and simmer until sauce has reduced sufficiently. Then pour over the chicken.

6. Surround with a border of plainly boiled rice and decorate with the cooked mushrooms.

Chicken Baked with Bacon and Mushrooms

4 lb (1.75 g) roasting chicken
8 rashers back bacon
½ lb (225 g) mushrooms
4 oz (100 g) butter
1 oz (25 g) plain flour
¼ pt (150 ml) stock
¼ pt (150 ml) single cream
salt and pepper

1. Set oven at 400°F (200°C) or Mark 6.

2. Divide the chicken up into 8 joints if your butcher has not already done it for you. Skin the joints.

3. Wash and slice the mushrooms. Lay a piece of chicken on each bacon rasher. Sprinkle half the given quantity of mushrooms on top, season with pepper and wrap the bacon around tightly.

4. Butter a shallow ovenproof dish with half the given butter. Arrange the chicken pieces in it and sprinkle over the remaining mushrooms. Dot with the rest of the butter and season lightly.

5. Cover the dish with foil and bake in the pre-set oven on centre shelf for 30–40 minutes.

6. When cooked, arrange the chicken pieces on a heated serving dish and keep warm. Tip the remaining liquor into a small pan and blend in the flour. Add the stock a little at a time, stirring well after each addition. Then add the cream. When sauce has reached a good consistency pour over the chicken and serve with creamed potatoes.

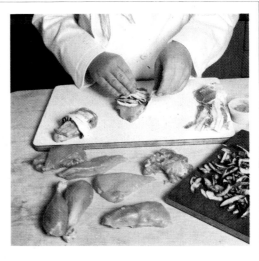

1. Place a portion of chicken on a rasher of bacon. Top with sliced mushrooms and wrap the bacon rasher round.

2. Place all the prepared chicken pieces in the baking dish. Scatter the remaining mushrooms over the top.

Chicken Baked with Bacon and Mushrooms.

Chicken Fricassée.

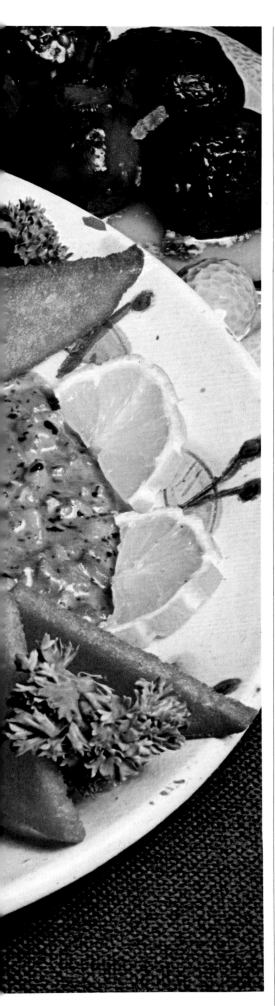

Chicken Fricassée

3½ lb (1.5 kg) roasting chicken
4½ oz (125 g) butter
thyme
marjoram
mace
nutmeg
1 onion
3 cloves
¼ lemon
¼ pt (150 ml) red wine
1 anchovy
1½ oz (35 g) plain flour
3 egg yolks
¼ pt (150 ml) double cream

For garnish
triangular croûtes
lemon slices
parsley sprigs

1. Skin and joint the chicken. Cut into small pieces. Place in a pan with 3 oz (75 g) of the butter, a pinch of thyme, a pinch of marjoram, a blade of mace, a pinch of nutmeg, the whole onion stuck with cloves, the lemon quarter, the wine, the anchovy, salt and pepper and the stock.

2. Bring to the boil, then simmer for 45 minutes, or until the chicken is tender.

3. Lift out the chicken pieces and place on a serving dish. Keep warm. Strain the liquor into a clean pan.

4. Work the remaining butter and flour together. Drop small pieces of this into the liquor, stirring over a gentle heat until the sauce has thickened.

5. Remove the pan from the heat. Beat the yolks with the cream, and add slowly to the sauce. Return the pan to a very gentle heat and stir for a few moments. Do not allow the sauce to boil or it will curdle.

6. Pour the sauce over the chicken piece. Garnish with triangular croûtes, slices of lemon and sprigs of parsley.

Chicken in Lemon Sauce

2½–3 lb (1kg) roasting chicken
salt and pepper
1 bayleaf
bouquet garni
2 lemons
2 oz (50 g) butter
2 oz (50 g) plain flour
½ pt (300 ml) single cream

1. Place the chicken in a pan with just enough water to cover. Bring to the boil and remove any scum that forms on the top. Add the seasoning and herbs. Slice the lemons and discard the pips. Add to the chicken. Simmer for 1¼ hours or until the chicken is tender.

2. Lift out the chicken and keep hot. Strain off ½ pt (300 ml) stock.

3. Melt the butter in a pan, stir in the flour and cook for a few minutes. Gradually stir in the stock. Bring to the boil, still stirring. Add the cream off the heat. Return to a gentle heat and stir until blended. Season as necessary.

4. Cut the chicken into joints and arrange on a hot serving dish. Pour over the lemon sauce and serve immediately.

Poultry and game

Paprika Chicken.

Paprika Chicken

3 lb (1.5 kg) roasting chicken
1½ oz (35 g) butter
1½ fl oz (35 ml) oil
1 large onion
1 tbsp (15 ml) mild paprika
4 tomatoes
½ pt (300 ml) chicken stock
salt and pepper
¼ pt (150 ml) soured cream

1. Divide the chicken into joints. Heat the butter and oil in a pan, add the chicken and brown evenly on all sides. Remove the joints and place in a flameproof casserole.

2. Peel and chop the onion into dice, place in pan fry gently until soft. Then work in the paprika with a wooden spoon. Add to the casserole with the chicken.

3. Pour over the chicken stock, cover and simmer on top of the stove. Meanwhile scald and skin the tomatoes. Chop roughly and remove the seeds. After about 20 minutes add these to the casserole and continue to cook until chicken is tender.

4. Arrange chicken joints on a warmed serving dish. Allow cooking liquor to bubble up well. Then remove from heat and stir in the soured cream. Pour over the chicken and serve with plainly boiled rice.

Miss Sue's Southern Fried Chicken

1 chicken cut into serving pieces
milk
4 oz (100 g) plain flour
½ tsp (2 ml) baking powder
salt and pepper
fat for frying

For cream gravy
1 tbsp (15 ml) plain flour
1 chicken bouillon cube
¼ pt (150 ml) milk
¼ pt (150 ml) single cream
salt and pepper

1. Dip the chicken joints in milk. Mix the flour, baking powder, salt and pepper. Coat the chicken as thickly as possible with this flour.

2. Pour 2 inches (5 cm) of fat into a deep wide pan with a lid. Heat the fat but do not let it smoke. Put in the chicken and fry for 20–30 minutes, or until tender and golden brown. For a crisp crust, cover the pan and cook half the required time, then remove the lid for the last half of cooking. For a tender crust, cook uncovered for half the time, then cover to finish the cooking.

3. Drain the chicken on absorbent paper and keep warm whilst making the gravy.

4. Pour off all but 2 tbsp (30 ml) fat from the pan. Stir in the flour over a moderate heat until blended and pale brown. Stir in the milk and cream. Heat through, stirring well. Season to taste.

Chicken Lyonnaise

1 boiling fowl weighing about 4–5 lb
  (1.75–2.25 kg)
½ lb (225 g) mushrooms
2 lb (900 g) carrots
2 lb (900 g) potatoes
20 baby onions
chicken stock to cover
bouquet garni
salt and pepper

1. Wipe the bird well. Then start to lift skin away from the flesh by pinching with the fingers to create a cavity in which to put the mushrooms.

2. Wash the mushrooms and slice them across the bottom to remove the stalks and some of the base of the mushrooms.

3. Peel the carrots and potatoes and cut into even size pieces if necessary. Peel the shallots and leave whole.

4. Push the mushrooms between the flesh and skin of the bird so that they cover the breast of the bird. Secure the flap of skin underneath with a small skewer.

5. Place the prepared bird in a deep flameproof casserole dish. Surround with the carrots, potatoes and onions and pour over sufficient stock to cover. Tuck in the bouquet garni and season with salt and pepper.

6. Simmer the casserole on top of the stove for about 1½–2 hours, or until the vegetables are tender and the chicken is cooked.

7. Dish up the chicken and vegetables on a heated serving dish. Skim off fat from the cooking liquor, boil to reduce strain and serve separately.

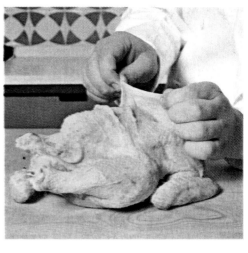

1. Pinch the chicken skin all over to help to loosen it from the flesh.

2. Push whole mushrooms under the skin.

3. Place the chicken and vegetables in a casserole and pour over the stock.

Poultry and game

Chicken Curry shown here with plainly boiled rice and chapatis. Other suitable accompaniments for a curry are mango chutney, sliced bananas, desiccated coconut, sliced cucumber in plain yoghourt, and curried lentils. Never serve wine with curry – try beer or iced water instead.

Chicken Curry

3 lb (1.5 kg) roasting chicken
3 cloves garlic
ground ginger
1 oz (25 g) curry paste
½ tsp (2 ml) crushed cardamoms
¼ pt (150 ml) wine vinegar
2 large onions
4 tbsp (60 ml) olive oil
salt

1. Divide the chicken into small joints. Peel and chop the garlic cloves and crush them with a pinch of ginger with a pestle and mortar.

2. Mix together with the curry paste, crushed cardamoms and vinegar. Place the chicken joints in a bowl and pour over the spicy mixture. Cover and leave to marinate for about 6 hours.

3. Peel and chop the onions into dice. Heat the oil in a pan and cook the onions gently until soft. Then add the chicken and the marinade. Cover and simmer slowly for about 1½ hours. Serve with plainly boiled rice and chapatis if available.

Chicken with Oregano

3¼ lb (1.5 kg) roasting chicken
1¼ oz (35 g) butter
1¼ fl oz (35 ml) oil
¼ pt (150 ml) dry white wine
½ pt (300 ml) white stock
½ tsp (2 ml) oregano
¼ pt (150 ml) single cream
salt and pepper

1. Joint the chicken into 4 portions.

2. Fry the joints in butter and oil until lightly browned.

3. Add the wine, stock and oregano. Cover and simmer until the chicken is tender. Take out joints and arrange on a serving dish.

4. Add the cream to the liquor in the pan. Increase the heat and reduce to the consistency of thick cream. Season and strain the sauce over the chicken joints.

Stuffed Roast Turkey

1 turkey
butter
salt and pepper

For sausagemeat stuffing
1½ lb (700 g) pork sausagemeat
1½ oz (35 g) butter
1 large onion
2 tsp (10 ml) dried mixed herbs
1 tbsp (15 ml) freshly chopped parsley
1 oz (25 g) fresh breadcrumbs
beaten egg
salt and pepper

For celery, apricot and walnut stuffing
1 small head of celery
2 oz (50 g) dried apricots
4 oz (100 g) walnuts
1½ oz (40 g) butter
2 onions
1¼ oz (35 g) fresh breadcrumbs
1 tbsp (15 ml) freshly chopped parsley
salt and pepper

For garnish
½ lb (225 g) streaky bacon rashers
watercress

1. Soak the dried apricots in water overnight.

2. Set oven at 325°F (160°C) or Mark 3.

3. Prepare the stuffings. Place the sausagemeat in a bowl. Peel and chop the onion into small dice. Melt the butter in a pan and fry the onion gently until soft and transparent.

4. Add the onion to the sausagemeat together with the herbs and breadcrumbs and mix well together. Add enough beaten egg to bind the mixture thoroughly and season with salt and pepper. Stuff into the carcass of the bird.

5. Peel and chop the onions into small dice. Melt the butter in a pan and cook the onions until soft.

6. Drain and cut the apricots into quarters. Wash and thinly slice the celery and chop the walnuts. Add the apricots, celery and walnuts to the pan with the onions and cook for about 4 minutes. Turn into a bowl and allow to cool. Then add the breadcrumbs, parsley and season with salt and pepper. Mix together well and stuff into the breast of the bird.

7. Brush the turkey with melted butter and sprinkle with salt and pepper. Wrap the bird loosely in transparent cooking foil and place in a roasting tin.

8. Roast in the pre-set oven for 20 minutes per lb (450 g) plus 30 minutes over. For the garnish, remove rind from bacon rashers, roll them up, place on skewers and cook them under the grill. Serve with Brussels sprouts and chestnuts, roast potatoes and cranberry sauce.

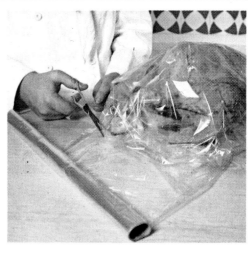

1. Take a large sheet of transparent foil. Brush it with melted butter and season it. Place the turkey on one end of the foil and bring the remaining foil up over the top of the bird.

2. Tuck the ends up under the turkey and place in a baking tin for roasting.

Poultry and game

Roast Stuffed Duck

1 large duck weighing about 5 lb (2.25 kg)
salt and pepper
clear honey

For stuffing
3 onions
2 oz (50 g) butter
6 oz (175 g) fresh breadcrumbs
2 tsp (10 ml) dried sage
1 tsp (5 ml) chopped parsley
salt and pepper
beaten egg

1. Set oven at 400°F (200°C) or Mark 6.

2. Now prepare the stuffing. Peel and slice the onions, place in a pan of salted water and boil for about 15 minutes. Drain, place in a bowl, add the butter and then the breadcrumbs, herbs and seasoning. Work in enough beaten egg to bind and then stuff mixture into the duck.

3. Pat the bird completely dry with a clean tea towel. Then rub in some salt and pepper. Prick the duck well with a fork and place on a grid which will sit over the top of your roasting pan. Spread the duck with clear honey and work in well with the fingertips. Roast in the pre-set oven for 15 minutes per lb (450 g) and 15 minutes over.

4. Serve apple sauce, peas and new potatoes with the roast duck.

ROASTING A DUCK

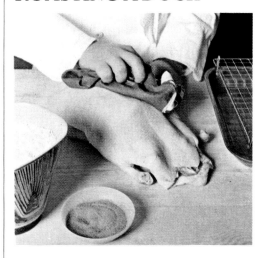

1. Gently pat the skin of the duck dry with a clean cloth.

2. Rub the bird with salt and pepper.

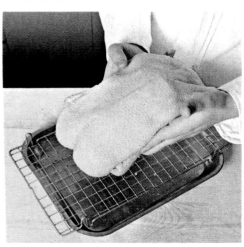

3. Place on a grid over a baking tin.

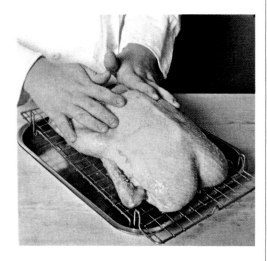

4. Rub honey all over the bird.

5. The cooked duck is a rich brown.

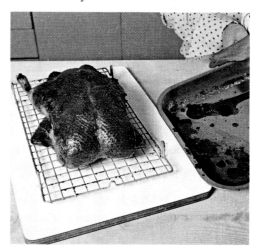

6. The succulent pan juices are used for making the accompanying sauce.

Duck with Grape Sauce.

Duck with Grape Sauce

1 duck weighing about 4 lb (1.75 kg)
salt and pepper
clear honey
1 tbsp (15 ml) plain flour
1 pt (600 ml) stock
½ lb (225 g) green grapes

1. Set oven at 375°F (190°C) or Mark 5.

2. Pat the skin of the duck completely dry with a clean tea towel. Then season with salt and pepper, prick the skin, and spread with honey rubbing in well with the fingertips.

3. Place the duck on a grid which will stand over your chosen roasting tin. Pour enough boiling water into the bottom of the pan just to cover and place the grid on top.

4. Roast the duck in the pre-set oven for 15 minutes per lb (450 g) and 15 minutes over.

5. Meanwhile peel and pip the grapes. If the skin is difficult to remove, cover them with very hot water, count to 12 and re-place the hot water with cold water before peeling.

6. When duck is cooked, place on a serving dish and keep warm. Skim the fat off the juices in the pan, then add the flour and blend in well with a wooden spoon. Stir in the stock and boil up to reduce. Season to taste and add about half the peeled grapes. Heat gently to warm through.

7. Pour the sauce around the duck and garnish with the remaining grapes. If liked the duck can be placed on a large deep fried croûte.

Poultry and game

Duck Cooked with Onions.

Duck in Cider

1 duck weighing about 4 lb (1.75 kg)
seasoned flour
2 oz (50 g) butter
½ pt (300 ml) dry cider
salt and pepper
6 small cooking apples
7 fl oz (200 ml) single cream

1. Set oven at 400°F (200°C) or Mark 6.

2. Divide the duck into joints and cover lightly with seasoned flour.

3. Melt butter in a pan and brown the duck pieces on all sides.

4. Place them in a casserole with the pan juices, pour over the cider and season with salt and pepper. Cover and cook in the pre-set oven until tender.

5. Peel and core the apples. When the duck is cooked take out and keep warm in a separate container. Now place the apples in the cooking liquid, turn oven down to 350°F (180°C) or Mark 4, cover and cook until tender.

6. Arrange the duck pieces on a warmed serving dish with the cooked apples. Strain the cooking liquid into a pan, allow to bubble up well, then stir in the cream. Pour sauce over the duck and serve with creamed potato.

Duck Cooked with Onions

1 duck weighing about 4 lb (1.75 kg)
1 oz (25 g) butter
16 shallots or small onions
sprigs of fresh rosemary
1 tbsp (15 ml) chopped parsley
1 pt (600 ml) stock
salt and pepper

1. Set oven at 375°F (190°C) or Mark 5.

2. Melt the butter in a pan, put in the duck and brown it on all sides. Remove from pan and place in an ovenproof casserole dish.

3. Peel the shallots and leave whole. Arrange them around the duck, add the herbs and seasoning and pour the stock over.

4. Cook in the pre-set oven for about 1½ hours. When duck is cooked, place on a warmed serving dish with the shallots. Strain the cooking liquid into a pan, remove the fat and boil up to thicken.

5. Pour a little of the sauce over the duck and the rest over the shallots. Serve with broad beans, croûtons and fresh rosemary for garnish.

Duck à l'Orange

1 duck weighing about 4 lb (1.75 kg)
plain flour
juice and rind of 2 oranges
2 tbsp (30 ml) wine vinegar
1 tsp (5 ml) sugar
1 tsp (5 ml) brandy
salt and pepper
watercress for decoration

1. Set oven at 350°F (180°C) or Mark 4.

2. Clean and dry the bird thoroughly and prick the skin all over with a fork. Place the bird in a large baking tin and rub all over with flour. Cook in the pre-set oven for about 1½ hours until browned.

3. Remove the duck from the oven, and keep warm while making the garnish. Cut one of the oranges into slices and grate the rind of the other. To make the sauce place the vinegar and sugar in a small pan over a low heat and when dissolved simmer for one minute. Add the juice of one orange and simmer quickly until it becomes syrupy; then throw in the grated rind, pour in the brandy and season.

4. Strain the sauce over the finished bird and arrange the orange segments and watercress around it.

1. Cut one of the oranges into slices.

2. Baste the duck frequently with the pan juices during cooking.

Duck à l'Orange.

Poultry and game

Pheasant with Onion Sauce.

Pheasant with Onion Sauce

1 pheasant
¼ lb (100 g) mushrooms
2 oz (50 g) butter
salt and pepper
3–4 rashers streaky bacon
beef dripping or pork fat for roasting
6 shallots or very small onions
milk

For onion sauce
6 onions
2 oz (50 g) butter
4 tbsp (60 ml) plain flour
1 pt (600 ml) milk
salt and pepper
2 tbsp (30 ml) double cream

For garnish
watercress

1. Set oven at 400°F (200°C) or Mark 6.

2. Wash and remove stalks from the mushrooms. Wipe out the insides of the pheasant, place the mushrooms inside together with the butter and some salt and pepper.

3. Wrap the breasts with the bacon rashers to prevent them drying out. Place them in a roasting tin with a little dripping or pork fat and roast in the pre-set oven for 45–55 minutes, basting frequently.

4. Peel the shallots, place them in a pan with milk to cover and simmer gently until tender.

5. Now prepare the sauce. Peel and slice the onions, place in a pan, cover with salted water and cook until tender. Then drain thoroughly and pass them through a sieve.

6. Melt the butter in a pan, remove from heat and blend in the flour. Return to heat and pour on the milk stirring continually. Simmer for 2–3 minutes, then add the sieved onions and season. Finally stir in the cream.

7. When pheasant is cooked remove mushrooms from the inside, skin the bird and place in a deep serving dish. Pour over the onion sauce and then decorate with the mushrooms and poached shallots. Garnish with watercress.

Roast Pheasant.

Roast Pheasant

1 brace of pheasant
6–8 rashers streaky bacon
2 oz (50 g) butter
salt and pepper
beef dripping or pork fat for roasting
2 tbsp (30 ml) plain flour

For gravy
stock made from:
    pheasant giblets
    1 carrot
    1 onion
    bouquet garni
1 tsp (5 ml) flour

For garnish
watercress

1. Set oven at 400°F (200°C) or Mark 6.

2. Wipe the insides of the birds and place a knob of butter, seasoned with salt and pepper in each one.

3. Wrap the breasts of each pheasant with the bacon rashers to prevent them drying out. Place them in a roasting tin with a little dripping or pork fat and roast in the pre-set oven for 45–55 minutes basting frequently.

4. About 10 minutes before the end of the cooking time, remove the bacon rashers and dredge the birds lightly with the flour. Then return them to the oven to brown.

5. While the pheasants are cooking make the stock. Place the giblets from the birds, a carrot, an onion and bouquet garni to flavour in a pan and cover with water. Simmer for 30–40 minutes.

6. When the birds are cooked, dish them up and keep warm. Pour the fat off from the roasting tin leaving sediment behind. Blend in the flour with a wooden spoon. Then add the stock and bring to the boil. Season as necessary and strain into a sauce boat.

7. Garnish the pheasants with watercress and serve with bread sauce.

Roast Grouse.

Roast Grouse

1 grouse
1 oz (25 g) butter
salt and pepper
2 rashers fat bacon
plain flour

For garnish
1 croûte same size as the grouse
liver from the grouse
butter
watercress

1. Set oven at 400°F (200°C) or Mark 6.

2. Wipe out the inside of the bird, season and place a nut of butter in it. Wrap the bacon rashers over the breast to keep it moist.

3. Place remaining butter in roasting tin with the grouse and roast in the pre-set oven for about 35 minutes. 10 minutes before the end of cooking time remove bacon from bird, dredge lightly with flour and baste. Return to oven to brown.

4. While grouse is cooking, sauté the liver lightly in a little butter, then mash with a fork and spread on the croûte. Place the cooked grouse on this and garnish with the bacon rashers and watercress. Other traditional accompaniments for roast grouse are rowan or redcurrant jelly, browned crumbs and game chips.

Bread Sauce

Basic Recipe

2 oz (50 g) fresh white
    breadcrumbs
1 onion
cloves
small bayleaf
½ pt (300 ml) milk
½ oz (15 g) butter
salt and pepper
1 tbsp (15 ml) cream

1. Peel the onion and stud with 2 or 3 cloves. Place in a pan with the milk and bayleaf. Bring to the boil, cover and leave to one side for 15 minutes.

2. Remove onion and bayleaf. Add breadcrumbs and bring slowly to the boil stirring continually. Add the butter and seasoning and allow to simmer gently. Finally stir in the cream.

Pigeons en Croûte.

Partridge with Mushrooms

1 partridge
salt and pepper
2 rashers bacon
2 oz (50 g) mushrooms
8 fl oz (200 ml) stock

For garnish
1 croûte same size as the partridge
watercress
game chips

1. Set oven at 375°F (190°C) or Mark 5.

2. Season and cover the partridge breast with bacon rashers. Stuff the bird with the unpeeled mushrooms.

3. Place in a baking tin and pour over half the stock. Roast in the pre-set oven for 35–40 minutes.

4. Remove the bacon rashers and set aside. Place the partridge on the croûte on a serving dish and keep warm. Take the mushrooms out of the bird and use 4 large ones as garnish. Chop up the remaining mushrooms and place in the baking tin.

5. Add the remaining stock and place over a fierce heat. Allow to bubble up until thickened, stirring continuously. Chop up the crispy bacon and add to the sauce.

6. Pour sauce over the bird and garnish with watercress and game chips.

Pigeons en Croûte

1 brace of pigeon
4 oz (100 g) puff pastry
salt and pepper
2 oz (50 g) mushrooms
beaten egg

1. Set oven at 400°F (200°C) or Mark 6.

2. Remove the breasts from the pigeons. Season the breasts.

3. Divide pastry into quarters and roll out each quarter very thinly.

4. Place each breast on a piece of pastry. Chop the mushrooms and sprinkle over the breasts. Wrap the pastry over each breast, sealing the edges with cold water.

5. Brush with beaten egg and place on a baking sheet. Bake in the pre-set oven for 30 minutes or until the pastry is golden brown.

Harvest Pie.

Pies and casseroles

Harvest Pie

2 lb (900 g) rabbit joints
seasoned flour
dripping for frying
1¼ lb (600 g) raw pork
2 rashers back bacon
2 tbsp (30 ml) parsley
2 tsp (10 ml) dried thyme
2 tsp (10 ml) dried sage
1 egg yolk
1 large onion
salt and pepper
cinnamon
½ pt (300 ml) stock
½ pt (300 ml) red wine
3 hard boiled eggs
½ lb (225 g) quantity savoury shortcrust
  pastry
beaten egg

1. Soak the rabbit joints overnight in a bowl of cold salted water.

2. Set oven at 325°F (160°C) or Mark 3.

3. Drain and dry the rabbit joints and dip them in seasoned flour. Heat the dripping in a pan and fry the joints until brown.

4. Take ¼ lb (100 g) of the pork and cut into cubes. Remove rind from bacon and chop the bacon. Pass pork and bacon through a mincer with the herbs. Add the egg yolk to bind and shape into sausages.

5. Cut the rest of the pork into cubes, roll in seasoned flour and brown lightly in the dripping. Peel and slice the onion.

6. Arrange rabbit joints, pork and onions in your chosen pie dish. Season with salt and pepper and a pinch of cinnamon. Lay the sausages on top and then pour over stock and wine. Cover and cook in the pre-set oven for about 1½ hours.

7. If the meat is tender at the end of this time, remove from oven and allow to cook a little. Turn oven up to 375°F (190°C) or Mark 5.

8. Roll out the pastry to cover the pie dish. Shell the hard boiled eggs and tuck them into the cooled casserole. Cover with the pastry lid using trimmings for decoration. Brush with beaten egg.

9. Bake in the pre-set oven for 30–40 minutes or until well browned.

MAKING PUFF PASTRY

*1 lb (450 g) self
    raising flour
1 lb (450 g) butter or
    margarine
1 fl oz (25 ml) lemon
    juice
7 fl oz (200 ml) ice cold
    water*

1. Sift flour onto a very cold work surface and make a well in the centre of the
flour. Cut 3 oz (75 g) chilled butter or
margarine into tiny pieces (keep remainder chilled) and place in centre of the well.
With one hand, begin to draw the flour
into the centre and rub in the butter until it
resembles very fine crumbs. Make a well
in the centre again, then pour in lemon
juice and a little of the cold water.

2. Using 2 knives, work the mixture from
the sides to the centre, adding a little water
from time to time, until a firm but smooth
dough is formed. Wrap in greaseproof
paper or foil and chill in refrigerator for
about 30 minutes.

3. Meanwhile shape remaining butter
into a small rectangle and reserve. Lightly
flour work surface again, then unwrap
chilled dough and roll out to a narrow
rectangle. Place the slab of butter in the
centre of the dough.

4. Make a parcel of the dough by folding
nearest pastry edge into the centre of the
butter. Fold the sides up and over, pressing down gently as you do so. Complete
by folding the edge furthest away into the
centre. Half turn the dough on the work
surface, then roll out again to the same
sized rectangle. Wrap again and chill in
refrigerator for about 30 minutes.

5. Return the dough to the floured work
surface again, unwrap and roll out, repeat-
ing this once more and always giving the
dough a half turn each time. Rewrap and
chill finally before use according to the
recipe. Puff pastry can be stored in the
refrigerator for up to a week.

1. Place the sifted flour on a cold work
surface – preferably marble. Put some of
the ice cold butter or margarine in the
centre of the flour.

2. Using really cold hands, draw a little
flour into the butter and start rubbing in
gently with just 2 fingers and thumb.

6. Take the remaining butter from the
refrigerator.

7. With a knife, pat the remaining butter
into a rectangle on the cold surface.

11. Make an indentation with your finger
in the top fold of the pastry. This will help
keep your place when rolling out.

12. Wrap in greaseproof paper and leave
in the refrigerator for 30 minutes. Take
out and place in the same position as

3. When the flour is rubbed in and the mixture resembles fine breadcrumbs, shape into a pile with a well in the centre.

4. Pour the lemon juice into the well with a little ice cold water. Using 2 knives, work the liquid into the mixture. Gradually add enough water to bind the mixture together into a dough.

5. Work the dough into a smooth ball with your hands. Sift a little flour over the dough, fold it in a clean cloth and leave in the refrigerator to rest.

8. Take the dough from the refrigerator and roll out into a rectangle on the lightly floured work surface. Place the rectangle of butter in the centre.

before. Roll, fold and turn, then repeat the process before refrigerating again. This rolling, folding, turning and refrigerating procedure has to be done 5 times before the pastry can be used.

9. Carefully wrap the pastry round the butter to form a neat rectangular parcel.

10. Turn the pastry 90°. Roll out as before and fold up into a parcel.

Pies and casseroles

Cornish Pasties

1 lb (450 g) quantity savoury shortcrust
 pastry, made without the cheese
2 potatoes
1 swede
8 oz (225 g) finely diced steak
5 tsp (25 ml) suet
salt and pepper
beaten egg

1. Set oven at 375°F (190°C) or Mark 5.

2. Roll out the pastry and cut 5 6 inch (15 cm) diameter circles.

3. Peel and finely dice the potatoes and the swede. Place in a bowl with the steak and the suet. Season and mix well.

4. Place a fifth of the meat and potato mixture on each pastry circle, leaving a generous border. Brush the borders with cold water and bring up the sides to meet over the centre. Seal the pastry edges together so that the pasties are standing on an oval base with the edges on top. If the edges are not sealed thoroughly the juices will run out during cooking and the filling will be dry when cooked.

5. Brush with beaten egg and place on a baking tray. Bake in the pre-set oven on the centre shelf for 30 minutes. Lower the temperature to 325°F (160°C) or Mark 3 and cook for a further 30 minutes.

Savoury Shortcrust Pastry

Basic Recipe

1 lb (450 g) plain flour
1 tsp (5 ml) salt
4 oz (100 g) butter or margarine
4 oz (100 g) lard
3 oz (75 g) grated Cheddar or
 Parmesan cheese
1 egg yolk
6–8 tbsp (90–120 ml) cold water

1. Sift the flour and salt into a large mixing bowl. Cut the butter or margarine and lard into small pieces and put into the bowl. Work into the flour with the fingertips until the mixture resembles fine breadcrumbs.

2. Stir in the grated cheese. Add the egg and a little water and stir to combine. Add more water gradually and stir until the dough begins to hold together.

3. Form dough into a ball with the fingers, turn out onto a floured board and knead lightly until smooth and free from cracks.

4. Wrap dough in foil and chill for at least an hour before using.

Veal and Mushroom Flan

8 oz (225 g) quantity savoury shortcrust
 pastry, made without cheese
2 oz (50 g) butter
1 oz (25 g) plain flour
½ pt (300 ml) stock
4 oz (100 g) mushrooms
8 oz (225 g) diced cooked veal

1. Set oven at 350°F (180°C) or Mark 4.

2. Line a flan dish with shortcrust pastry and bake blind.

3. Melt 1 oz (25 g) butter in a pan, stir in the flour and cook for a few minutes, stirring. Gradually stir in the stock and cook gently until thickened.

4. Slice and lightly fry the mushrooms in the remaining butter. Add to the sauce. Fold in the cooked veal and mix well.

5. Spoon the filling into the flan case and place in the pre-set oven for 30 minutes.

Cornish Pasties.

LINING A FLAN AND BAKING IT BLIND

1. Roll out the pastry and lift over the flan ring, using the rolling pin. You can use either a plain or fluted edged ring.

2. Press the pastry against the sides and base with the knuckles.

3. Roll the rolling pin over the flan to cut off the surplus pastry.

4. This provides the flan with a neat edge when it is cooked.

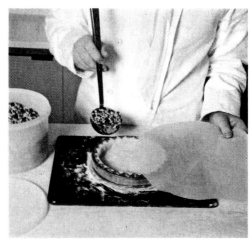

5. Baking blind means cooking the flan without a filling. It is necessary to weight the pastry down with dried beans or rice otherwise the pastry base will be bumpy with air bubbles.

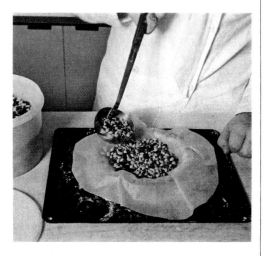

6. Place a circle of greaseproof paper in the flan ring. Spoon in beans or rice.

7. Fill the pastry case with beans.

8. After baking, lift up the greaseproof paper and beans. Leave the beans to cool and then store for further use. The flan ring is removed and the case is left to cool before filling.

Pies and casseroles

Steak and Kidney Pudding.

Steak and Kidney Pudding

1½ lb (700 g) stewing steak
6 oz (175 g) ox kidney
seasoned flour
½ lb (225 g) carrots
½ lb (225 g) onions
Worcestershire sauce
1 tsp (5 ml) tomato purée
stock

For suet crust
10 oz (275 g) self raising flour
salt
6 oz (175 g) suet
5 fl oz (125 ml) cold water

1. Set oven at 350°F (180°C) or Mark 4.

2. Trim stewing steak of any excess fat and gristle and cut into cubes. Chop up kidney and turn both in seasoned flour.

3. Peel and chop carrots into dice. Peel and slice the onions finely. Place all these ingredients in a casserole dish. Season with a few drops of Worcestershire sauce and the tomato purée. Pour over enough stock to cover. Cover with lid and cook in the pre-set oven for about 1¼ hours. Then allow to cool.

4. Meanwhile prepare suet crust. Sift the flour with a pinch of salt into a bowl. Stir in the suet and then mix to a firm dough with the cold water. Take two thirds of the pastry and roll out into a circular shape.

5. Grease the pudding basin well. Fold pastry in half and make a dart which tapers to a point where the pastry is folded. Now roll out the dart, open out the pastry and line it into the basin. Work up the edges of the pastry so it stands ½–1 inch above the rim of basin.

6. Fill the cooled steak and kidney mixture into the basin. Roll out the remaining pastry to form the lid. Damp the edges, put on the lid and then pinch edges well together. Cover with foil making a large pleat in the centre to allow for expansion.

7. Steam for 2 hours.

Variation:
Steak and Kidney Pie. Use the same steak and kidney mixture and cook in a casserole in the oven as described above. Then, using a 1¼ lb quantity of puff pastry, line a pie dish, fill with meat mixture and cover with a pastry lid. Brush with beaten egg and bake in the oven at 400°F (200°C) or Mark 6 for 45 minutes until golden brown.

Chicken Pie

3 lb cooked chicken
4 leeks
16 fl oz (450 ml) stock
1 tsp (5 ml) sugar
salt
2 oz (50 g) cooked ham
1 tbsp (15 ml) chopped parsley
6 oz (175 g) quantity puff pastry
beaten egg
4 tbsp (60 ml) double cream

1. Wash and slice the leeks, and put in a pan with the stock. Bring to the boil and simmer for 15–20 minutes.

2. Set oven at 400°F (200°C) or Mark 6.

3. Cut the chicken into bite size pieces and arrange in a deep pie dish. Pour over the leeks and stock. Sprinkle with the sugar and a pinch of salt. Place thin slices of ham over the top.

4. Roll out pastry to 1 inch (2.5 cm) larger than the pie dish. Cut off a border to fit round the rim of the pie dish. Cover the pie dish, seal the edges to the rim, cut a cross in the centre and brush with beaten egg.

5. Place the pie in the pre-set oven and bake for an hour.

6. Heat the cream in a pan and pour through the cross in the centre. Serve immediately.

Shepherd's Pie

1¼ lb (700 g) cold cooked lamb
1 large onion
2 tbsp (30 ml) freshly chopped parsley
4 oz (100 g) cooked gammon
½ pt (300 ml) stock
salt and pepper

For potato topping
2 lb (900 g) potatoes
1½ oz (40 g) butter
warmed milk
salt and pepper
beaten egg

1. Set oven at 375°F (190°C) or Mark 5.

2. Peel the potatoes and cut into even size pieces. Place in a pan of cold, salted water, bring to the boil and simmer until tender.

3. Meanwhile pass the cold lamb, with the onion, peeled and sliced, through the mincer. Place in a bowl, season with salt and pepper and add the parsley.

4. Now mince up the cooked gammon, place in a pan with the stock and simmer gently for a few minutes. Then add to the minced lamb and mix together well.

5. Place filling in chosen pie dish. Drain the potatoes when cooked, return them to pan and set over the heat briefly to dry off any excess moisture. Season, add butter and a little warmed milk and mash them well until creamy and smooth.

6. Spoon potato over the meat filling and decorate the top with a knife. Then brush with a little beaten egg. Bake in the pre-set oven for about 45 minutes until golden brown.

Shepherd's Pie.

Ham and Vegetable Cream Flan

6–8 oz (175–225 g) cooked ham or
  gammon
¾ lb (350 g) puff pastry
beaten egg
1 small cooked cauliflower
4 oz (100 g) cooked French beans
4 oz (100 g) cooked peas
¾ pt (450 ml) mornay sauce
1 tbsp (15 ml) freshly grated Parmesan
  cheese
1 oz (25 g) butter

Ham and Vegetable Cream Flan.

1. First prepare the pastry case. This can, of course, be made up the day before. Set the oven at 425°F (220°C) or Mark 7.

2. Roll out the pastry to a long rectangular shape ½ inch (1 cm) deep. Trim the rectangle off neatly. It should measure 5 inches by 15 inches (12×37cm).

3. Place on a well dampened baking tray. Mark an inner rectangle on the pastry with the back of a knife about ¾ inch (2 cm) from the outer edge. Take care not to cut right through pastry. Decorate the outer edge with diagonal lines and brush the whole with beaten egg.

4. Chill in the refrigerator for 10–15 minutes, then bake in the pre-set oven for 25–30 minutes until well risen and a good colour.

5. Slide onto a rack to cool. While still warm go over the marked inner rectangle with a sharp knife. Then using a metal spatula lift out the inner panel and reserve for a lid. Scoop out some of the soft centre.

6. Have ready a fresh batch of mornay sauce. Chop ham into dice removing any excess fat. Divide the cauliflower into flowerets removing any green leaves. Chop up the French beans. Mix the ham and vegetables into the warm sauce folding over carefully so as not to break up the vegetables.

7. Pile into the pastry case, sprinkle with the Parmesan cheese and dot with butter. Cover with foil and place in the oven for about 10 minutes to heat through. Place the pastry lid on a separate baking sheet in the bottom of the oven to warm.

8. Serve very hot with the lid in position.

Chicken Puff

6 oz (175 g) cooked chicken
¾ lb (350 g) puff pastry
beaten egg
4 oz (100 g) cream cheese
salt and pepper
2 tsp (10 ml) paprika
4 tbsp (60 ml) single cream
2 eggs
¼ pt (150 ml) milk

1. First prepare the pastry case. This can of course be made up the day before. Set the oven at 425°F (220°C) or Mark 7.

2. Roll the pastry out into a square ½ inch (1.5 cm) deep. Trim off to measure approximately 9 inches (22 cm) square. If liked roll out the pastry trimmings into strips 1 inch (2.5 cm) wide and twist into straws to use for decoration.

3. Place pastry square on a dampened baking sheet. Mark an inner square on it with the back of a knife about ¾ inch (2 cm) from the edge. Decorate the outer edge

MAKING A RECTANGULAR PUFF PASTRY CASE

with a knife and brush with beaten egg.

4. Chill in the refrigerator for 10–15 minutes, then brush with beaten egg and bake in the pre-set oven for 25–30 minutes until well risen and a good colour. Bake the decorative pastry straws at the same time or a separate baking sheet.

5. Slide onto a rack to cool. While still warm cut around the marked inner square with a knife and then ease out with a metal spatula and reserve for decoration. Scoop out some of the soft centre.

6. Reduce oven temperature to 325°F (160°C) or Mark 3.

7. Cut the chicken into dice removing any skin. Place the cream cheese in a bowl, season with salt and pepper and half the given paprika. Beat well with a wooden spoon, then add the chicken and the cream.

8. Break the eggs into a separate bowl, season with salt and pepper, and whisk in the milk. Add a third of this to the chicken and cheese and mix in well.

9. Pile chicken into the pastry case, then pour the remaining egg mixture on top and cover with a piece of foil.

10. Bake in the pre-set oven for about 10–12 minutes, or until egg has just set. Then turn up the oven to 400°F (200°C) or Mark 6 and place flan in oven without foil to brown. At the same time divide pastry lid into 4 diagonally and place on a separate baking sheet with the pastry straws to heat.

11. Sprinkle the finished dish with the remaining paprika, garnish with parsley and decorate with the pastry pieces.

1. Roll out the pastry to a rectangle measuring 12½ by 7 by ¾ inches (31 × 18 × 2 cm).

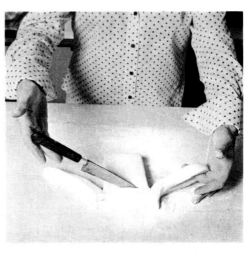

2. Fold it over so that the cut ends are on top of each other. Make the frame by cutting off a 1 inch (2.5 cm) border so that the rectangle is smaller but still in the same proportions.

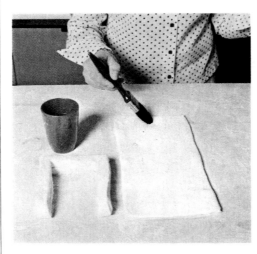

3. Roll out the rectangle to its former size and brush with cold water.

4. Open the frame out and lay over the base. Prick the surface of the base.

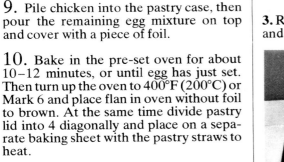

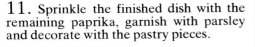

5. Place the pastry case on a floured baking sheet and decorate the edges.

133

Pies and casseroles

Sausage and Potato Pie.

Sausage and Potato Pie

1 lb (450 g) cooked pork sausages
1¼ lb (700 g) waxy potatoes boiled in their
  skins
1¼ lb (600 g) quantity puff pastry
2 shallots or small onions
3 tbsp (45 ml) chopped chives
2 rashers streaky bacon
salt and pepper
2 eggs
3 tbsp (45 ml) cream

1. Set oven at 375°F (190°C) or Mark 5.

2. Roll out half the given quantity of puff pastry quite thinly and line into your chosen pie dish or tin.

3. Slice up the sausages diagonally. Skin the cold, cooked potatoes and chop into dice. Peel and chop the shallots up finely. Cut rind off the bacon and chop bacon.

4. Layer the diced potato and sliced sausages in the pie dish. Sprinkle with the shallots, bacon and chives. Season with salt and pepper.

5. Break the eggs into a bowl and whisk up with the cream. Pour this into the pie, reserving a little.

6. Roll out the rest of the pastry for the pie lid. Dampen the edges with cold water before sealing firmly. Use any trimmings for decoration and brush with the reserved egg and cream mixture.

7. Bake in the pre-set oven for about 45 minutes or until golden brown. This dish can be served hot or cold.

Veal, Ham and Egg Pie

1 lb (450 g) pie veal
1½–2 lb (700–900 g) pork
salt and pepper
mace
2 onions
2 cooking apples
2 hard boiled eggs
½ pt (300 ml) plus 2 tbsp (30 ml) stock
½ oz (15 g) gelatine

For raised pie pastry
15 oz (425 g) plain flour
salt and pepper
6 fl oz (175 ml) milk and water mixed in
  equal quantities
5 oz (150 g) lard
beaten egg

1. Set oven at 400°F (200°C) or Mark 6.

2. Prepare the ingredients for the filling. Remove any excess fat or gristle from pork and veal and chop into dice. Season with salt and pepper and a pinch of mace.

3. Peel and chop the onions. Peel and slice the apples, removing the core.

4. Prepare the pastry. Sift the flour with salt and pepper and set in a warm place. Measure the lard, milk and water into a small pan and bring slowly to the boil so that the fat melts in the liquid.

5. Pour into the centre of the sifted flour and beat well with a wooden spoon. Turn onto a board and knead lightly.

6. Roll out the pastry reserving about a quarter for the lid. Line the rest into a greased pie tin. Layer the meat, onions and apples into the lined tin. When it is half full, halve the eggs and arrange them lengthwise along the pie. Then continue to layer the ingredients to the top. Sprinkle over the 2 tbsp (30 ml) stock.

7. Have the pastry lid ready. The filling should not quite come up to the top rim of the pastry. These edges should be folded over on top of the meat. Brush pastry edges with cold water and then lay the lid on top. Pinch the edges to decorate and then brush lid with beaten egg.

8. Roll out the pastry trimmings to a strip about 2 inches (5 cm) wide. With a knife fringe the pastry along one side, brush with beaten egg and roll up to form a tassel. Make a hole in the centre of the pie lid and place the pastry tassel over it.

9. Place the pie in the centre of the pre-set oven and bake for 20 minutes. Then lower the heat to 350°F (180°C) or Mark 4 and bake for a further 2–2½ hours.

10. When the pie is cooked, heat the remaining stock in a pan and dissolve the gelatine in it. Leave to cool a little until it begins to thicken, then pour into the hole in the lid and leave to cool.

1. Line the baking tin with warm pastry.

2. Half fill with meat mixture, then arrange the hard boiled eggs on it.

3. Add the remaining meat. Moisten the pastry rim with a little stock and then push the rim over the meat. Brush the edge with cold water.

4. Put the pastry lid in position and decorate the edges with pastry pincers.

5. Make a fringe out of a 2 inch (5 cm) wide strip of paste.

6. Brush with beaten egg.

7. Roll up the fringe to make a tassel.

8. Make a hole in the centre of the pastry and place tassel in position. Brush the top of the pastry with beaten egg.

Chicken Waterloo.

Chicken Waterloo

3 lb (1.5 kg) roasting chicken
3 carrots
1 large onion
2 leeks
4 parsley stalks
salt and pepper
1 pt (600 ml) chicken stock
2 oz (50 g) butter

To finish
2 oz (50 g) kneaded butter
4 fl oz (100 ml) double cream
freshly chopped parsley

1. Set oven at 325°F (160°C) or Mark 3.

2. Peel and slice the carrots into thin rounds. Peel and chop the onion into small dice. Wash and trim the leeks, removing most of the green leaves. Slice up finely.

3. Melt half the butter in a pan, add the chopped vegetables, parsley stalks and seasoning, cover and cook for a few minutes. Then pour over half the stock and simmer until very tender.

4. Meanwhile divide the chicken into joints. Melt the remaining butter in another pan and lay the chicken pieces in, skin side downwards, to brown.

5. Pass the cooked vegetables and stock through a sieve to purée them. Place browned chicken joints in a casserole. Add the purée and the remaining stock. Cover and cook in the pre-set oven for about an hour or until the chicken is tender.

6. Arrange the chicken joints on a warmed dish. Thicken the sauce with the kneaded butter, then stir in the cream. Pour over the chicken and sprinkle with chopped parsley before serving.

Pot Roast of Beef with Prunes.

Pot Roast of Beef with Prunes

3 lb (1.5 kg) joint topside beef
dripping for frying
12 prunes
tea
3 onions
1 clove garlic
salt and pepper
¼ pt (150 ml) red wine
2 oz (50 g) mushrooms
3 oz (75 g) black olives
1 oz (25 g) kneaded butter
2 tbsp (30 ml) freshly chopped parsley

1. Soak the prunes overnight in freshly made tea.

2. Set oven at 325°F (160°C) or Mark 3.

3. Heat the dripping in a pan, place the joint of beef in it and brown well on all sides. Lift out and place in a deep casserole.

4. Peel and slice the onions, peel and crush the garlic with a little salt. Fry lightly in the dripping and meat juices, and add to the casserole.

5. Pour over the red wine, season with salt and pepper and cook in the pre-set oven for 2–3 hours, or until meat is really tender.

6. Meanwhile wash the mushrooms and chop roughly. Drain the prunes. Remove stones from the olives and prunes.

7. During last 30 minutes of cooking time, add the mushrooms, olives and prunes to the casserole dish.

8. When meat is cooked, lift out onto a warmed serving dish, skim any fat from the cooking liquor and thicken with the kneaded butter. Pour around the joint and sprinkle with chopped parsley.

Pies and casseroles

Beef Goulash.

Beef Goulash

3 lb (1.5 kg) beef for stewing
oil for frying
1½ lb (700 g) onions
4 tbsp (60 ml) mild paprika
2 tbsp (30 ml) plain flour
1 clove garlic
1 tsp (5 ml) caraway seeds
2 tbsp (30 ml) tomato purée
1¼ pt (750 ml) stock
bouquet garni
salt and pepper

1. Set oven at 325°F (160°C) or Mark 3.

2. Trim the meat of any excess fat and gristle, and cut into large cubes. Melt a little oil in a frying pan and brown the meat in it quickly. Then place in a large casserole.

3. Peel and slice the onions, place in the pan and fry slowly. After 3 or 4 minutes, stir in the paprika, then the flour and blend in well.

4. Peel and crush the garlic clove with the

caraway seeds with a pestle and mortar. Add these to the pan followed by the tomato purée and the stock. Bring to the boil and then pour over the meat in the casserole.

5. Mix ingredients well together, tuck in the bouquet garni and season lightly with salt and pepper. Cool in the pre-set oven for 2½–3 hours until meat is quite tender. Remove bouquet garni and serve with plainly boiled rice.

Braised Oxtail

2 oxtails
seasoned flour
dripping for frying
1 lb (450 g) onions
1 lb (450 g) carrots
salt and pepper
stock
2 tbsp (30 ml) tomato purée
Worcestershire sauce
bouquet garni

This is a dish which is inclined to be fatty, so if possible we would recommend that you cook it the day before you plan to serve it. Overnight the fat will rise to the surface and then can be easily skimmed off before reheating.

1. Set oven at 325°F (160°C) or Mark 3.

2. Divide the oxtails into joints or get your butcher to do it for you. Roll the pieces in seasoned flour.

3. Heat some dripping in a large frying pan and brown them evenly all over. Lift out and place in a deep casserole.

4. Peel and slice the onions. Peel and chop the carrots into rounds. Add these to the casserole dish, season with salt and pepper and pour over enough stock to cover. Stir in the tomato purée and a sprinkling of Worcestershire sauce to flavour. Finally tuck in the bouquet garni.

5. Cook in the pre-set oven for about 3 hours. The meat is cooked when it falls easily away from the bone. Then leave to cool and skim off the fat as described above. Reheat well before serving. Remove bouquet garni before serving.

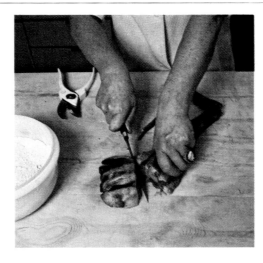

1. Cut through the oxtail joints.

2. Dip the pieces of meat in seasoned flour to coat thoroughly.

3. Shake off the surplus flour.

4. Fry the floured meat pieces in a little fat or oil and butter.

5. Cook over a brisk heat until the meat is evenly browned.

Pies and casseroles

Pork Cooked in Cider

3 lb (1.5 kg) pork
seasoned flour
oil for frying
½ lb (225 g) carrots
2–3 leeks
1 tsp (5 ml) powdered rosemary
salt and pepper
¾ pt (450 ml) stock
¼ pt (150 ml) dry cider

1. Set oven at 325°F (160°C) or Mark 3.

2. Trim and chop pork into chunks. Coat in seasoned flour. Heat a little oil in a frying pan and brown the meat evenly.

3. Peel the carrots and slice into rounds. Wash and trim the leeks, discarding the green part, and slice also into rounds.

4. Place the browned meat in a casserole dish, add the vegetables, season with the rosemary, salt and pepper. Pour over the stock and cider and cover tightly. Cook in the pre-set oven for 2–2½ hours. Serve if liked with cauliflower.

Pork Cooked in Cider.

Cassoulet

1½ lb (700 g) white haricot beans
½ lb (225 g) gammon
4 cloves garlic
1 small duck
dripping
3 onions
salt and pepper
bouquet garni
¾ lb (350 g) garlic sausage
½ lb (225 g) tomatoes
breadcrumbs

1. Soak the beans overnight in a bowl of water. Soak the gammon in a separate container.

2. Drain the beans and place in the pan with plenty of fresh warm water. Bring them very slowly to the boil – taking about 30 minutes. Cover and simmer very gently for about 1 hour.

3. Peel and finely chop the garlic. Place the beans and the soaked gammon in a large flameproof casserole. Add the garlic and enough water to cover well. Cover and simmer gently for 1–1½ hours.

4. Divide the duck into joints. Melt a little dripping in a frying pan and brown the duck pieces in it.

5. Drain the gammon and beans, reserving the cooking liquor. Return the beans and gammon to the casserole, add the duck and season with salt and pepper. Peel and slice the onions and add these together with the bouquet garni. Pour over some of the reserved cooking liquor, cover and simmer very slowly for 3–4 hours. Add more cooking liquor and water as necessary.

6. Roughly chop the tomatoes, and after 2½ hours of the cooking time add these together with the garlic sausage.

7. Set oven at 375°F (190°C) or Mark 5.

8. When the beans are tender take out the gammon and garlic sausage, slice up and return to the casserole. Sprinkle the top with the crumbs.

9. Place the casserole in the pre-set oven and cook for a further hour to brown.

Cassoulet.

Pies and casseroles

Chicken Cooked with Tarragon

3 lb (1.5 kg) roasting chicken
2 oz (50 g) butter
salt and pepper
1 clove garlic
¼ lb (100 g) mushrooms
6 shallots or small onions
2 tbsp (30 ml) finely chopped tarragon
bouquet garni
1 pt (600 ml) stock
1 oz (25 g) kneaded butter

1. Set oven at 325°F (160°C) or Mark 3.

2. Melt the butter in a pan and when foaming put in the chicken, breast side downwards. Brown the bird all over on a slow heat for about 15 minutes, turning as necessary.

3. Peel and crush garlic clove with a little salt. Wash and roughly chop the mushrooms. Peel the shallots and leave whole.

4. Place the browned chicken in a deep casserole dish. Add the tarragon and garlic and season lightly with salt and pepper. Arrange the mushrooms and shallots round it. Pour over the stock and tuck in the bouquet garni.

5. Cook in the pre-set oven for about 1¼ hours. Lift chicken, mushrooms and onions onto a heated serving dish. Remove bouquet garni, thicken the cooking liquor with kneaded butter and pour over.

Kneaded Butter

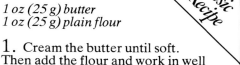

1 oz (25 g) butter
1 oz (25 g) plain flour

1. Cream the butter until soft. Then add the flour and work in well until it forms a smooth paste. Divide up into small pieces and use as required to thicken sauces and casseroles.

2. If liked you can make up kneaded butter in larger quantities and store in the refrigerator for future use.

Chicken Cooked with Tarragon.

Spicy Beef Casserole

5 lb (2.25 kg) beef for stewing
seasoned flour
dripping
3 carrots
3 large onions
1 pt (600 ml) stock
4 tbsp (60 ml) black treacle
2 bayleaves
allspice
3 tbsp (45 ml) brandy
3 anchovy fillets
1 tbsp (15 ml) wine vinegar
2 tbsp (30 ml) plain flour
½ pt (300 ml) single cream

1. Set oven at 325°F (160°C) or Mark 3.

2. Trim the excess fat from the meat and cut into cubes. Roll in seasoned flour.

3. Melt some dripping in a frying pan and add the meat to brown. Then place in a large casserole dish.

4. Peel and chop the onions and carrots. Add a little more dripping to the pan and lightly fry the vegetables. Add them to the casserole.

5. Pour stock into a pan, bring to the boil and then add treacle, bayleaves, a pinch of allspice and the brandy. Pour half of this into the casserole.

6. Chop up the anchovy fillets finely and add these to the rest of the stock in the pan. Blend them in well using a wooden spoon. Then add the vinegar and pour into casserole.

7. Cover and cook in the pre-set oven for about 3 hours or until tender. When the meat is tender lift out into a warmed serving dish. Then blend the flour into the cream and stir into the casserole. Bring back to the boil and simmer gently. Pour over the meat and serve with baked potatoes in their jackets.

Carbonnade of Beef

2¼ lb (1.25 kg) beef for stewing
seasoned flour
dripping
2 onions
12 shallots
1 pt (600 ml) light ale
1 tbsp (15 ml) brown sugar
1 tsp (5 ml) wine vinegar
bouquet garni
salt and pepper

1. Set oven at 325°F (160°C) or Mark 3.

2. Trim off any excess fat from the meat, cut into cubes and coat in seasoned flour.

3. Melt a little dripping in a frying pan, add the meat and brown overall. Put to one side.

4. Peel and slice the onions finely. Peel the shallots but leave whole. Turn the sliced onions in seasoned flour, add a little more dripping to the pan if necessary and fry the onions gently.

5. Have ready a large casserole dish. Cover the bottom with half the onions, then add half the meat followed by the rest of the onions and the remaining meat. Top with the shallots.

6. Pour over the beef, sprinkle with the sugar and wine vinegar and tuck in the bouquet garni. Season lightly with salt and pepper.

7. Cook in the pre-set oven for about 2½-3 hours. Remove bouquet garni before serving with creamed potatoes.

Irish Stew

2¼ lb (1.25 kg) scrag or middle neck of
    lamb
1 lb (450 g) onions
1½ lb (700 g) potatoes
1½ pt (900 ml) stock or water
salt and pepper

1. Set oven at 325°F (160°C) or Mark 3.

2. Trim the meat and cut into pieces. Peel and thickly slice the onions and potatoes.

3. Layer the meat and vegetables into a casserole dish starting and finishing with potatoes. Season well with salt and pepper.

4. Pour over the stock or water, cover and cook in the pre-set oven for at least 2 hours. The potatoes will pulp down to thicken the gravy.

Hunter's Hot Pot

8 oz (225 g) pork loin
2 pork kidneys
3 onions
12 fl oz (300 ml) lager
12 fl oz (300 ml) stock
1 tsp (5 ml) castor sugar
black pepper
1 bayleaf
1 lb (450 g) potatoes
1½ oz (35 g) butter
1½ oz (35 g) oil

1. Set oven at 325°F (160°C) or Mark 3.

2. Slice the onions thinly and fry gently in oil and butter until soft. Take out and set aside.

3. Skin and slice the kidneys, thinly slice the pork loin. Brown both in the pan in which the onions were fried. Remove the meat and set aside.

4. Still using the same pan, pour in the lager and stock with the sugar. Bring to the boil and then strain off the liquor.

5. Peel and thinly slice the potatoes. Place the kidneys, pork, onions, and potatoes in layers in the casserole. Put the bayleaf on top and pour in the liquor then finish with a thick layer of potato.

6. Cover with a lid and cook in the pre-set oven for 1½ hours. Increase the heat to 425°F (220°C) or Mark 7. Remove the lid and cook until the potato topping is brown and crisp.

Bouquet Garni

Basic Recipe

This bunch of herbs traditionally consists of 2-3 parsley stalks, a sprig of thyme and a bayleaf. The herbs can either be tied together with string, or tied up in a piece of muslin. A sprig of marjoram or a few leaves of chives can be added if wished.

Carbonnade of Beef.

143

Special Omelet with Mushrooms.

Eggs and cheese

Special Omelet with Mushrooms

6 eggs
3 oz (75 g) butter
salt and pepper

For filling
6 oz (175 g) mushrooms
1 shallot
2½ fl oz (75 ml) white wine
salt and pepper
2 tbsp (30 ml) single cream

To finish
¼ pt (150 ml) single cream
2 tbsp (30 ml) freshly grated Parmesan
*   cheese*
6 leaves Emmenthal cheese

1. First prepare the filling. Wash and chop the mushrooms into dice. Peel and grate the shallot. Place both in a pan season with salt and pepper and pour over the wine and cream. Simmer gently for 5–6 minutes.

2. Break the eggs into a basin and whisk them with a fork. Cream the butter and drop half of it into the eggs. Season and whisk again.

3. Have the omelet pan heating on a low heat. Also turn on the grill to heat. Toss butter into the pan, turn up heat and when melted and foaming pour in the eggs. Stir briefly with the back of a fork.

4. When the eggs have begun to set add half of the prepared filling. Fold over the omelet with a palette knife and turn onto a warmed flameproof dish. Pour over the remaining filling. Add the cream, scatter over the grated Parmesan and cover with the leaves of Emmenthal.

5. Place under the hot grill to brown before serving.

MAKING OMELETS

Making an Omelet

Basic Recipe ☆

4 eggs
1½ oz (40 g) butter
salt and pepper

1. Break the eggs into a basin and beat them well with a fork.

2. Cream the butter and drop a third of it into the egg. Season with salt and pepper and beat again.

3. While you are doing this have the pan heating over low heat. Now turn up the heat and toss in the butter.

4. When all the butter is melted and foaming tip in the egg mixture. Leave for a few seconds, then stir slowly with the back of a fork.

5. Cook for another few seconds, then flip over a third of omelet with a palette knife.

6. Have ready a warmed plate and turn the omelet onto it making a second fold.

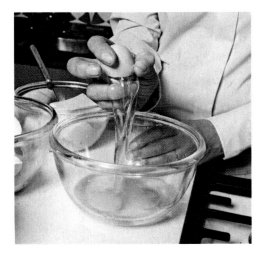

1. Break the eggs into a bowl.

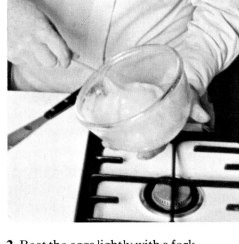

2. Beat the eggs lightly with a fork.

5. Melt some more butter in an omelet pan over a fierce heat.

6. Pour in the egg and butter mixture.

9. You can also use a fork to fold it.

10. Hold the pan at right angles to the serving dish and slide the omelet onto the dish, folding as you slide.

3. Soften some butter with the fingertips and drop pieces into the eggs. Season.

4. Beat in the butter.

7. Work the mixture for a few seconds with the back of a fork.

8. As it sets on the base, but is still moist in the centre, shake the pan to partly fold the omelet.

Take care of your omelet pan. Never wash it or use it for cooking anything else. To clean after use, wipe it while it is still hot with a clean cloth or kitchen paper. Prepare an old pan for omelet making by heating the pan and wiping it with raw pork fat immediately before use. To season a brand new pan, place it over a very low heat and half fill with coarse salt. Leave for 2 days then discard the salt. Wipe the pan vigorously with a cloth while it is still very hot. This treatment will prevent your omelets sticking to the pan.

Eggs Benedict

8 thick slices cooked ham
8 crumpets
2 tbsp (30 ml) butter
8 eggs

For hollandaise sauce
3 egg yolks
1 tbsp (15 ml) water
4 oz (100 g) softened butter
¼ tsp (1 ml) salt
cayenne pepper
1 tsp (5 ml) lemon juice
1 tbsp (15 ml) single cream

1. To make the sauce, beat the yolks and water until pale and thick in a basin set over a pan of hot water. Beat in the butter in small pieces. Continue beating until the sauce thickens. Add salt, pinch of cayenne pepper and lemon juice. Beat in cream. Keep warm.

2. Grill the ham for 3 minutes on each side. Toast the crumpets and spread with butter. Poach the eggs lightly.

3. Arrange a slice of ham on each buttered crumpet. Top with a poached egg and spoon a little sauce over.

Florentine Eggs

large packet frozen spinach
2 oz (50 g) softened butter
¼–½ tsp (1–3 ml) grated nutmeg
salt and pepper
6 eggs
6 tbsp (90 ml) single cream
2 oz (50 g) grated Cheddar cheese

1. Set oven at 350°F (180°C) or Mark 4.

2. Thaw and drain the frozen spinach. Brush the insides of 6 individual soufflé dishes with ½ oz (15 g) butter or margarine. Mix the spinach with nutmeg, salt and pepper. Beat in the remaining butter.

3. Divide spinach between the dishes and hollow out the centres. Break an egg into each hollow and pour a tbsp cream over. Sprinkle the cheese over the top and season.

4. Place in a baking tin half filled with water. Cover with foil. Bake in pre-set oven for 20–25 minutes until eggs are set.

Eggs and cheese

Chicken Liver Omelet

6 eggs
3 oz (75 g) butter
salt and pepper

For filling
6 oz (175 g) chicken livers
1 small onion
1 oz (25 g) butter
1 fl oz (25 ml) oil
¼ pt (150 ml) good stock
2 tbsp (30 ml) sherry
4 fl oz (100 ml) cream
salt and pepper

1. First prepare the filling. Chop up the chicken livers and peel and chop the onion. Heat the butter and oil together in a pan, add liver and onions, and brown well.

2. Pour over the stock and sherry and simmer for a few minutes. Then add the cream and cook briskly to reduce liquid sufficiently and thicken. Season.

3. Break the eggs into a bowl, beat them with a fork, add half the butter and season.

4. Toss butter into heated omelet pan, and when foaming and melted pour in the egg mixture. Stir with the back of a fork and when it has begun to set add half the prepared filling. Fold over with a palette knife and turn omelet onto a heated serving dish. Cover with rest of filling and serve.

Crab Omelet

6 eggs
3 oz (75 g) butter
salt and pepper

For filling
6 oz (175 g) mixed white and brown
  crabmeat
½ oz (15 g) butter
½ oz (15 g) plain flour
¼ pt (150 ml) white wine
salt and pepper
juice ½ lemon
¼ pt (150 ml) cream
chopped parsley

1. First prepare the filling. Melt the butter in a pan, add the flour and blend well together. Pour in the wine stirring continually. Add the crabmeat and the lemon juice and season with salt and pepper.

2. Simmer briefly, then add the cream.

3. Break the eggs into a bowl, beat with a fork, add half the given quantity of butter and season with salt and pepper.

4. Add remaining butter to the warmed pan and when foaming, add the eggs. When the mixture has begun to set, add a spoonful of the prepared filling. Fold the omelet over and turn onto a warmed serving dish. Pour over the rest of the crab sauce, sprinkle with chopped parsley and serve immediately.

Eggs Baked with Ham and Tomatoes

5 eggs
4 oz (100 g) cooked ham
4 oz (100 g) cooked pork
1 onion
½ lb (225 g) tomatoes
2 oz (50 g) butter
1 oz (25 g) plain flour
¼ pt (150 ml) stock
salt and pepper
chopped parsley

1. Set oven at 350°F (180°C) or Mark 4.

2. Remove any excess fat from ham and pork and chop into dice. Peel and slice the onion. Scald, skin and roughly chop the tomatoes.

3. Melt the butter in a pan and add the diced meat and onion. Cook for a few minutes and then work in the flour.

4. Add the chopped tomatoes and the stock and cook until all the ingredients are well blended. Season with salt and pepper.

5. Turn the mixture into a shallow ovenproof dish. Break the eggs on top and cook in the pre-set oven for 8–10 minutes.

Chicken Liver Omelet.

Eggs Baked with Ham and Tomatoes.

Eggs and cheese

Egg and Onion Flan.

Egg and Onion Flan

½ lb (225 g) quantity savoury shortcrust
    pastry
3 eggs
1 lb (450 g) onions
1 rasher bacon
salt and pepper
1 oz (25 g) butter
1 fl oz (25 g) oil
3 tbsp (45 ml) chopped chives
¾ pt (450 ml) milk

1. Set oven at 400°F (200°C) or Mark 6.

2. Roll out the pastry and line into a flan
ring or dish. Chill in the refrigerator for
about 30 minutes. Now line the pastry
with a piece of greaseproof paper and fill
with uncooked rice or beans.

3. Bake the flan case in the pre-set oven

for about 15 minutes, or until the pastry is
just set but not coloured. Remove beans
and greaseproof paper. Reduce oven
temperature to 375°F (190°C) or Mark 5.

4. Separate 2 of the eggs. Place the 2
yolks in a bowl with the third egg, season
lightly with salt and pepper and whisk
together. Then add the milk.

5. Chop the onions. Heat the butter and
oil in a pan, add the onions and cook until
soft and transparent. Chop the bacon and
fry. Leave to cool and then add to the egg
mixture with the chives.

6. Whip up the egg whites until stiff and
fold them into the egg and onions. Tip into
the flan case and cook in the pre-set oven
for 5 minutes. Then reduce heat to 325°F
(160°C) or Mark 3 and continue to cook
for a further 30 minutes.

Quiche Lorraine

6 oz (175 g) quantity savoury shortcrust
    pastry
1 onion
½ oz (12 g) butter
3 oz (75 g) bacon
3 oz (75 g) grated Cheddar cheese
2 eggs
¼ pt (150 ml) milk
¼ pt (150 ml) single cream
salt and pepper

1. Set oven at 400°F (200°C) or Mark 6.

2. Line a 7 inch (18 cm) flan ring with
pastry and bake blind.

3. Chop the onion and fry in butter until
soft. Remove the rind from the bacon.
Chop the bacon and fry. Arrange bacon
and onion in the flan case. Sprinkle with
grated cheese.

4. Whip eggs, milk and cream. Season
and strain into the flan. Bake in the pre-set
oven for 30–35 minutes, covering with
foil if necessary to prevent overbrowning.

Cheese and Leek Flan

6 oz (175 g) quantity savoury shortcrust
    pastry
2 leeks
2 oz (50 g) Parmesan or Cheddar cheese
½ pt (300 ml) creamy milk
2 egg yolks
salt and pepper

1. Set oven at 375°F (190°C) or Mark 5.

2. Make up pastry and line a 7 inch (18
cm) diameter flan ring. Prick base and
chill. Top and tail leeks, then chop them
and cook in boiling salted water until tender. Grate cheese.

3. Mix egg yolks into milk, add cheese
and season with salt and pepper. Sprinkle
a thick layer of chopped, cooked leeks
over the base of the flan case, pour over
custard mixture and bake flan in the pre-
set oven for 30 minutes, until filling is set.

Note: Extra cheese sauce can be served
with this flan, which is also good served
with small potatoes baked in their jackets.

Cheese and Leek Flan.

Eggs and cheese

Hot Cheese Puffs.

Hot Cheese Puffs

4 eggs
4½ oz (125 g) plain flour
4 fl oz (100 ml) single cream
2 fl oz (50 ml) beer
salt
1 oz (25 g) butter
grated rind of 1 lemon
olive oil for frying
1 tbsp (15 ml) Parmesan cheese

For sauce
1¼ oz (35 g) butter
1½ oz (35 g) plain flour
¼ pt (150 ml) white wine
¼ pt (150 ml) good stock
¼ pt (150 ml) cream
2 oz (50 g) Parmesan cheese
1 oz (25 g) grated Gruyère or Emmenthal
   cheese
4 oz (100 g) Demi-Sel cream cheese
salt and pepper

1. Separate the eggs, place the yolks in a basin and whisk them together.

2. Add the flour, cream and beer a little at a time beating well. Season with salt.

3. Melt the butter in a pan and blend in the lemon rind. Whisk into the batter.

4. Whip the egg whites until stiff and fold them into the batter.

5. Have ready a heated heavy based frying pan. Heat a little olive oil in it and then add about 4 tbsp (60 ml) of the batter. When the bottom has set, flip over with a spatula and cook on the other side. Keep the puffs warm in the oven while you cook the rest and make the sauce.

6. To prepare the sauce, melt the butter in a pan and blend in the flour with a wooden spoon. Pour in the wine, bring to the boil and beat until smooth. Then add the stock in the same manner. Pour in the cream and add the grated Parmesan. Allow sauce to bubble up until thick and creamy. Then add the Gruyère and the cream cheese a little at a time. Season to taste.

7. Spread each puff with a little of the sauce and pile them up on a warmed serving dish, pour over the remaining sauce and sprinkle the top with grated Parmesan. Brown under the grill.

Potted Cheese with Herbs.

Potted Cheese with Herbs

½ lb (225 g) grated Cheddar cheese
3 oz (75 g) butter
1 tsp (5 ml) each of fresh chopped
   chives, tarragon, chervil, sage, thyme,
   and parsley
1 tbsp (15 ml) double cream
2 tbsp (30 ml) sherry
salt and pepper
clarified butter

1. Place the grated cheese, butter, herbs, cream and sherry in the top of a double saucepan. Set over low heat and stir until all the ingredients melt and turn into a thick cream.

2. Season to taste. Then pour the mixture into small jars and allow to cool. When cold cover each one with ¼ inch (½ cm) layer of clarified butter and seal with lid. Keep in the refrigerator. Serve with fingers of hot buttered toast.

MAKING PANCAKES

4 oz (100 g) plain
*   flour*
salt
1 egg
½ pt (300 ml) milk
a little oil or lard for greasing
*   the pan*

1. Mix the flour and a pinch of salt. Make a well in the centre of the flour and break in the egg.

2. Add half the milk and gradually work the flour into the milk, beating until the mixture is smooth. Add the remaining liquid gradually and beat until it is well mixed in and the surface is covered with tiny bubbles.

3. Heat a little oil or lard in a 7 inch (18 cm), heavy based, flat frying pan until it is really hot, making sure that all the surface of the pan is greased. Pour off any surplus oil and reserve for using before the next pancake is cooked.

4. Pour a little of the batter into the pan, tilting it so that just a thin layer of batter covers the base. Cook over a low heat until the underside of the pancake is golden brown. Turn it over by tossing it or using a palette knife and cook until the second side is golden. Turn out onto greaseproof paper.

5. Make 7 other pancakes from this amount of batter, greasing the pan each time. If they are to be served immediately keep them warm between 2 plates in a warm oven.

Note: Cooked pancakes may be kept wrapped in greaseproof paper in an ordinary refrigerator for up to a week. Reheat them on both sides in a hot frying pan, without any fat.

1. Take the pan off the heat and pour a little batter in on one side.

2. Tip the pan to spread the batter thinly over the base. Cook on a low heat.

3. When the underside has set, slide a spatula underneath the pancake.

4. Lift carefully and turn the pancake over. Cook the second side for a moment. If the pancake is thick enough to toss, it is too thick.

5. Slide the cooked pancake out onto a piece of oiled greaseproof paper. Hold the edge of the pancake as it slides out.

6. You can store pancakes stacked on individual squares of oiled greaseproof paper. Wrap the stack in foil and keep in the refrigerator. Reheat in a low oven.

Cheese Crêpes

For batter
4 oz (100 g) plain flour
salt
1 egg
1 egg yolk
½ pt (300 ml) milk
1 tbsp (15 ml) salad oil

oil for frying
10–12 strips Emmenthal cheese
8 fl oz (225 ml) single cream
black pepper
3 oz (75 g) freshly grated Parmesan cheese
butter

1. Set oven at 375°F (190°C) or Mark 5.

2. First prepare the pancakes. Sift the flour into a bowl with a pinch of salt, make a well in the centre, add the egg and egg yolk and begin to add the milk slowly, stirring all the time. When half the milk has been added, stir in the oil and beat mixture until smooth.

3. Add the remaining milk and leave to stand for 30 minutes before using.

4. Heat a frying pan over low heat, then add a very little oil just to cover pan. Pour off any excess. Add about 2 tbsp (30 ml) of batter to the centre of the pan. Tip the pan so that the batter covers the base. When lightly browned on the underside flip over and cook the other side. Lay the cooked pancakes on a rack while you cook the remainder.

5. Lay a finger of Emmenthal cheese inside each pancake and roll up. Arrange them in an ovenproof dish.

6. Pour over the cream, sprinkle with Parmesan cheese and season with black pepper. Cook in the pre-set oven for about 15 minutes and serve immediately.

Cheese Crêpes.

MAKING CREAM CHEESE

2 pt (1 l) milk
4 tsp (20 ml) rennet

1. Pour the milk into a saucepan and place over a very low heat until quite hot.

2. Leave to cool down to blood temperature. Then tip it into a basin and add the rennet. Leave to set in a cool place (not the refrigerator).

3. When the milk has set take a large piece of muslin, double it over and lay it into a large sieve with the edges hanging well over the rim.

4. Spoon the milk into the muslin. Then tie the 4 corners of the muslin cloth together securely to make a handle.

5. Hang the muslin bag in a convenient place to drip for the next 48 hours. At the end of this time the dripping will have stopped. The cheese should then hang in a draughty place for another 24 hours to let it dry out. It will then be ready to use.

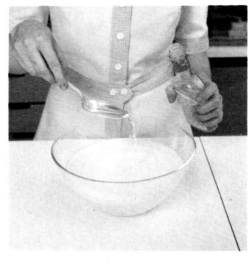

1. Pour the heated milk, or milk and cream, into a large bowl. Add the rennet. Leave to set in a cool place.

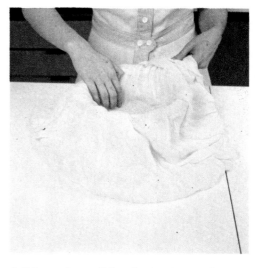

2. Line a sieve with a double layer of clean butter muslin.

4. Tie up the 4 corners of the muslin to make a handle and hang the muslin bag up to drip for 48 hours. It will need another 24 hours hanging in a draughty place before it is ready.

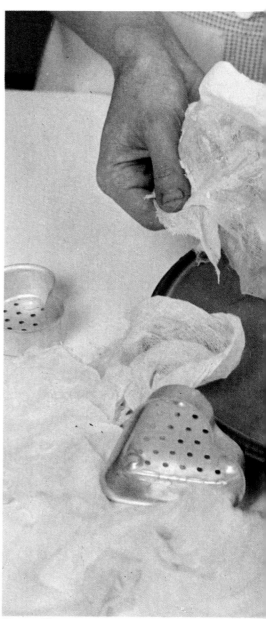

Cream Cheese.

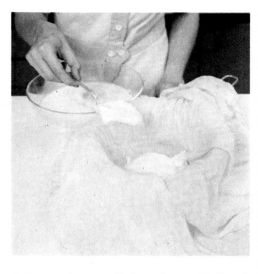

3. Spoon the set milk into the muslin lined sieve set over a bowl.

Swiss Fondue

12 oz (350 g) Emmenthal cheese
10 oz (300 g) Gruyère cheese
1 clove garlic
½ oz (12 g) plain flour
¼ pt (150 ml) dry white wine
1 tsp (5 ml) lemon juice
1¼ fl oz (35 ml) kirsch
grated nutmeg
black pepper

1. Rub the inside of a fondue pan or any heavy based pan with the halved clove of garlic.

2. Grate the cheese and mix with the flour. Put into the pan with the wine and lemon juice. Slowly bring to the boil, stirring continuously.

3. Add the kirsch and a pinch of nutmeg and pepper. Bring back to the boil. When the fondue is thick and creamy, it is ready to serve with cubes of French bread. Keep the fondue simmering during the meal. To eat, dip the bread into the fondue, using long forks.

Cheese Ramekins

2 eggs
2 oz (50 g) grated Cheddar cheese
salt and pepper
½ pt (300 ml) milk
2 slices bread
butter for frying
8 anchovy fillets
paprika pepper

1. Set oven at 375°F (190°C) or Mark 5.

2. Beat the eggs lightly, then add the grated cheese, seasoning and milk and set aside.

3. Cut the bread into cubes and fry in butter until crisp. Cut the anchovies in small pieces.

4. Butter 6 individual soufflé dishes. Divide the croûtons and anchovies between the dishes. Pour the egg mixture over. Place in a baking tin half filled with water and bake in the pre-set oven for 15–20 minutes or until firm and golden brown.

5. Dust with paprika pepper and serve.

Cheese Mousse

3 oz (75 g) cottage cheese
3 oz (75 g) Parmesan cheese
¼ pt (150 ml) milk
2 eggs
juice and rind of 1 lemon
¼ pt (150 ml) double cream
1 tsp (5 ml) powdered gelatine
cayenne pepper
nutmeg
salt

1. Separate the eggs and whip the cream.

2. Warm the milk to blood temperature. Place the egg yolks in a bowl, pour over the milk and beat gently.

3. Now add the cottage cheese and Parmesan cheese, the lemon juice and rind and the whipped cream. Blend well together.

4. Dissolve the gelatine as directed on the packet. When it begins to thicken, add to the egg and cheese mixture and beat again.

5. Whip the egg whites until stiff and fold them in. Season with a pinch of cayenne, a pinch of grated nutmeg and salt.

6. Turn into an oiled mould and place in the refrigerator to set. Serve garnished with pretzels if liked.

Cheese Fingers

8 oz (225 g) quantity puff pastry
10 oz (300 g) Roquefort cheese
1 beaten egg

1. Set oven at 425°F (210°C) or Mark 7.

2. Roll out the pastry to a thin rectangle. Brush half the pastry with water and lay slices of cheese on it. Cover the remaining pastry, pressing down well. Cut out 8 fingers and place on a baking sheet. Brush with beaten egg.

3. Bake in the pre-set oven for 15–20 minutes.

Farfalle with Bolognese Sauce.

158

Pasta and rice

Cook pasta in plenty of boiling water. Cover the pan and simmer until barely tender. To test if pasta is cooked try a piece between your teeth; it should be just firm – 'al dente'. Spaghetti takes 12–15 minutes, macaroni 10–12 minutes, tagliatelli 10–12 minutes, conchiglie 12–15 minutes, farfalle 10–12 minutes, fettucine 8–10 minutes, linguine 8–10 minutes, rigatoni 12–15 minutes. Strain off at once and rinse with hot water. Just before serving, drain and toss in butter.

Bolognese Sauce

4 oz (100 g) unsmoked streaky bacon
1 onion
1 carrot
2 stalks celery
1 oz (25 g) butter or margarine
2 tbsp (30 ml) olive oil
½ lb (225 g) minced lean beef
4 oz (100 g) chicken livers
1 tbsp (15 ml) tomato purée
sugar
½ pt (300 ml) beef stock and ¼ pt (150 ml)
  dry white wine, or ¾ pt (450 ml) stock
½ tsp (2 ml) dried oregano
½ tsp (2 ml) dried basil
salt and pepper

1. Cut the rinds off the bacon and discard. Dice bacon finely. Peel the onion and carrot and chop finely with the celery.

2. Heat the butter or margarine and oil in a pan, add the bacon and fry until crisp and golden. Remove from the pan with a slotted spoon and set aside.

3. Add the vegetables to the pan and fry gently for about 5 minutes until lightly coloured. Add the beef and fry for a further 10 minutes until browned, turning and stirring occasionally.

4. Meanwhile, chop the chicken livers and stir into the beef. Return the bacon to the pan and stir in the tomato purée and sugar. Add the remaining ingredients and stir well to mix.

5. Simmer the sauce for 25–30 minutes until thick and reduced, stirring occasionally. Taste for seasoning.

6. Serve hot on a bed of freshly cooked spaghetti or pasta bows, with grated Parmesan cheese served separately.

Pasta and rice

Spaghetti with Pesto

1 lb (450 g) spaghetti

For pesto
1 oz (25 g) fresh basil leaves
2 cloves garlic
2 oz (50 g) pine nuts
salt
2 oz (50 g) freshly grated Parmesan cheese
4 fl oz (100 ml) olive oil

1. First prepare the pesto. Peel and roughly chop the garlic cloves and place them in a mortar with the basil leaves. Pound well together with a pestle. Then add the pine nuts and a little salt and continue to pound.

2. Now add the grated cheese and work in until the mixture becomes a thick purée.

3. Begin to add the olive oil, a little at a time. Stir continually to make sure that the oil completely amalgamates with the purée.

4. Have ready a very large pan of boiling salted water. Plunge in the pasta and bring back to the boil as quickly as possible giving it a quick stir to make sure none has stuck to the saucepan. Continue to boil steadily for about 12 minutes until pasta is 'al dente' when tested. Drain immediately and turn into a heated serving dish, adding a knob of butter if liked.

5. Serve the pesto with the spaghetti.

Variation:
Walnuts may be used instead of pine nuts.

Tagliatelle with Tomato Sauce

½ lb (225 g) green tagliatelle
1 tsp (5 ml) vegetable oil
grated Parmesan cheese

For sauce
2 lb (900 g) ripe tomatoes
1 onion
1 clove garlic
salt
2 fl oz (50 ml) olive oil
2 tsp (10 ml) finely chopped fresh oregano,
or 1 tsp (5 ml) dried oregano
sugar
pepper

1. Skin the tomatoes chop the flesh roughly. Peel the onion and chop finely. Peel the garlic and crush with ½ tsp (2 ml) salt.

2. Heat the oil in a pan, add the onion and garlic and fry gently for about 5 minutes until lightly coloured. Add the chopped tomatoes to the pan with the oregano, a pinch of sugar and pepper to taste. Simmer gently for about 20 minutes until the sauce is thick and reduced, stirring occasionally. For a smooth sauce, you can liquidize it and then reheat, but this is not essential.

3. Meanwhile, put the tagliatelle in a large pan of boiling salted water with the vegetable oil. Cook for 8–10 minutes until tender, then drain and arrange in a warmed serving dish. Taste sauce for seasoning and pour over the tagliatelle. Serve hot with grated Parmesan cheese served separately.

Spaghetti with Pesto.

Veal and Mushroom Sauce

1 onion
1 carrot
2 stalks celery
1 oz (25 g) butter or margarine
2 tbsp (30 ml) olive oil
2 oz (50 g) mushrooms
4 oz (100 g) minced lean veal
2 large tomatoes
1 tbsp (15 ml) plain flour
7½ fl oz (225 ml) chicken stock
¼ pt (150 ml) dry white wine
1 tsp (5 ml) finely chopped fresh oregano, or
½ tsp (2 ml) dried oregano
salt and pepper

1. Peel the onion and chop finely. Peel the carrot and dice finely with the celery. Wipe the mushrooms clean with a damp cloth, but do not peel. Chop finely.

2. Heat the butter or margarine and oil in a pan, add the vegetables and fry gently for about 5 minutes until lightly coloured. Add the veal and fry for a further 10 minutes until browned, turning and stirring constantly.

3. Meanwhile, skin the tomatoes and chop the flesh roughly. Stir into the veal until evenly mixed. Sprinkle the flour into the pan and cook for 1–2 minutes, stirring constantly. Stir in the stock gradually with a wooden spoon, then add the wine, oregano and salt and pepper to taste.

4. Simmer sauce for 25–30 minutes until thick and reduced, stirring occasionally. Taste for seasoning. Serve hot on a bed of freshly cooked pasta shells, with grated Parmesan cheese served separately.

Conchiglie with Veal and Mushroom Sauce.

Pasta and rice

MAKING RAVIOLI

8 oz (225 g) plain flour
salt
2 oz (50 g) butter
2–3 fl oz (50–75 ml) cold water
beaten egg

For meat filling
6 oz (175 g) cooked minced beef
1 tbsp (15 ml) grated onion
butter
6 oz (175 g) cooked, well drained spinach
2 oz (50 g) cream cheese
2 oz (50 g) freshly grated Parmesan cheese
1 beaten egg
nutmeg
salt and pepper

For cheese filling
4 oz (100 g) cottage or cream cheese
4 oz (100 g) cooked, well drained spinach
1 oz (25 g) freshly grated Parmesan cheese
1 tsp (5 ml) basil or marjoram
nutmeg
salt and pepper

1. First prepare the paste. Sift the flour together with a generous pinch of salt into a bowl. Rub in the butter and then work in sufficient water to achieve a firm paste.

2. Place on a floured surface and knead well. Then divide paste in half.

3. Roll out the first piece very thinly. Dust with flour, set aside and cover with a clean cloth. Roll out the second piece keeping the surface well floured to prevent it from sticking to the rolling pin. If liked mark out the paste before you add the filling into 1¼ inch (3 cm) squares.

4. To prepare the meat filling, sauté the grated onion lightly in a little butter. Place the cooked mince in a bowl, add the onion, spinach, cream cheese and grated Parmesan. Mix together well and bind with the beaten egg. Season with salt and pepper and a pinch of nutmeg.

5. For the alternative cheese filling, place the cottage cheese or cream cheese, spinach, Parmesan and herbs in a bowl together. Cream well together and add seasoning and a pinch of nutmeg.

6. Spoon one of the fillings into a piping bag fitted with a plain nozzle. Pipe dots of filling onto the paste at regular intervals. Flatten the little piles of filling slightly with a knife dipped in cold water. Brush the paste in between the filling with beaten egg.

7. Lay the other sheet of paste carefully over and press down between the stuffing.

8. Cut the filled ravioli into squares with a knife or pastry wheel. Cover with a floured cloth until ready to cook.

9. Toss them into a large pan of boiling salted water and boil for 4–5 minutes.

Cappalletti with Meat Sauce.

Meat Sauce

½ lb (225 g) minced beef
1 onion
1 carrot
1 small stalk celery
3 oz (75 g) mushrooms
1 oz (25 g) butter
1 tbsp (15 ml) freshly chopped parsley
1 tbsp (15 ml) plain flour
2 tsp (10 ml) tomato purée
3 fl oz (75 ml) white wine
½ pt (300 ml) good stock
salt and pepper

1. Peel and chop onion and celery into dice. Wash and chop up celery. Wash and slice the mushrooms including the stalks.

2. Melt the butter in a pan and fry the onion in it. Add the other vegetables and the parsley and lightly brown.

3. Add the minced meat and brown it well. Then sprinkle over the flour and blend in. Stir in the tomato purée followed by the wine and the stock. Season with salt and pepper and simmer gently uncovered for about 30–40 minutes.

Lasagne Verde al Forno

1 lb (450 g) fresh lasagne verde
1 pt (600 ml) béchamel sauce
nutmeg
Bolognese sauce
butter
freshly grated Parmesan cheese

1. Set oven at 375°F (190°C) or Mark 5.

2. Cook the lasagne in a pan of boiling salted water for about 5 minutes. Do not overcrowd the pan. Drain and place in a bowl of cold water.

3. Prepare the béchamel sauce and flavour it with a pinch of nutmeg. Prepare the Bolognese sauce.

4. Drain and dry the lasagne. Butter a deep ovenproof dish. Now layer in the ingredients beginning with a layer of meat sauce followed by the béchamel sauce and then the pasta. Continue until the dish is full and finish with a layer of béchamel sauce over the meat sauce. Sprinkle with the Parmesan cheese. Bake in the pre-set oven for 25–30 minutes.

1. Thinly roll out the first piece of paste and mark into squares with a little metal wheel.

2. Fill a piping bag with the chosen filling and pipe blobs of it in each paste square.

3. Flatten the blobs slightly with a knife which has been dipped in water.

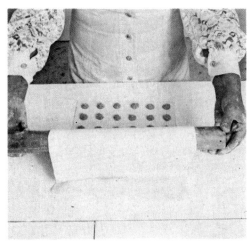

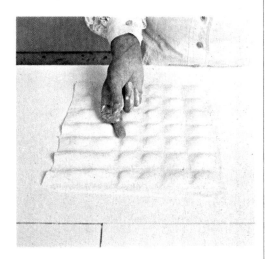

4. Brush the paste with beaten egg.

5. Using a rolling pin, lift the second piece of paste and place over the first.

6. Press into shape with a finger.

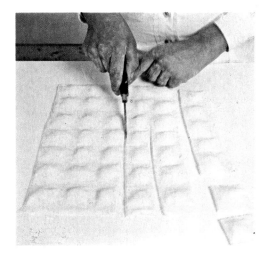

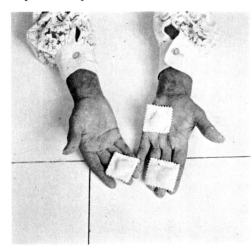

7. Using a knife or metal wheel, cut ravioli into squares.

8. Ravioli ready for boiling.

Pasta and rice

Cannelloni with Veal and Mushroom Stuffing

10 cannelloni tubes or pasta squares
salt
water
2 tbsp (30 ml) oil
1 small onion
1 clove garlic
½ lb (225 g) finely minced lean veal
4 oz (100 g) mushrooms
2 tbsp (30 ml) tomato purée
¼ tsp (1 ml) sugar
½ tsp (2 ml) dried oregano
pepper
a little stock or water
1 small egg
1 oz (25 g) softened butter or margarine

To serve
spinach and cheese sauce
grated Parmesan cheese

1. Set oven at 350°F (180°C) or Mark 4.

2. Put the cannelloni or pasta squares in a large pan of boiling salted water with 1 tsp (5 ml) oil. Cook for 8–10 minutes until tender. Lift out with a slotted spoon and leave to drain.

3. Peel the onion and chop finely. Peel the garlic and crush with ½ tsp (2 ml) salt. Heat the remaining oil in a pan, add the onion and garlic and fry gently for about 5 minutes until lightly coloured. Add the veal and fry gently for a further 10 minutes until browned, stirring constantly.

4. Meanwhile, wipe the mushrooms clean with a damp cloth, but do not peel. Chop finely. Stir into the pan with the tomato purée, sugar, oregano and pepper to taste. Stir well to combine. Moisten with a little stock or water, cover with a lid and simmer gently for 10 minutes, stirring occasionally. Remove from the heat, taste for seasoning and stir in the egg.

5. Spoon prepared filling into cannelloni tubes or divide equally amongst squares of pasta and roll up. Brush the inside of a shallow ovenproof dish with butter or margarine. Place the cannelloni in the dish in 2 layers.

6. Spoon over spinach and cheese sauce and bake in pre-set oven for about 15 minutes until the sauce is bubbling. Serve hot straight from the baking dish, with grated Parmesan cheese served separately.

Spinach and Cheese Sauce

4 oz (100 g) frozen chopped spinach
2 oz (50 g) grated Parmesan cheese
1 pt (600 ml) béchamel sauce
salt and pepper
½ oz (15 g) butter or margarine

1. Put the frozen spinach in a colander or sieve and leave to thaw and drain.

2. Stir the spinach and cheese into the hot béchamel sauce over gentle heat. Simmer until the cheese melts, stirring constantly.

3. Add salt and pepper to taste, then beat in the butter or margarine. Use immediately.

Cannelloni with Spinach and Cheese Sauce.

Mushroom Sauce

1 onion
1 clove garlic
salt
2 oz (50 g) butter or margarine
1 tbsp (15 ml) olive oil
6 rashers unsmoked streaky bacon
½ lb (225 g) button mushrooms
2 tsp (10 ml) plain flour
4 tbsp (60 ml) stock
¼ tsp (2 ml) oregano
pepper

To finish
1 oz (25 g) butter or margarine
2 oz (50 g) button mushrooms
2 tbsp (30 ml) fresh double cream
1–2 tbsp (15–30 ml) finely chopped
*   fresh parsley*
grated Parmesan cheese

1. Peel the onion and chop very finely. Peel the garlic and crush with ½ tsp (2 ml) salt. Heat the butter or margarine and oil in a pan, add the onion and garlic and fry gently for about 5 minutes until lightly coloured.

2. Meanwhile, cut the rinds off the bacon and discard. Dice bacon finely, then add to the pan and fry until golden.

3. Wipe the mushrooms clean with a damp cloth, but do not peel. Slice finely, then add to the pan. Fry until lightly coloured and the juices run, turning occasionally.

4. Sprinkle the flour over the mushroom mixture and cook for 1–2 minutes, stirring constantly. Stir in the stock with a wooden spoon, then add the oregano and pepper to taste. Simmer gently.

5. Melt the 1 oz (25 g) butter or margarine in a separate pan. Add cleaned, whole mushrooms and fry until lightly coloured. Stir in the cream and parsley, then remove from the heat.

6. Serve hot mushroom sauce on a bed of freshly cooked pasta and top with mushrooms, cream and parsley. Serve immediately with grated Parmesan cheese served separately.

FRYING RICE

½ lb (225 g) long grain rice
1 shallot or small onion
2 oz (50 g) butter
1½ pt (900 ml) stock

1. Set oven at 425°F (220°C) or Mark 7.

2. Peel and chop the shallot. Melt the butter in a frying pan, add the shallot and cook for a few minutes, then add the rice. Cook until all the butter has been absorbed.

3. Tip into an ovenproof dish, pour over the stock, cover and cook in the pre-set oven for about 20 minutes.

4. The cooked pilaf can be dotted with butter and sprinkled with grated cheese before serving.

1. Fry raw rice in sizzling butter, with a finely chopped onion, until the butter is completely absorbed.

2. If using the oven, turn the mixture into a casserole.

3. Pour on hot stock and cook until the liquid is absorbed.

Pasta and rice

Jambalaya, a Creole dish popular in the Southern States of America. The name Jambalaya comes from the Spanish 'jamon' meaning ham, one of the basic ingredients. The dish can also contain shrimps, crab or chicken.

Jambalaya

8 oz (225 g) Italian rice
2 Spanish onions
1 green pepper
1 clove garlic
salt and pepper
2 oz (50 g) butter
6 oz (175 g) uncooked gammon
6 tomatoes
dried thyme
dried basil
1 tsp (5 ml) paprika
6 drops Tabasco sauce
¼ pt (150 ml) white wine
1 pt (600 ml) stock
freshly grated Parmesan cheese

1. Peel and chop the onions. Halve the green pepper, remove core and seeds and chop into dice. Peel and crush the garlic clove with a little salt. Chop the gammon into dice and scald, skin and roughly chop the tomatoes.

2. Melt the butter in a frying pan, add the onion, pepper and crushed garlic and cook until tender. Then add the rice and cook until faintly coloured.

3. Add the gammon, tomatoes, and a pinch each of thyme and basil. Sprinkle over the paprika and Tabasco sauce, and pour in the wine.

4. Simmer until all the wine has evaporated. Then tip it all into a flameproof casserole dish and pour over half the given stock. Cover and cook on top of the stove.

5. Stir the rice from time to time and add more stock as necessary until the rice grains are just tender.

6. Sprinkle with Parmesan cheese before serving.

Risotto with Mushrooms.

Risotto with Mushrooms

12 oz (350 g) Italian rice
1 shallot or small onion
6 oz (175 g) mushrooms
1½ oz (40 g) butter
6 fl oz (175 ml) white wine
1¼–1½ pt (750–900 ml) stock
1½ oz (40 g) freshly grated Parmesan cheese

1. Peel and chop the shallot. Wash and slice the mushrooms thinly.

2. Melt the butter in a large frying pan add the shallot and cook gently until soft and transparent. Then add the sliced mushrooms followed by the rice.

3. Cook until all the butter has been absorbed, then pour over the wine and simmer until evaporated.

4. Now begin to add the stock about ¼ pt (150 ml) at a time. As soon as the stock is absorbed by the rice add some more. The rice should take 20–30 minutes to cook. At the end of that time the grains should be just tender and the risotto creamy.

5. Fork in the Parmesan cheese, cover and leave for a few minutes. Then turn into a heated dish and serve.

Rice with Lentils

1 lb (450 g) long grain rice
½ lb (225 g) lentils
1 onion
2 oz (50 g) butter
1 tsp (5 ml) ground turmeric
salt
2–3 pt (1.25–1.75 l) stock

1. Peel and chop up the onion. Melt the butter in a flameproof casserole, add the onion and cook for 5 minutes, then add the rice and lentils, and cook for a few minutes.

2. Sprinkle over the turmeric and season well with salt. Pour over 2 pt (1.25 l) of the stock, cover and simmer.

3. When all the liquid has been absorbed and rice is still firm, add some more stock. Continue to cook until rice is tender. Serve with mango chutney.

Pasta and rice

Seafood Pilaf

1 onion
1 green pepper
1 pimiento
¼ lb (225 g) mushrooms
2 oz (50 g) butter
1 lb (450 g) brown rice
saffron
2 pt (1 l) white stock
½ lb (225 g) cooked smoked haddock
1 pt (600 ml) shrimps or prawns
1½ oz (40 g) chopped almonds
4 tomatoes

1. Peel and chop the onion. Cut pepper and pimiento in half, remove core and seeds and cut into strips. Wash and slice the mushrooms.

2. Melt the butter in a frying pan. Add the onion and cook until soft. Then add the rice and cook for a few minutes, stirring to prevent over browning.

3. Turn into flameproof casserole and add the chopped pepper, pimiento and mushroom reserving a little of each.

4. Mix a pinch of saffron in some water, pour over and then add the stock. Cover and cook on top of the stove until rice is tender. Add more liquid if necessary.

5. Flake the cooked haddock and remove any bones. Peel the shellfish leaving the heads on some for decoration. Scald and skin the tomatoes.

6. When rice is cooked fork in the flaked haddock and some of the shellfish. Tip the rice onto a serving dish and decorate with the reserved mushrooms, peppers, pimientos and shellfish. Sprinkle with the chopped almonds and garnish with the whole tomatoes.

Kedgeree

1 lb (450 g) smoked haddock
2 eggs
4 oz (100 g) rice
2 oz (50 g) butter
chopped parsley

1. Cook and flake the haddock. Hard boil the eggs. Boil the rice.

2. Melt the butter and add to the rice. Fork in the haddock. Chop one egg and add to the rice mixture. Mix well and arrange on a hot serving dish.

3. Garnish with the sieved yolk of the second egg and sprinkle with a little chopped parsley.

Paella.

Paella

3 lb (1.5 kg) roasting chicken
¼ pt (150 ml) olive oil
½ lb (225 g) lean raw pork
½ lb (225 g) chipolata sausages
1 Spanish onion
1 pimiento
4 cloves garlic
saffron
¾ lb (350 g) tomatoes
1½ lb (700 g) long grain rice
2 pt (1 l) white stock
1 pt (600 ml) mussels
½ pt (300 ml) prawns
6 oz (175 g) cooked French beans
6 oz (175 g) cooked peas

Seafood Pilaf.

of the stove until rice is tender. Add more liquid if necessary.

6. Decorate the finished dish with the reserved prawns and arrange some of the mussels around the edge of the dish.

Note: ½ lb (225 g) of squid and a small lobster may be added to this dish. The squid should be washed and cleaned as usual and added to the pan at the same time as the pork and sausages. The lobster should be cooked as usual and the lobster meat added towards the end of cooking time.

Risotto Milanese

8 oz (450 g) Italian rice
1 small onion
2 oz (50 g) butter
1 clove garlic
⅓ tsp (2 ml) salt
saffron
salt and pepper
1¼ pt (750 ml) stock
2 tbsp (30 ml) grated Parmesan cheese

1. Soak a pinch of saffron in 2 tbsp (30 ml) hot water for 30 minutes.

2. Chop the onion and fry gently in half the butter for 5 minutes. Add the rice and fry for a further 5 minutes.

3. Add this with a third of the stock. Season and simmer, stirring occasionally until the rice thickens. Add more stock, and continue to cook until all the stock is absorbed.

4. Add the remaining butter and the grated Parmesan cheese. Mix well. Cover the pan, take it off the heat and leave for 5 minutes.

5. Stir with a fork and turn out onto a hot serving dish.

1. Divide the chicken into small joints. Heat approximately half the oil in a large frying pan. Add the chicken joints and brown them evenly.

2. Chop pork into dice and add to the pan with the sausages. Cook gently until the chicken is at least half cooked.

3. Meanwhile peel and chop the onion into dice. Halve the pimiento, remove core and seeds and cut into strips. Crush the garlic with a little salt and blend a generous pinch of saffron into it. Scald, skin and roughly chop the tomatoes.

4. Remove chicken, pork and sausages from the pan and set to one side. Add the remaining oil and then the chopped onion. Cook until tender, then add the rice and fry until the grains turn white. Then add the chopped pimiento, the crushed garlic and saffron, chopped tomatoes and some of the stock. Simmer for a few minutes and then turn into a large, shallow, flameproof casserole dish.

5. Have ready the mussels, well scrubbed and washed, and the prawns peeled. Reserve a few prawns with their heads on for decoration. Add the shellfish to the casserole together with the peas and beans. Season with salt and pepper and add the rest of the stock. Cover and simmer on top

Casseroled Onions.

Vegetables and salads

Casseroled Onions

2 lb (900 g) small onions
stock
3 oz (75 g) sultanas
2 tbsp (30 ml) brown sugar
salt and pepper
arrowroot to thicken

1. Set oven at 325°F (160°C) or Mark 3.

2. Peel the onions and leave whole. Place them in a casserole and add sufficient stock to cover. Sprinkle over the sultanas and sugar, and season with salt and pepper.

3. Cook in the pre-set oven for about 1¼ hours until onions are tender.

4. Mix some arrowroot with a little water and pour this into the casserole to thicken.

Turnips in Mustard Glaze

2 lb (1 kg) young turnips
2 oz (50 g) butter
¼ pt (150 ml) stock
1 tsp (5 ml) brown sugar
salt and black pepper
2 tsp (10 ml) Dijon mustard
2 tbsp (30 ml) chopped parsley

1. Peel the turnips and leave whole unless very large. Fry in butter for about 10 minutes, turning frequently, so that they become golden brown all over.

2. Lower the heat and add the stock, sugar and seasoning. Cover the pan and simmer for 20 minutes or until tender.

3. Remove turnips from the pan. Stir mustard into pan juices. Return turnips to pan and coat with the mustard glaze. Sprinkle with parsley and serve.

Vegetables and salads

Vegetable Fritters

1 small cauliflower
1 large aubergine
3–4 courgettes
1 onion
oil for deep frying
salt and pepper
freshly chopped parsley

For fritter batter
2 oz (50 g) plain flour
salt
2 tsp (10 ml) salad oil
2½ fl oz (60 ml) water
1 egg white

1. First prepare the batter. Sift the flour with a pinch of salt. Add the oil and water very gradually, stirring all the time. Then beat to a smooth consistency. Leave to stand for about 30 minutes.

2. Wash and slice the aubergine thinly. Spread the slices on a board and sprinkle them with salt. Leave for about 30 minutes to draw out the liquid.

3. Wash and trim the cauliflower. Cut into quarters and place in a pan of cold salted water. Bring to the boil and simmer gently for a few minutes. Then drain well and allow to cool. When cold divide into flowerets.

4. Wash, top and tail the courgettes. Slice into rounds. Peel and slice the onion.

5. Whip the egg white until stiff, then fold it into the batter mixture. Dip the prepared vegetables in the batter and then deep fry in the hot oil, taking care not to add too many to the pan at once. Drain on absorbent paper, sprinkle with salt and pepper, and serve garnished with parsley.

Vegetable Fritters.

MAKING DUCHESS POTATOES

1¼ lb (700 g) potatoes
salt and pepper
2 oz (50 g) butter
2 eggs

Basic Recipe

1. Peel the potatoes and cut into even pieces. Place them in a pan of cold salted water, bring to the boil and cook for about 15–20 minutes or until tender.

2. Set oven at 400°F (200°C) or Mark 6.

3. Drain well, return to the pan and set over the heat for a minute to dry off any excess moisture. Then pass the potatoes through a sieve and season well with salt and pepper.

4. Beat in half the given quantity of butter and the eggs so that the potato is a good piping consistency.

5. Spoon the potato into a piping bag fitted with a rosette nozzle. Pipe whirls of potato onto a buttered baking sheet. Melt the remaining butter and brush each potato pile with this. Bake in the pre-set oven for about 10 minutes until browned.

1. For pyramids, use a fluted nozzle and hold the piping bag vertically.

2. For rings, use a fluted nozzle and hold the pipe at an angle.

4. Use a knife to emphasize the shape.

5. For balls, just use a piping bag without any nozzle.

7. For galettes, shape little rounds with floured hands.

8. Brush the galettes with beaten egg.

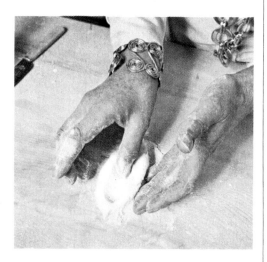

3. For boats, shape the mixture with lightly floured hands.

6. Pipe a large ball and a small ball, indent the top of the larger one and place the smaller one on top.

9. Make a crisp cross pattern with a knife on the top.

Stuffed Onions

6 Spanish onions

For meat sauce
½ lb (225 g) minced beef
1 onion
1 carrot
3 oz (75 g) mushrooms
½ oz (15 g) butter
1 tbsp (15 ml) oil
2 tbsp (30 ml) plain flour
1 tbsp (15 ml) tomato purée
Worcestershire sauce
¾ pt (450 ml) stock
salt and pepper

For meat filling
4 oz (100 g) minced beef
oil for frying
1 tsp (5 ml) dried thyme
2 tsp (10 ml) tomato purée
salt and pepper
beaten egg

1. Peel the onions and leave whole. Place in a pan of salted water and simmer until tender.

2. Meanwhile make up the sauce. Peel and chop the onion, carrot and mushrooms. Heat the butter and oil in a pan, add the vegetables and cook for a few minutes. Then add the minced beef and brown thoroughly.

3. Sprinkle over the flour and blend in well. Stir in the tomato purée and a few drops of Worcestershire sauce. Pour in the stock and season with salt and pepper. Simmer for 20–25 minutes.

4. Set oven at 350°F (180°C) or Mark 4.

5. Now prepare the meat filling. Heat a little oil in a pan and add the meat. Season with the thyme, tomato purée and salt and pepper, and cook until tender.

6. Drain the onions and allow to cool a little. Then remove the centres which you can chop up and add to the meat filling. Pile a little of the filling into each onion, place them in a shallow ovenproof dish and cook in the pre-set oven for about 15 minutes.

7. Pour the hot sauce into a warmed serving dish, arrange the stuffed onions in it and serve piping hot.

Dauphine Potatoes

8 oz (225 g) creamed potatoes
salt and pepper
oil for frying

For choux paste
2 oz (50 g) butter or margarine
¼ pt (150 ml) water
3 oz (75 g) plain flour
2 eggs plus 1 egg yolk

1. Sieve the creamed potatoes, season and keep warm.

2. Put the butter or margarine in a pan with the water and heat until melted. Sift the flour and stir in over a low heat. Beat the eggs and the extra yolk into the flour paste.

3. Blend the potato purée with the choux paste.

4. Deep fry small balls of the mixture in hot oil until golden brown. Drain on absorbent paper and serve immediately.

Creamed Carrots

2 lb (900 g) carrots
1 oz (25 g) butter
salt and pepper
2 fl oz (50 ml) single cream
chopped parsley

1. Peel or scrape the carrots, top and tail them and cut into rounds.

2. Place them in a pan of cold, salted water. Bring to the boil and simmer until tender.

3. Drain and pass through a sieve. Then return to the pan and place over low heat to drive off any excess moisture. Beat in the butter and season well with salt and freshly ground black pepper.

4. Stir in the cream and serve sprinkled with chopped parsley.

MAKING FRENCH FRIED POTATOES

1½ lb (700 g) potatoes
oil for deep frying
salt

1. Peel and cut potatoes into chips. Dry off thoroughly in a clean cloth before frying.

2. Heat fat to a medium temperature – about 350°F (180°C). Lower the raw chips in gently and fry for about 4–5 minutes until just soft but not coloured.

3. Lift out, drain well and set aside. The chips do not need to be fried again immediately.

4. Reheat the frying oil to about 390°F (200° C). Return the chips to the pan and fry briskly until deep golden brown. Drain them on absorbent paper, turn onto a warmed serving dish and sprinkle with salt.

1. Lower the basket of raw French fries into lightly heated oil.

2. Cook until they are soft and only lightly coloured.

3. Heat the oil to smoking hot. Lower the basket again and fry for a few moments until golden.

4. Drain on absorbent paper.

French Fried Potatoes.

Ratatouille

1 large onion
3 pimientos
1 clove garlic
olive oil
4 courgettes
2 aubergines
2 large tomatoes
salt and pepper
parsley

1. Peel and slice the onion finely. Remove core and seeds from pimientos and cut flesh into strips. Peel and chop garlic clove and crush with a little salt in a pestle and mortar.

2. Take a heavy bottomed pan, add sufficient olive oil to cover the base of it and heat gently. Now add the onion, pimiento and garlic and cook over a low heat for about 5 minutes, taking care not to let them brown.

3. Meanwhile prepare the courgettes and aubergines. Wash the courgettes, top and tail them and slice into rounds. Wipe the aubergines and chop into rough dice. Add these vegetables to the pan and allow to simmer gently with the lid on for 10–12 minutes.

4. Skin the tomatoes. Place them in a bowl, cover them with boiling water and allow to stand for a minute. Drain and peel away the skins. Chop roughly and remove seeds.

5. Add tomatoes to the pan, cover and continue to cook gently until all the vegetables are soft. Adjust seasoning with salt and pepper. Sprinkle with fresh chopped parsley before serving.

Casserole of Broad Beans

2 lb (900 g) shelled broad beans
3 small carrots
3 onions
2 cloves garlic
salt and pepper
¼ lb (100 g) belly pork
2 tsp (10 ml) brown sugar
¾ pt (450 ml) boiling water
bouquet garni

For garnish
grilled tomatoes
watercress

1. Set oven at 325° F (160° C) or Mark 3.

2. Peel and chop the carrots into dice. Cook in boiling salted water for about 10 minutes.

3. Remove skins from beans if necessary.

4. Peel and slice the onions. Peel the garlic cloves and crush with a little salt.

5. Remove rind from belly pork and cut into thin strips. Heat a frying pan and toss in the belly pork. Fry gently until well browned.

6. Add the beans, carrots, onions, crushed garlic, sugar and pour over the boiling water.

7. Tip into a casserole dish, tuck in the bouquet garni and season with salt and pepper. Cover and cook in the pre-set oven until vegetables are tender.

8. Serve garnished with grilled tomatoes and watercress.

Casserole of Broad Beans.

Vegetables and salads

Savoury Courgettes and Tomatoes

4 courgettes
3 tomatoes
1 tbsp (15 ml) freshly grated Parmesan
* cheese*

For courgette filling
4 tbsp (60 ml) white breadcrumbs
2 tbsp (30 ml) grated Gruyère
1 oz (25 g) butter
1 clove garlic
salt and pepper

For tomato filling
4 tbsp (60 ml) white breadcrumbs
1 tbsp (15 ml) mixed fresh herbs – parsley,
* chives or tarragon*
1 oz (25 g) butter
1 clove garlic
salt and pepper

1. Wash, top and tail the courgettes and cook in boiling salted water for about 10 minutes. Halve them and scoop out the seeds in the centre.

2. Mix together the courgette seeds with the breadcrumbs and grated cheese. Crush the garlic clove with a little salt and blend this into the butter. Then use to bind the stuffing mixture and season with salt and pepper. Fill this mixture into the courgettes.

3. Slice tomatoes in half and scoop out core and seeds. Mix this into the breadcrumbs and fresh herbs. Peel and crush the garlic clove with a little salt and then cream with the butter. Melt in a small pan and then mix into the crumb mixture. Pile onto the tomatoes.

4. Sprinkle the courgettes and tomatoes with Parmesan cheese and brown them under the grill before serving.

Red Cabbage

1 red cabbage
2 onions
2 oz (50 g) butter
4 tbsp (60 ml) brown sugar
½ lb (225 g) apples
¼ pt (150 ml) chicken stock
¼ pt (150 ml) red wine
3 tbsp (45 ml) wine vinegar
salt
black pepper

1. Shred the cabbage finely and blanch in boiling water.

2. Slice the onions and fry in butter until soft and transparent. Stir in the sugar and allow to caramelize but not burn.

3. Add the drained cabbage, chopped apple, stock, wine and vinegar. Mix well and season. Cover and cook gently for 1½ hours or until the cabbage is soft and the liquid absorbed.

Celery with Almonds

1 head celery
2 oz (50 g) butter
2 oz (50 g) blanched, slivered almonds
2 shallots or 1 small onion
salt
black pepper
¼ pt (150 ml) single cream

1. Cut the celery into 1 inch (2 cm) pieces.

2. Sauté the almonds in butter until crisp and golden. Lift out and set aside.

3. Chop the shallots or onion and fry with the celery and seasoning for 15 minutes in a covered pan. Stir frequently.

4. Stir in the cream and continue to cook for a further 20 minutes or until the celery is tender.

5. Stir in the almonds and cook gently for 5 minutes.

French Beans with Garlic

2 lb (900 g) French beans
2 oz (50 g) butter
1 clove garlic
salt and pepper
freshly chopped parsley

1. Wash the beans well, discarding any old ones. You can test these by doubling them over. If they are soft and pliable rather than crisp then they should be discarded.

2. Gather up a handful and top and tail them with a pair of scissors. Continue until all the beans are trimmed.

3. Plunge into a pan of salted boiling water and cook until just tender. If they are very young this should only take 10 minutes but if they are bigger it could take 20 minutes.

4. Peel and crush the garlic clove with a little salt. Work it into the butter. When cooked, drain beans immediately and return to the hot pan. Toss in the garlic flavoured butter and season.

5. Dish up on a warmed dish and sprinkle with freshly chopped parsley.

1. A bean which does not snap in half when you bend it is too old to eat.

2. Gather up a handful of beans holding them so that the tips are level.

3. Snip off the tips at both ends.

French Beans with Garlic.

Vegetables and salads

Fennel au Gratin. Fennel is a bulbous white root that looks a little like a fat celery heart. It has a pleasant flavour of anise, which is stronger in the raw vegetable. The leaves of the fennel plant can be chopped and used in sauces in place of parsley. Although fennel is considered an unusual vegetable nowadays, it is of ancient origin and was very popular until the last century.

Fennel au Gratin

4 small heads fennel
1 lemon
1 oz (25 g) butter
salt and pepper
1 tbsp (15 ml) freshly grated Parmesan
  cheese

1. Trim off some of the hard outer leaves. Then peel back some of the leaves and rub fennel all over with cut lemon. Leave to stand for about 10 minutes.

2. Plunge into salted boiling water and cook gently for 30–40 minutes. Drain when tender, return to the warm pan and toss in the butter.

3. Turn into a warmed serving dish and sprinkle with the Parmesan cheese. Brown under the grill before serving.

Beans with Peppers

1 green pepper
1 shallot
1 clove garlic
2 tbsp (30 ml) oil
1 tbsp (15 ml) butter
1 lb (450 g) French beans
2 tsp (10 ml) dried basil
salt
black pepper
4 tbsp (60 ml) grated Parmesan cheese

1. Slice the green pepper, chop the onion and crush the garlic. Fry these gently in oil and butter.

2. Prepare the beans and add to the pan. Sprinkle with basil and seasoning, and mix well.

3. Pour on ¼ pt (150 ml) boiling water. Cover the pan and cook for 10 minutes, or until the beans are tender and the liquid has evaporated.

4. Stir in the Parmesan cheese, heat through and serve.

Cauliflower au Gratin.

Cauliflower au Gratin

1 large cauliflower
1 pt (600 ml) mornay sauce
fine breadcrumbs
1 tbsp (15 ml) freshly grated Parmesan
  cheese

1. Wash the cauliflower thoroughly in salted water. Trim the stalk and cut off some of the outer green leaves. Divide the cauliflower into even size flowerets and boil in salted water for about 15 minutes, or until just tender.

2. Meanwhile make up the mornay sauce.

3. Drain the cauliflower thoroughly. Have ready a buttered ovenproof dish. Arrange the cauliflower in it and pour over the sauce. Sprinkle with bread-crumbs and grated Parmesan cheese and brown under the grill before serving.

Sautéed Mushrooms in Cream Sauce

½ lb (225 g) mushrooms
1½ oz (40 g) butter
3½ fl oz (100 ml) dry white wine
3½ fl oz (100 ml) stock
5 fl oz (150 ml) single cream
salt and pepper
6 tbsp (90 ml) chopped chives

1. Wash and roughly chop the mushrooms.

2. Melt the butter in a frying pan, add the mushrooms and fry gently for 2 or 3 minutes.

3. Stir in the wine and let it bubble up before adding the stock. Simmer for a couple of minutes.

4. Now pour in the cream and simmer until a thick creamy consistency is obtained.

5. Season with salt and pepper, and add the chopped chives.

6. This delicious creamy mixture can be served on star shaped croûtes.

1. Add the mushrooms to the pan.

2. Fry gently until butter is absorbed.

Sautéed Mushrooms in Cream Sauce.

3. Pour in the wine, allow to bubble up. When the liquid is absorbed, add the stock and let it bubble up and become absorbed as before.

4. Add the single cream.

5. Work the mixture together until it is thick and creamy.

6. The mixture is ready when it leaves thick streaks across the pan base when you scrape a spoon across it.

7. Season and add chives.

Deep Fried Aubergines.

Deep Fried Aubergines

3 large aubergines
salt and pepper
4 tbsp (60 ml) plain flour
cold water
oil for frying
paprika
freshly grated Parmesan cheese

1. Wipe the aubergines and slice up fairly thinly. Lay the pieces on a board and sprinkle them with salt. Leave for about 30 minutes. The salt removes excess moisture and any bitterness from the aubergines.

2. Meanwhile prepare the batter. Sift the flour into a bowl and fill a jug with cold water. Now begin to add the water to the flour very gradually and beating all the time. The batter is ready when it is the consistency of thin cream.

3. Wipe the water and salt from the aubergines with a clean cloth. Dip the slices in the batter and then deep fry in the hot oil until tender and well browned.

4. Drain on absorbent paper, then arrange in a warmed serving dish. Season each layer lightly with paprika, salt and pepper and sprinkle over a little Parmesan cheese. Brown under the grill before serving.

1. Slice the aubergines and spread out on a wooden board.

2. Scatter with plenty of salt. Leave for 30 minutes.

3. Wipe each slice with a clean cloth. This removes any bitterness.

Vegetables and salads

Stuffed Cabbage Leaves

1 green cabbage
melted butter

For stuffing
6 oz (175 g) long grain rice
½ oz (15 g) butter
1 tsp (5 ml) paprika
1 oz (25 g) currants
salt and pepper
1 tbsp (15 ml) freshly chopped parsley

1. First prepare the stuffing. Tip the rice into a large pan of boiling salted water and cook for about 12 minutes. Strain and tip into a bowl.

2. Chop the currants up finely and add these to the rice with the butter, paprika and parsley. Season with salt and pepper.

3. Wash and trim tough outer leaves from the cabbage. Cut away the stalk. Place in a large pan of boiling salted water and boil gently until just tender. Drain and then begin to peel away the leaves.

4. Spoon some of the stuffing mixture on to each leaf and then roll up like a parcel.

When the leaves become too small, use 2 leaves overlapping. Arrange them in an ovenproof serving dish and cover with melted butter.

5. If necessary, reheat in a low oven before serving.

Bean Sprouts with Ginger

2 tsp (10 ml) chopped root ginger
4 sliced spring onions
4 tbsp (60 ml) oil
1 lb (450 g) bean sprouts
1½ tbsp (22 ml) soy sauce

1. Briskly fry the ginger and spring onions in oil, stirring continuously for 30 seconds.

2. Add the bean sprouts and cook for a minute, stirring.

3. Add the soy sauce, lower the heat and cook, still stirring, for about 4 minutes.

Stuffed Cabbage Leaves.

1. Trim the asparagus spears to equal lengths. Scrape the lower ends.

2. Place upright, tips uppermost, in the asparagus container.

3. Lower the inner pot into the outer pot. Fill the outer pot with boiling salted water. Cover the lid and cook.

Greek Salad

1 crisp lettuce
2 green peppers
6 tomatoes
2 tsp (10 ml) oregano
salt and pepper
12 black olives
4–6 oz (100–175 g) cottage cheese
¼ pt (150 ml) soured cream

1. Wash and trim the lettuce. Halve the peppers, remove core and seeds and cut into thin strips. Scald, skin and roughly chop the tomatoes. Stone the olives.

2. Arrange the lettuce leaves on a flat serving dish. Place the tomatoes and green peppers on top, sprinkle with oregano and season well with salt and pepper.

3. Place the cottage cheese in spoonfuls over the salad, dot with the soured cream and finally add the olives.

Pepper Salad

12 oz (350 g) green peppers
1½ lb (700 g) small ripe tomatoes
4 fl oz (125 ml) salad oil
1 tbsp (15 ml) wine vinegar
chopped chives and parsley to garnish
salt and black pepper

1. Cut peppers in half, scoop out seeds and cut flesh into strips. Slice tomatoes, leaving the skins on.

2. Put the peppers and tomatoes in a bowl, sprinkle with salt and pepper, add oil, then vinegar and mix well. Sprinkle chives and parsley over to garnish and adjust seasoning, if necessary.

Note: This simple salad is suitable for serving with a selection of cold meats, or poultry.

Carrot and Walnut Salad, with Beetroot and Onion Salad in the background.

Carrot and Walnut Salad

3–4 carrots
8 walnuts
2½ fl oz (65 ml) fresh orange juice
4 fl oz (100 ml) mayonnaise
salt and pepper

1. Peel carrots and cut into julienne (matchstick size) strips, using a mandoline grater. Crack walnuts, cut into quarters. Beat the orange juice into the mayonnaise.

2. Mix the walnuts with the carrot sticks in a bowl and season. Spoon over the dressing and toss the salad just before serving.

Note: About ¼ pt (150 ml) French dressing can be used as an alternative to mayon-naise. Flavour with the grated rind of half an orange, if liked.

Beetroot and Onion Salad

1 large cooked or 4 small beetroots
1 large or 2 medium Spanish onions,
  or a bunch of spring onions
1 tbsp (15 ml) wine vinegar
¼ pt (150 ml) strong stock

1. Rub skin off the beetroot, if not already peeled. Cut into thin sticks, each about 1½ inch (4 cm) long and put into a bowl with the wine vinegar.

2. Peel onion and cut into thin rings. Add to beetroot and chill while bringing the stock to the boil. Pour over the beetroot and onions and serve.

Vegetables and salads

Potato Salad with Garlic

3 lb (1½ kg) potatoes
1 large clove garlic
1–2 tsp (5–10 ml) Dijon mustard
1 fl oz (25 ml) white wine vinegar
3 fl oz (75 ml) salad oil
1 large crust of brown or white bread
7½ fl oz (225 ml) stock

1. Boil or steam the potatoes in their skins. Peel the garlic clove and cut in half.

2. Peel the potatoes and cut into dice. Rub the salad bowl thoroughly (preferably a wooden one for this classic salad) with the cut clove of garlic, then add the mustard and some of the vinegar. Adding oil and vinegar alternately, whisk together until a thick French dressing consistency is achieved and the oil is totally absorbed into the mixture.

3. Crush the rubbed garlic and spread it over the crumb side of the bread crust. Cut crust into julienne (matchstick size) strips and place in salad bowl. Stir in the dressing until well coated. Add the potatoes and toss. When coated with dressing, bring the stock quickly to the boil, and pour over the potatoes. Toss again and serve on a bed of crisp lettuce leaves and garnished with a sprinkling of paprika, a little chopped parsley and a few black olive slices.

Variation:
This salad can be turned into a substantial snack by the addition of matchstick thin strips of continental garlic sausage, salami, chipolatas or Frankfurters. It is good served with watercress or crisp curly endive.

Potato Salad with Garlic.

Salad Marguerite

cooked cauliflower or carrots
small can French beans
small can asparagus tips
can potatoes
a little French dressing
mayonnaise to garnish
1–2 cooked egg whites

1. Break cooled cauliflower into flowerets. Dice French beans, asparagus tips and potatoes. Slice cooked carrots, if using and toss in a little French dressing.

2. Arrange in a bowl, smooth over top and make up just enough mayonnaise to coat the surface. Decorate with strips of egg white and slices of cooked carrot.

American Salad

1 clove garlic
½ pimiento
½ green pepper
6 green olives
6 black olives
2 crisp lettuce hearts from a Webb's, Iceberg
   or Cos lettuce
5 tomatoes
3 eggs
5 fl oz (150 ml) wine vinegar
paprika
7 fl oz (200 ml) salad oil
1 tbsp (15 ml) sweet pickle
2 bananas
a few flaked almonds
salt and pepper

1. Crush garlic clove with a little salt; scoop out seeds and core from the pimiento and the pepper; chop up olives; wash lettuce leaves; scald, skin and slice tomatoes and hard boil eggs.

2. In a bowl, pour the vinegar, add the garlic, paprika and oil. Whisk until blended and season with salt and pepper. Cut pimiento and pepper into strips and add, with the olives and sweet pickle. Toss until coated thoroughly with dressing. Leave to chill.

3. On a bed of lettuce leaves, arrange slices of tomato and hard boiled egg. Peel the bananas at the last minute and chop. Add to the platter. Garnish with flaked almonds and pour over chilled savoury dressing. Serve with French bread.

Vegetables and salads

Mimosa Salad.

Mimosa Salad

4 oz (100 g) peas
4 oz (100 g) French beans
2–3 sticks celery
6–8 spring onions
8 oz (225 g) potatoes
mayonnaise

For garnish
6 eggs
4 oz (100 g) button mushrooms
a little salad oil to moisten
½ tomato

1. Cook peas and drain, if not from a can. Cut French beans into small slices and cook. Wash and chop celery. Wash spring onions and slice, discard tough, dark green stems. Cut potatoes into dice and cook. Make up mayonnaise. Chop mushrooms very finely and soak in a little oil.

2. Mix together salad vegetables, adding just enough basic mayonnaise to bind well. Spoon into a bowl and smooth over top. Mark surface into 6 equal sections, using a knife.

3. Hard boil the eggs and remove the yolks. Push the yolks through a strainer and chop up the whites very finely.

4. Sprinkle the whites, then the yolks, over the top of the salad to decorate, starting from the edge and working to the centre. Fill the remaining 2 sections with the drained, oiled mushrooms and place a tomato in the centre of the dish to garnish.

Note: The Mimosa of the title refers to the hard boiled egg yolk garnish. This is a special party version of the dish. Usually, the egg yolks are sprinkled liberally over a green salad mixture.

Salade Basquaise

2 large pimientos
4 oz (125 g) rice
4 oz (125 g) French beans
1 shallot or onion
black olives
green olives
4 oz (100 g) peas
small can tuna fish or small can shrimps
chopped fresh thyme, if available, or ½ tsp
  (2 ml) dried thyme
mayonnaise
salt and pepper

1. Cut pimientos in half lengthwise and remove core and seeds. Cook rice and drain; rinse in cold water, spread out on a baking tray or flat dish and leave to dry. Cook French beans – if not from a can – and cut into neat dice. Peel and grate shallot or onion. Stone and dice olives. Cook peas and drain – if not from a can. Drain and flake tuna fish or chop shrimps.

2. Mix together the rice, beans, grated onion, diced olives, peas and fish. When thoroughly mixed, season and bind with a little mayonnaise and pile into pimiento halves. Sprinkle with thyme and serve.

Note: Extra mayonnaise may be served separately. Alternatively, bind the salad ingredients together with a little French dressing and omit the mayonnaise.

Cauliflower Salad

1 cauliflower
salt
8 anchovy fillets
2 shallots
8 tbsp (120 ml) olive oil
3 tbsp (90 ml) lemon juice
½ tsp (2 ml) French mustard
black pepper

1. Boil the cauliflower in 1 inch (2 cm) of salted water for 8 minutes only. Drain and break into flowerets. Place in a bowl.

2. Finely chop the anchovy fillets and the shallots, and place in a small pan with the olive oil, the lemon juice, the mustard and the black pepper. Bring this mixture slowly to the boil. Pour the hot dressing over the cauliflower.

3. Chill well before serving.

Wilted Salad with Bacon Dressing

½ clove garlic
1 cos lettuce
4 rashers bacon
1 tbsp (15 ml) wine vinegar
1 hard boiled egg
2 tbsp (30 ml) chopped parsley
salt
black pepper

1. Warm the salad bowl and rub the garlic clove around the bowl. Wash and dry the lettuce, tear into small pieces and put in the bowl.

2. Dice the bacon and cook gently in the butter for 10 minutes. Pour the bacon and melted fat over the lettuce.

3. Add the vinegar to the pan in which the bacon was cooked. Heat it through and sprinkle over the lettuce.

4. Chop the hard boiled egg. Toss the salad, add the chopped hard boiled egg, parsley and seasoning, and toss again. Serve immediately.

Coleslaw

1 lb (450 g) cabbage
2 carrots
1 crisp apple
2 shallots
3 tbsp (45 ml) cider vinegar
½ pt (300 ml) mayonnaise
¼ pt (150 ml) soured cream
1 tbsp (15 ml) sugar
1 tsp (5 ml) celery seed
6 drops Tabasco sauce
salt
pepper

1. Shred the cabbage, grate the carrots and the apple. Finely chop the shallots.

2. Place the prepared vegetables in a large bowl with the cider vinegar.

3. Mix the mayonnaise and soured cream together. Add the remaining ingredients.

4. Pour the dressing over the vegetables and toss thoroughly so that every shred of cabbage is coated.

5. Chill well before serving.

Caesar Salad

6 slices of bread from a standard sandwich
  loaf
1 small crisp lettuce
2 cloves garlic
4 anchovy fillets
milk
8 fl oz (225 ml) salad oil
1 level tsp (5 ml) English mustard powder
salt and pepper
3 fl oz (75 ml) white wine vinegar
1 egg
5 oz (125 g) hard or Parmesan cheese

1. Remove crusts from bread and cut into dice. Wash and tear lettuce leaves into strips.

2. Peel and crush garlic cloves. Soak anchovy fillets in a little milk to remove excess saltiness. Grate cheese.

3. In half the oil, fry the bread croûtons until browned and crisp, then drain on absorbent paper.

4. Place lettuce in a salad bowl with the crushed garlic. Drain and chop anchovy fillets and add to salad.

5. Sprinkle over mustard, season with salt and pepper if needed, and toss salad in the remaining oil. When the ingredients are well coated, add the vinegar and continue tossing the salad.

6. Lightly boil the egg for 1–2 minutes in boiling water, then break it into the salad bowl. Add grated cheese and, finally, the croûtons of bread. Serve immediately.

Waldorf Salad

5 apples
4 sticks celery
5 tbsp (75 ml) mayonnaise
salt
pepper
nutmeg
1 oz (25 g) chopped walnuts

1. Peel the apples and cut into cubes. Slice the celery and mix with the apples and mayonnaise.

2. Season and add a pinch of nutmeg. Sprinkle with chopped walnuts and serve immediately.

Hamburgers with a choice of barbecue sauces, Chilli Barbecue Sauce (left and in the background) and Apple Barbecue Sauce.

Snacks and savouries

Hamburgers

1 lb (450 g) lean minced steak
1 onion
1 tbsp (15 ml) olive oil
½ oz (15 g) butter
3 drops Tabasco sauce
1 tsp (5 ml) Worcestershire sauce
1 level tsp (5 ml) dried mixed herbs
salt and pepper
2 egg yolks
fresh breadcrumbs for binding
seasoned flour
oil for frying

1. Fry grated onion in oil and butter until soft and transparent.

2. Mix the minced steak, sauces, herbs, seasoning and cooked onion in a bowl.

3. Now add the egg yolks and, if the mixture becomes too soft, a few fresh breadcrumbs.

4. Turn the mixture out onto a clean working surface and divide into 6 even size round flat cakes. Dip each one in seasoned flour and then fry in a little oil.

Chilli Barbecue Sauce

12 oz (350 g) onions
½ small dried chilli
6 tbsp (90 ml) olive oil
2 tbsp (30 ml) wine vinegar
1 tsp (5 ml) Tabasco sauce
1 tsp (5 ml) salt
1 tsp (5 ml) dry mustard
1 tbsp (15 ml) brown sugar
4 tbsp (60 ml) water
4 tbsp (60 ml) lemon juice
grated rind 1 lemon

1. Chop the onions and pound the chilli.

2. Place all the ingredients in a pan. Bring to the boil and simmer 15 minutes.

Apple Barbecue Sauce

1 lb (450 g) apple purée
1 tsp (5 ml) brown sugar
1 tsp (5 ml) mixed spice
½ tsp (2.5 ml) dry mustard
1 tbsp (15 ml) wine vinegar

Simply mix the ingredients and heat.

Snacks and savouries

1. Sharpen a very clean garden stake to a point with a Stanley knife.

2. Thread the sausages onto the stake, brush them with oil and prick with a fork. Lay the stake across the barbecue, turning so that the sausages cook evenly.

Hot Dogs with Fried Onion Rings.

Hot Dogs

1 lb (450 g) fresh frankfurters or large pork
  sausages if preferred
6–8 rolls
butter for spreading
a little made English mustard

For fried onion rings
1 large onion
a little plain flour mixed with water
oil for frying

1. Grill or fry the frankfurters.

2. Split the rolls down the middle, butter them and spread with a little mustard.

3. Peel and slice the onion into thin rings. Mix some flour and water together in a bowl to a creamy consistency. Then dip the onion rings in the mixture and shallow fry until crisp and brown.

4. Fill the prepared rolls with the cooked frankfurters and garnish with the onion rings.

Bacon and Mushroom Bread Snack

1 small round loaf or cottage loaf
1 egg
2¼ fl oz (75 ml) milk
4 or 6 rashers back bacon
1 oz (25 g) butter or margarine
1 oz (25 g) cooking oil
6 oz (175 g) mushrooms
1 oz (25 g) plain flour
English mustard
¼ pt (150 ml) brown stock
salt and pepper
spring onions

1. Cut base crust off small round loaf and hollow out until a bread 'shell' is left. Invert and cut top into v-shapes to decorate, if liked.

2. Whisk egg with milk and dip bread in the mixture until thoroughly coated. Deep fry in hot fat until browned and crisp. Drain on absorbent paper and keep hot while preparing filling. Wipe and slice the mushrooms.

3. De-rind bacon rashers, stretch a little by running the back of a knife along them, and fry in a little extra fat, if necessary. When cooked, roll up each rasher into a 'curl', and keep hot.

4. Add the extra butter or margarine and oil to the pan. Add the sliced mushrooms, stalks and all, and sauté over low heat until cooked. Sprinkle over flour and stir until absorbed; add a pinch of mustard then gradually add the stock, stirring well between each addition. Season with salt and pepper. If the mixture is too runny, turn up heat and boil to reduce liquid a little.

5. Heap the mixture inside the bread case, top with bacon rolls and serve hot, garnished with spring onions.

Variation:
A sprinkling of dry sherry poured in just before serving gives the sauce a particularly rich flavour.

Scrambled Eggs with Shrimps

2 slices white bread, each ½ inch (1 cm)
*   thick, cut from the length of a medium*
*   sized loaf*
a little oil or butter for frying
1 oz (25 g) butter or margarine
¼ pint (150 ml) peeled shrimps
3 eggs
2–3 tbsp (30–45 ml) milk
salt and pepper

1. Trim the bread slices with a fancy pastry cutter and fry them in oil or butter until golden brown. Drain on absorbent paper and keep hot.

2. Melt the butter or margarine in a pan over low heat, break eggs into a bowl, add milk and whisk briskly.

3. Season with a little white pepper and pour eggs into pan, stirring continuously with a wooden spoon until lightly cooked.

4. As soon as they are lightly set, take pan off heat and stir in half the shrimps. Adjust seasoning and heap onto the fried bread base and decorate with the remaining shrimps.

Variation:
2 oz (50 g) smoked eel makes a luxury variation of this simple dish. A few snipped chives add a colourful and tasty garnish, too.

Croque Monsieur

For each portion:
2 slices white bread from a standard
*   sandwich loaf*
½ oz (15 g) butter
1 slice cooked ham to fit bread slice
2 slices Gruyère or Emmenthal cheese to fit
*   bread slice*

1. Trim crusts from bread slices, lightly spread with butter.

2. Lay a slice of cheese on one slice of the buttered bread, place the slice of ham on top, add the second slice of cheese and top with the second slice of buttered bread.

3. Grill on both sides until toasted and golden brown, and the cheese is melted. Eat immediately.

Bacon and Mushroom Bread Snack.

Scrambled Eggs with Shrimps.

Snacks and savouries

Block Buster.

Block Buster

1 French stick
butter for spreading

For filling
a selection of cold meats including ham,
*   liver sausage, salami, mortadella*
slices of Cheddar, Dutch Gouda or
*   Emmenthal cheese*
green and black olives
gherkins
pickled onions
sliced tomatoes

For garnish
sprigs of watercress and endive

1. Split the French stick lengthwise and butter on the inside.

2. Fill the loaf generously with all, or a selection of the given ingredients and garnish with watercress and endive.

Club Sandwiches

18 slices white bread for toasting
butter for spreading

For filling
8 oz (225 g) cooked chicken or turkey
8 oz (225 g) streaky bacon
3 eggs
3 large tomatoes
½ cucumber
1 crisp lettuce heart preferably the Webb's
*   variety*
6 fl oz (175 ml) mayonnaise
salt and pepper

1. Cut the cold chicken or turkey into thin slices. Grill the bacon slowly taking care not to overcook it. Hard boil the eggs.

2. Wash the lettuce heart and divide up. Slice the cucumber and tomatoes.

3. Now toast the bread lightly and butter each slice. Make up 6 3 decker sandwiches dividing the ingredients evenly between each. Season each with salt and pepper and add a little mayonnaise. Serve immediately for a lunch or suppertime snack.

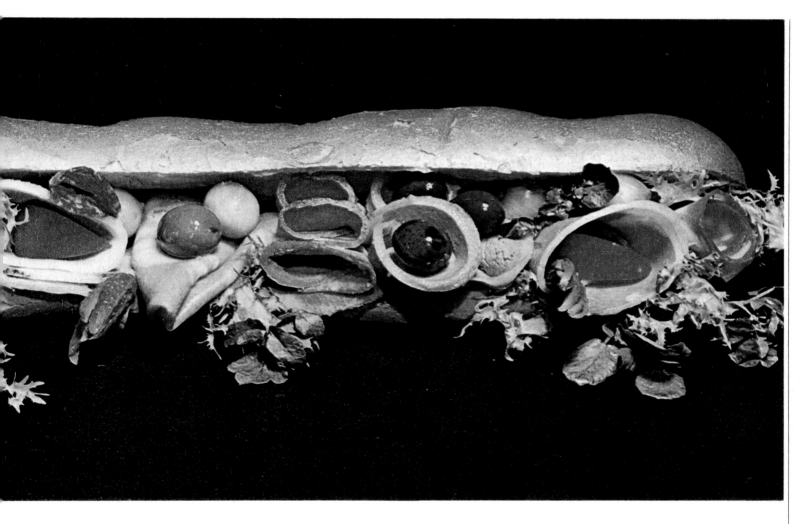

Club Sandwiches.

To cut thin slices of bread; spread each slice with soft butter before you cut it, then dip a very sharp knife in hot water, shake off the surplus water, and then with this hot, moist knife you will be able to cut very thin slices of bread. Cut off the crusts if you wish.

Snacks and savouries

Savoury Tartlets Provençale

*8 oz (225 g) quantity savoury shortcrust
   pastry*
dried rice or beans for baking blind

For filling
1 large onion
3 pimientoes
1 clove garlic
olive oil for frying
2 medium size courgettes
1 medium size aubergine
2 large tomatoes

salt and pepper
freshly grated Parmesan cheese

1. Set the oven at 350°F (180°C) or
Mark 4.

2. Roll the pastry out thinly and line into
tartlet moulds. Leave to chill in the refrigerator.

3. Now prepare the vegetables for filling.
Peel and slice the onion finely. Remove
core and seeds from pimientoes and cut
flesh into strips. Peel and chop garlic clove
and crush with a little salt. Top and tail the
courgettes and slice into rounds. Chop the
aubergine into rough dice. Scald and skin
the tomatoes, chop roughly and remove
the seeds.

4. Heat some olive oil in a heavy based
pan, add the onion, pimiento and garlic
and cook over low heat for about 5 minutes, taking care not to let them brown.

5. Add the courgettes and aubergines to
the pan and allow to simmer gently with
the lid on for 10–12 minutes.

6. Finally add the chopped tomatoes and
continue to cook gently until all the vegetables are soft.

7. Prick small holes with a fork on the
base of the tartlets. Put a piece of foil in
each and bake in the pre-set oven on the
shelf above centre for 20 minutes, removing foil after 15 minutes.

8. Spoon some filling into each of the
tartlets, sprinkle with Parmesan cheese
and brown under the grill before serving.

Cheese and Potato Croquettes

10 oz (275 g) potatoes
1 oz (25 g) butter or margarine
6 oz (175 g) Gruyère or Cheddar cheese
2 egg yolks
2 oz (50 g) plain flour
2 oz (50 g) fresh white breadcrumbs
1 egg
salt and pepper
oil

1. Peel and boil potatoes. Mash well or
push through a sieve. When cool, beat in
the butter or margarine and chill. Grate
cheese. Sift flour and beat egg. Put flour,
egg and breadcrumbs in separate dishes.

2. Beat cheese and egg yolks into the
cooled potato and seasoning. Chill.

3. Roll out mixture into a long thin strip
about 1½ inches (4 cm) in diameter and cut
into 4 inch (10 cm) lengths. Dip each croquette into first flour, then beaten egg,
then roll thoroughly in breadcrumbs. Chill
each coated croquette in the refrigerator
until firm. Deep fry in oil until golden
brown.

Savoury Tartlets Provençale.

Fried Camembert

1 whole Camembert cheese
1 beaten egg
fine breadcrumbs
oil

1. Unwrap the Camembert, which should be soft and ready to eat. Carefully scrape away any excess white powdery substance clinging to the rind of the cheese.

2. Cut the cheese in half, then into quarters and then each quarter into 2 so that you have 8 pieces altogether.

3. Dip the pieces in the beaten egg and then turn in the breadcrumbs, making sure that they are completely covered. Then deep fry in oil until golden brown.

Savoury Cutlets

6 ½ inch (12 mm) slices of cold cooked
  chicken or turkey
cold mashed potato made with:
  ½ lb (225 g) potatoes
  1 small egg yolk
  a little butter
  salt and pepper
2 tbsp (15 ml) tomato purée
1 beaten egg
fine breadcrumbs
oil

1. Peel and boil the potatoes until tender. Drain and return to pan over heat to dry off any excess moisture. Press the potatoes through a sieve into a bowl. Beat in the butter and egg yolk and season with salt and pepper. Leave to cool.

2. Using a pastry cutter of your choice, stamp out a cutlet from each slice of meat. Then spread the cutlets with a little tomato purée.

3. Top each with some cold mashed potato, dip in beaten egg and roll in breadcrumbs. Deep fry in oil until crisp and brown.

Fried Camembert.

Savoury Cutlets.

Provençale Onion Flan.

Quick Pizza Napolitana.

Provençale Onion Flan

6 oz (175 g) basic shortcrust pastry
1¼ lb (675 g) onions
2 cloves garlic
16–20 anchovy fillets
32 black olives
1¼ oz (75 ml) oil
1¼ oz (75 g) butter or margarine

1. Set oven at 375°F (190°C) or Mark 5.

2. Make up pastry. Peel and slice onions into very thin rings. Peel and chop garlic finely. Slice anchovy fillets into very thin strips. Soak in a little milk. (Stone black olives, if not already pitted.)

3. Roll out pastry very thinly and line into a shallow 10 inch (25 cm) flan ring. Prick the base with a fork and chill. Heat oil and butter in a frying pan and fry onion rings with garlic over a low heat until transparent, but not brown. Turn into pastry case and smooth over. Make a neat lattice pattern of drained anchovy strips and place an olive in each square.

4. Bake in the pre-set oven for about 30–35 minutes until pastry is golden brown and topping is cooked.

Note: The quantity of half butter and half oil – if butter is used – stops the butter from browning too quickly and burning.

Quick Pizza Napolitana

12 oz (350 g) bread dough or basic puff
pastry
2–3 oz (50–75 g) Emmenthal or
Mozzarella cheese
4 oz (100 g) pitted green and black olives
8 anchovy fillets
4 tomatoes
dried mixed herbs or dried basil
oil
black pepper

1. Set oven at 400°F (200°C) or Mark 6.

2. Roll out the dough to a circle about ¼ inch (½ cm) thick and place on a floured baking sheet.

3. Grate the cheese. Slice anchovy fillets in half and soak in a little milk, if liked, to remove excess saltiness. Scald, skin and de-seed tomatoes.

4. Sprinkle the dough round with grated cheese, dot the surface with olives. Drain and arrange anchovy fillets between the olives. Slice the tomatoes and scatter slices over surface. Add a generous pinch or two of dried mixed herbs, or basil, and sprinkle surface with drops of cooking oil. Grind over some black pepper, and bake the pizza in the pre-set oven until dough or pastry is golden brown and cooked – about 20–30 minutes.

Note: If dough has not been proved twice, leave pizza for 10–15 minutes in a warm place to rise a little before cooking. A bread mix, ready baked, may be used for this pizza, in which case, bake case before filling, then slide pizza under grill to cook the topping until cheese bubbles.

Pineapple Cream.

Desserts and puddings

Pineapple Cream

1 large can crushed pineapple in syrup
3 egg yolk quantity confectioners' custard
¼ pt (150 ml) double cream
¾ oz (20 g) powdered gelatine
3 tbsp (45 ml) cold water

1. Strain the pineapple, place pulp in a blender and blend thoroughly. Beat in the confectioners' custard.

2. Whip the cream until very stiff.

3. Dissolve the gelatine in water and stir into the pineapple mixture. Carefully fold in the whipped cream.

4. Pour into a lightly oiled mould and leave to set.

5. Unmould into the centre of a flat oval dish and serve with fresh pineapple if desired.

Vanilla Cream

1 pt (600 ml) milk
4 level tbsp (60 ml) castor sugar
2 separated eggs
vanilla essence
4 level tsp (20 ml) powdered gelatine
2 tbsp (30 ml) water

1. Heat together the milk, sugar, beaten egg yolks and a few drops of vanilla essence to make a custard and leave to cool.

2. Dissolve the gelatine in the water and add to the custard mixture.

3. Whisk the egg whites stiffly and fold lightly into the cool custard mixture.

4. Pour into a decorative mould or glass dish and leave to set.

5. Turn out just before serving. Serve with lemon wedges, stewed fruit or jam.

Note: Do not worry when this mixture separates out. The finished dessert should be in layers with jelly on the top and the custard underneath.

Desserts and puddings

Cherry Cream.

Cherry Cream

¾ oz (20 g) gelatine
4 tbsp (60 ml) cold water
1 lb (450 g) tin stoned black cherries or 1 lb
    (450 g) fresh stoned black cherries of
    which 6 oz (175 g) have been liquidized
    to give approx 6 fl oz (175 ml) of juice.
¼ pt (150 ml) sweet white wine or water
½ pt (300 ml) whipping cream or double
    cream
1 tbsp (15 ml) kirsch
extra whipped cream for decoration if
    liked.

1. Dissolve the gelatine in the cold water.
Strain on the juice from the tin of cherries
or that extracted from the fresh cherries.
Stir in the wine or water and allow to cool.

2. Whip the cream lightly and then whip
it quickly into the juice.

3. Pour into a lightly oiled 1½–1¾ pt (1 l)
ring mould and leave to set.

4. Turn out onto a large round flat plate
and fill the centre with the stoned cherries.
Sprinkle kirsch onto the cherries if liked.
Decorate with piped cream and cherries
or serve it plain.

Marie Louise Pudding

4 oz (100 g) cooking chocolate
2 6 inch (15 cm) rounds of swiss roll sponge
¾ lb (350 g) cooking chocolate
4 egg yolks
½ pt (300 ml) lightly whipped double cream
1 tbsp (15 ml) rum
1 tsp (5 ml) orange flower water
1 tsp (5 ml) rose water
¼ pt (150 ml) double cream

1. First prepare the chocolate case in
which the chocolate cream is to be served.
Use a loose based cake tin 6 inches (15
cm) diameter and 3 inches (7.5 cm) deep.
Line it at the bottom and sides with car-
tridge paper. When it fits exactly with a 1
inch (2.5 cm) overlap at the sides, remove
the paper and stick onto it matching
shapes in waxed paper. Fit these back into
the tin.

2. Melt the 4 oz (100 g) cooking chocolate in the top of a double saucepan and tip
half of it into the tin. Tilt the tin in all
directions until the base and sides are well
coated. Leave in a refrigerator to set and
then repeat the process with the remaining
melted chocolate.

3. Leave to set again and then gently
ease the case out of the tin by pushing up
the base. Carefully remove the paper and
place on serving dish.

4. Place the circles of sponge in the
chocolate case.

5. Melt the remaining cooking chocolate
until smooth and thick. Allow to cool.

6. Beat the eggs and cream together well
in a large bowl.

7. Add the softened chocolate to the
eggs and cream beating well all the time.

8. Add the rum, orange flower water and
rose water and continue beating until the
consistency of stiff whipped cream.

9. Fill the prepared chocolate case and
level off the top.

10. Decorate with piped whipped cream
and keep refrigerated until served.

Apricot Cream

¾ pt (450 ml) apricot purée
16 soaked apricot halves if dried, or 8 whole
*   fresh small apricots, split and stoned*
7 fl oz (200 ml) single cream
¼ pt (150 ml) milk
1 oz (25 g) powdered gelatine
2 tbsp (30 ml) cold water
4 oz (100 g) cream cheese
castor sugar for sweetening to taste
1 tbsp (15 ml) apricot brandy

1. If using dried apricots for the purée, soak them in cold strained tea for a minimum of 36 hours – then they will not require cooking.

2. Mix the apricot purée with the cream and milk and blend in well. Check for sweetness and add a little castor sugar.

3. Dissolve the gelatine in the water, in a cup placed in a pan of gently boiling water. Add apricot brandy if being used. Beat this into the apricot mixture.

4. Pour into a decorative mould of 1¾ – 2 pt (1 – 1¼ l) capacity and leave to set.

5. Mix the cream cheese with castor sugar to taste. Put into a piping bag and pipe it into the reserved whole apricots, sandwiching them together.

6. Unmould the cream onto chosen dish; place the apricots around the base.

Little Pots of Chocolate

4 oz (100 g) plain chocolate broken into
*   pieces*
2 tbsp (30 ml) single cream
4 separated eggs
double cream for decoration

1. Place the chocolate in the top of a double saucepan over hot water. Add the cream and heat until the chocolate has melted. Beat well, remove from heat. Add the unbeaten egg yolks one at a time beating well between each addition.

2. Whisk the egg whites until very stiff and fold gently and evenly into the mixture. Divide into glasses and refrigerate.

3. Before serving, pipe a spiral of whipped double cream on top of each.

Apricot Cream.

Desserts and puddings

Crème Caramel

4½ oz (125 g) castor sugar
¼ pt (150 ml) water
1 pt (600 ml) milk
4 lightly whisked eggs

1. Set oven at 325°F (170°C) or Mark 3. Put the tins being used – either a 6 inch (15 cm) cake tin or 6 ¼ pt (150 ml) individual tins or moulds – in a warm place.

2. Put 4 oz (100 g) of the sugar and all the water into a small, preferably heavy based pan and put over a low heat until the sugar has dissolved. Bring to the boil without stirring it until it turns a rich golden brown colour. Pour the caramel into the large tin or divide it between the individual tins, turning each tin until the bottom is completely covered. Leave to cool.

3. Warm the milk, add the remaining ½ oz (15 g) sugar and the lightly whisked eggs. Strain this mixture over the caramel.

4. Place in a shallow tin like a roasting tin with sufficient cold water in it to come half way up the tin containing the crème caramel. This is to prevent the crème caramel boiling during cooking which spoils its smooth texture. Bake in the pre-set oven for about an hour until set. Small tins will need only 45 minutes.

5. Leave in the tin until quite cold – preferably the next day – before turning it out onto the serving dish.

Crème Brûlée

½ pt (300 ml) double cream
½ pt (300 ml) single cream
1 vanilla pod
1 level tbsp (15 ml) castor sugar
4 egg yolks

For caramel topping
3 level tbsp (45 ml) castor sugar

1. Put the creams and vanilla pod in the top of a double saucepan.

2. Heat through slowly until the cream reaches scalding point about 125°F (52°C). Remove vanilla pod.

3. Cream the castor sugar with the egg yolks until they look thick and pale.

4. Pour the cream onto the egg yolks, mix together well, and return to the top of the double pan. Continue to heat, but do not boil, until the mixture coats the back of a wooden spoon.

5. Strain the custard into a 1½ pt (900 ml) shallow ovenproof serving dish. Leave to cool and then refrigerate overnight or for a minimum of 6 hours. This ensures a firm set.

6. Pre-set the grill to hot.

7. Sprinkle the sifted castor sugar evenly all over the top of the chilled cream. Place under the grill for as short a time as possible just until the sugar caramelizes.

8. Remove from the grill and chill for 2–3 hours before serving.

Mont Blanc

2 egg whites
4 oz (100 g) castor sugar
food colouring
1½ lb (700 g) chestnuts or an 8 oz (225 g)
   can chestnut purée.
3 tbsp (45 ml) Marsala
approx 1 oz (25 g) icing sugar
¼ pt (150 ml) stiffly whipped double cream

1. Set oven at 275°F (140°C) or Mark 1.

2. Whisk the egg whites until stiff, add nearly half the sugar and whisk again until stiff. Lightly fold in the remaining sugar.

Crème Caramel.

At this stage add any colouring you desire. Put the meringue into a piping bag fitted with a large star pipe.

3. Line a large baking sheet with lightly oiled greaseproof paper and mark on it a circle 7 inches (18 cm) in diameter. Pipe a ring of meringue about 2 inches (5 cm) high around the circle and smooth the remainder evenly over the base.

4. Bake the meringue in the pre-set oven for about an hour or until it is crisp and dry. Carefully peel off the paper and leave the meringue case to cool completely on a wire rack.

5. If using fresh chestnuts place a few at a time into a deep fat frying basket and lower them into the hot oil causing them to split. When they are cool remove the shell and inner skin. Place in a pan, cover with boiling water and simmer until they are tender. Drain them and rub them through a sieve.

6. Add the Marsala and enough sifted icing sugar to sweeten and bring out the flavour – about 1 oz (25 g). The mixture should be very stiff and rather dry.

7. Beat in the stiffly whipped cream until blended thoroughly.

8. Place the mixture in a piping bag with a narrow writing pipe. Push the mixture through this pipe into the meringue case forming a mound of long squiggles.

Nesselrode Pudding

18 chestnuts
4 egg yolks
½ pt (300 ml) milk
1 vanilla pod
¼ pt (150 ml) canned pineapple syrup
2 oz (50 g) diced citron peel
3 oz (75 g) crystallized pineapple or fresh
*   pineapple shredded and simmered for 7*
*   minutes in the pineapple syrup*
3 oz (75 g) glacé cherries or angelica
2 oz (50 g) seeded raisins
3 fl oz (75 ml) maraschino
½ pt (300 ml) whipped double cream

1. Nick the chestnuts and boil them until tender. Peel off and discard the inner and outer skins, and rub them through a sieve to form a purée.

Nesselrode Pudding.

2. Place the purée in the top of a double saucepan over hot water with the egg yolks, milk, crushed vanilla pod and pineapple syrup. Stir over heat until the mixture thickens to a thick smooth custard consistency. Turn it into a bowl. If there are any lumps at all in it pass it through a sieve as you turn it into the bowl.

3. In a separate bowl mix together the diced citron peel, the crystallized pineapple roughly cut or the cooled and well drained stewed pineapple, the cherries, raisins and maraschino. Cover the bowl tightly with foil and leave for 4 hours.

4. Place the bowl of custard mixture covered with foil into the freezer or freezing compartment of the refrigerator and freeze until the edges are firm and the centre is just beginning to set.

5. Scrape out into a bowl, beat well and fold in the fruit and maraschino.

6. When all ingredients are blended well together fold in the whipped cream until smoothly blended in.

7. Place in a decorative mould cover with foil and freeze until required.

8. Just before serving pour hot water onto the bottom of the mould for an instant to unmould it. Place on a serving dish and decorate with cherries or angelica.

Desserts and puddings

Lemon Sorbet

8 oz (225 g) castor sugar
1 pt (600 ml) water
rind and juice of 4 lemons

1. Dissolve the sugar in the water over a low heat.

2. Add the very thinly pared lemon rind, bring mixture to the boil and boil for 10 minutes. Allow to cool and stir in the lemon juice.

3. Strain the mixture into ice cube trays and leave in the freezing compartment of the refrigerator until half frozen, i.e. edges crystallized but centre not set.

4. Turn into a large bowl and fold in the egg whites thoroughly.

5. Turn into a plastic container with a well fitting lid and freeze until required.

Lemon Sorbet.

Floating Island

2 egg whites
4 oz (100 g) castor sugar
1 pt (600 ml) milk
1 vanilla pod
1 tbsp (15 ml) castor sugar
1 level tbsp (15 ml) cornflour
1 oz (25 g) castor sugar

1. Whisk egg whites until very stiff, add half the sugar and whisk again to its former stiffness. Lightly fold in remaining half of sugar with a metal spoon.

2. Place the milk in a wide shallow pan like a frying pan. Add the vanilla pod and 1 tbsp (15 ml) castor sugar and heat until very hot but not boiling.

3. Using a tablespoon, scoop up a heaped spoonful of the meringue, slide it into the hot vanilla flavoured milk and leave to poach until set – about 4 minutes. Continue to do this until the surface of the pan is covered with half submerged ovals of meringue. Turn them over and repeat on the underside. Remove with a slotted spoon onto greaseproof paper and repeat the process until all the meringue is used up.

4. Blend the cornflour to a paste with very little cold water. Beat it with the egg yolks and the 1 oz (25 g) sugar until thick and creamy. Slowly beat in the milk the meringues were poached in. Place in the top of a double saucepan and bring to the boil stirring all the time until it has the consistency of fairly thick custard. Turn the mixture into chosen serving dish.

5. Pile the meringues up in the centre to make a floating island in the custard.

Redcurrant Jelly Glaze

Basic Recipe

12 oz (350 g) jar redcurrant jelly
2½ fl oz (60 ml) water

1. Heat the redcurrant jelly in the water in a pan over a very low heat until the jelly has completely dissolved.

2. Work the glaze through a sieve and pour into clean dry airtight containers for storage. Reheat gently before use.

Floating Island – a sea of soft, rich vanilla custard, topped with an island of meringues – makes a sumptuous dessert.
Serve this classic French pudding with sponge fingers or crisp 'cigarette' biscuits, and sprinkle a little chocolate vermicelli
over the top. Sometimes this dish is known as Snow Eggs.

Desserts and puddings

Peach Melba.

Peach Melba

2 large peaches
juice of 1 lemon
approx ¾ pt (450 ml) vanilla ice cream

For Melba sauce
8 oz (225 g) fresh or frozen raspberries
juice of 1 lemon
3 oz (75 g) castor sugar
2 tbsp (30 ml) kirsch or cold water.

1. Plunge the peaches into boiling water for a few seconds so that the skin can be easily removed.

2. Cut them in half, remove the stone, and rub the flesh well with lemon juice to keep them a pleasant colour.

3. Put to one side one raspberry per person for decoration. Simmer together the sauce ingredients for 5 minutes then strain through a sieve and chill.

4. Assemble the sweet by placing a large scoop of vanilla ice cream in each individual glass sundae dish.

5. Place one peach half on top, rounded side up and coat with a chilled raspberry sauce.

6. Decorate with whipped cream and flaked almonds and raspberries if liked.

Chocolate Ice Cream

4 oz (100 g) cooking chocolate
¼ pt (150 ml) water
1 pt (600 ml) milk
4 egg yolks
4 oz (100 g) castor sugar
½ pt (300 ml) double cream

1. Place the chocolate and water in the top of a double saucepan with the outer pan half full of boiling water. Keep over the heat and stir until the contents are thoroughly blended.

2. Infuse the milk with a vanilla pod by heating the milk slowly to boiling point with the vanilla pod in it.

3. Remove vanilla pod, wipe and store it. Add the milk to the chocolate mixture.

4. Whip the egg yolks and sugar together until pale and very fluffy and add to the rest of the ingredients in the double saucepan. Stir over heat until the mixture is thick and very smooth. Cool until below blood heat.

5. Reserve a little double cream for decoration. Whip the remainder into the ice cream and freeze into desired shape.

6. Just before serving turn it out onto chosen dish.

7. Whip the cream for decoration until stiff and pipe small rosettes around the base of the ice cream and around the top. Chocolate shapes may also be used for decoration if desired.

Baked Alaska

1 sponge cake round
½ lb (225 g) fresh ripe strawberries or
*   raspberries or other fruit*
vanilla ice cream
3 egg whites
6 oz (175 g) castor sugar

1. Set oven at 450°F (230°C) or Mark 8.

2. Place the sponge cake on a heat resistant dish. Arrange the chosen fruit on top with a little juice to moisten the sponge.

3. Make the meringue and put into a piping bag with a rosette pipe attached. Place the ice cream on top of the fruit. Pipe the meringue mixture all over so that the cake, fruit and ice cream are completely covered, taking the meringue right down to the dish.

4. Place in the pre-set oven for 2–3 minutes or until the outside of the meringue just begins to brown.

5. Decorate with crystallized violets and rose petals and serve at once.

1. Arrange fruit on the sponge base.

2. Place very firm ice cream on top.

3. Pipe meringue all over so that the alaska is masked in meringue.

4. Place in a very hot oven to brown.

Baked Alaska.

Black Cherries Jubilee.

Blackcurrant and Raspberry Water Ice.

Black Cherries Jubilee

1 lb (450 g) stoned black cherries
3 tbsp (45 ml) sifted icing sugar
5 oz (150 g) blackcurrant jelly
2 tbsp (30 ml) kirsch

1. Set oven at 275°F (140°C) or Mark 1.

2. Retain any juice resulting from stoning the cherries. Place the stoned cherries and the juice in a covered casserole. Add the icing sugar. Cook in the pre-set oven for about an hour until the juices are drawn out of the fruit, then take out and leave to one side.

3. Melt the blackcurrant jelly in the top of a double saucepan and add the kirsch. Put to one side off the heat to cool and thicken.

4. Strain the cherries over a bowl and gently stir them into the cooled sauce. Serve the strained cherry juice in a separate jug. Taste and gently stir in more icing sugar if necessary.

Blackcurrant and Raspberry Water Ice

½ lb (225 g) blackcurrant purée made from fresh raw blackberries rubbed through a sieve. Reserve about 1 oz (25 g) for final decoration.
½ lb (225 g) raspberry purée made from fresh raspberries rubbed through a sieve. Reserve about 1 oz (25 g) for final decoration.
1 pt (600 ml) stock sugar syrup, simmered on for a further 5 minutes than usual.

1. Mix the purée together and beat in the syrup.

2. Turn into a wetted 2 pt (1 l) mould and freeze.

3. Turn out onto a large round flat dish and keep chilled until served.

4. Decorate around the base with the reserved fresh blackcurrants and raspberries and a sprig of fresh raspberry leaves on top.

Desserts and puddings

Pineapple Ninon

1 pineapple
sifted icing sugar
8 oz (225 g) vanilla ice cream
4 oz (100 g) almond paste
chantilly cream
½ lb (225 g) whole strawberries

1. Cut the top off the pineapple. Dig out all the flesh and chop it up. Dust the inside of the pineapple with icing sugar. Put all but 2 tbsp (30 ml) of pineapple flesh into the pineapple.

2. Pack vanilla ice cream tightly into the pineapple case. Cover with foil and freeze until just before serving.

3. Roll out the almond paste and line 7 tartlet tins with it. Leave to set for 24 hours.

4. Put a spoonful of pineapple flesh in each tartlet. Fill a piping bag, fitted with a rosette nozzle, with chantilly cream and pipe over tarts and pineapple top. Decorate with strawberries. Arrange almond tarts around the pineapple.

Special Fruit Salad

1 medium pineapple
1 lb (450 g) blackberries
½ lb (225 g) strawberries
1 oz (25 g) sifted icing sugar
kirsch (optional)

1. Remove green top from pineapple with a straight cut so that the tuft will stand steadily on its own. Place it at the centre back of a circular dish for decoration.

2. Cut the pineapple into 3 pieces. First cut right through from top to base ½ inch (1 cm) left of centre. Then cut top to base right through ½ inch (1 cm) right of centre so that you end up with 1 large wedge of pineapple 1 inch (2.5 cm) thick, and 2 pineapple 'shells'. Remove all pineapple flesh from shells, dice it and return it to shells. Cut the slice of pineapple from top to base and halve each slice centrally. Place these strips of pineapple across the shells.

3. Fill the spaces in between the strips with strawberries and blackberries and pile blackberries up the centre front of the pineapple tuft. Sprinkle the icing sugar all over the fruit and sprinkle on a few drops of kirsch if used. Chill in the refrigerator until required.

Strawberry and Orange Surprise

1 lb (450 g) strawberries
1 orange
2 tbsp (30 ml) castor sugar
¼ pt (150 ml) whipped double cream

1. Wash and hull the strawberries and place to one side in a bowl.

2. Grate the orange rind carefully ensuring none of the pith is removed and squeeze the juice from half the orange into a small bowl. Add the sugar and rind and stir until the sugar melts.

3. Fold the cream into the orange syrup and pour over the strawberries. Cover and chill before serving.

Pineapple Ninon.

Glazed Pears.

Glazed Pears

6 large firm eating pears
juice of 2 lemons
1 lb (450 g) castor sugar
¾ pt (450 ml) water
4 oz (100 g) redcurrant jelly
1 tbsp (15 ml) arrowroot
2 tbsp (30 ml) cold water

1. Peel the pears from bottom to tip, leaving them whole and leaving the stalk intact. Rub well with lemon juice so they keep their colour. Place pears upright in a saucepan into which they just fit so they will not fall over when cooking.

2. In another pan dissolve the sugar in the water, stir in the redcurrant jelly and pour over the pears.

3. Simmer the pears until they are tender – about 20 minutes. Lift them out into the serving dish still keeping them upright and reserving the liquid.

4. While they are cooling, blend the arrowroot with the 2 tbsp (30 ml) of cold water and gradually add to the redcurrant syrup in the pan stirring all the time. Bring to the boil and then simmer until sauce thickens.

5. Pour over the pears and chill well before serving. May be accompanied by unsweetened whipped cream if desired.

Desserts and puddings

Black Mountain Pudding

2 lb (900 g) blackcurrants
½ pt (150 ml) water
approx ½ thinly sliced sandwich loaf
granulated sugar to taste
arrowroot
fruit juice
cream

1. Put the fruit in a saucepan, add the water and cover the pan. Simmer for 6–7 minutes and strain.

2. Either work the fruit with a little of the juice through a blender or else rub through a sieve. If the blender is used, it is important to remember to strain the pulp to remove any small pips. Add the rest of the juice.

3. Pour a little of the purée into a bowl. Cut away the bread crusts and place 2 slices on top of this. Then add more purée.

4. Continue in this fashion until the dish is full and you have at least ¼ pt (150 ml) of the purée remaining. Ensure that each layer is well soaked in the purée.

5. Cover by placing a small plate on top, and pressing it down on the bread. Place a 2 lb weight on top of this. Leave until the following day.

6. To make a sauce: Add a little water to ¼ pt (150 ml) reserved purée. Slake the arrowroot with the fruit juice and add to the purée. Bring to the boil, stirring continuously. Pour off and allow to cool.

7. Turn the pudding out onto a plate or flat dish and spoon the sauce all over it, followed by the cream if desired.

This pudding is also delicious if raspberries, loganberries or blackberries are substituted for the blackcurrants, although the initial simmering time should be a few minutes less.

Plum Sponge Flan

For sponge
5 oz (150 g) self raising flour
1 level tsp (5 ml) cream of tartar
11 oz (300 g) castor sugar
9 fl oz (250 ml) water
7 very stiffly whipped egg whites
7 egg yolks
2 tbsp (30 ml) cooking brandy

For filling
3 egg quantity confectioners' custard
1½ lb (700 g) cherry plums
6 fl oz (175 ml) stock sugar syrup
redcurrant glaze

1. Set oven at 350°F (180°C) or Mark 4.

2. Sift the flour, cream of tartar and salt into a large bowl.

3. Place the sugar and water in a thick pan over a low heat for the sugar to dissolve.

4. Bring it to the boil and simmer strongly until a big bubble is formed when you dip in a slotted spoon and blow hard through the perforations.

5. Pour the syrup onto the very stiffly whipped egg whites and beat continuously for 5 minutes.

6. Whip the egg yolks and stir in the brandy. Very slowly beat the egg yolk mixture into the meringue mixture. Fold in the flour.

7. Turn into a 10 inch (25.5 cm) diameter flan case or 2 5 inch (12.5 cm) flan cases if preferred. Bake in the pre-set oven until the sponge is just springy under very light pressure.

8. Allow it to become completely cold before turning it out onto a serving dish.

9. Cover the base with confectioners' custard.

10. Poach the cherry plums in the stock sugar syrup over a very low heat. Drain over a jug and place them over the custard in the flan. Brush with warm redcurrant glaze.

11. Serve the strained sugar syrup separately in a jug.

Plum Sponge Flan.

Desserts and puddings

French Apple Flan.

French Apple Flan

1 lb (450 g) quantity sweet shortcrust pastry
3 egg quantity confectioners' custard
6 cooking apples
2 oz (50 g) castor sugar
redcurrant jelly glaze

1. Set oven at 375°F (190°C) or Mark 5.

2. Roll the pastry thinly and line a 9 inch (23 cm) flan ring.

3. Cover the base with the confectioners' custard.

4. Peel and thinly slice the apples. Then cover the flan with overlapping sheets of apple. Dust with sifted castor sugar.

5. Bake in the pre-set oven until the pastry edges are lightly brown and the edges of the apple rings are quite brown – approximately 15–20 minutes.

6. Remove from oven and immediately brush the entire surface including edges of flan case with redcurrant glaze.

7. When it is cold, transfer to serving dish using 2 metal slices underneath to prevent it splitting. Remove flan ring.

Sweet Shortcrust Pastry

Basic Recipe

1 lb (450 g) self raising flour
8 oz (225 g) unsalted butter
4 oz (100 g) castor sugar
cinnamon
2 egg yolks
approx 6 tbsp (90 ml) ice cold water

1. Sift the flour into a bowl. Cut in the butter with a round bladed knife, and, once evenly coated with flour, rub in lightly with the fingertips until mixture has turned into fine crumbs.

2. Add the castor sugar and a pinch of cinnamon and mix in well.

3. Make a well in the centre of the mixture, add egg yolks and at least two thirds of the water and work in using a fork. Add more of the water if necessary until the mixture forms a firm dough.

4. Turn out onto a floured board and knead lightly until smooth. Wrap the pastry in a polythene bag or a piece of greaseproof paper and leave in the refrigerator for at least one hour before rolling out.

Cherry Pie

8 oz (225 g) sweet shortcrust pastry
1 lb (450 g) cooked, stoned red cherries
2 tbsp (30 ml) castor sugar
1 tbsp (15 ml) melted butter
1 tbsp (15 ml) tapioca
almond essence
1 egg white
extra castor sugar for dusting

1. Set oven at 400°F (220°C) or Mark 6.

2. Make the sweet shortcrust pastry and line a 7–8 inch (18–20 cm) diameter deep pie dish with half of it.

3. Strain the cherries and place in a bowl with 8 fl oz (220 ml) cherry juice. Add the sugar, melted butter, tapioca and a few drops of almond essence. Mix together and leave aside to stand for about 15 minutes.

4. Pour the cherry filling into the pie dish and cover with the remaining pastry, sealing the edges well.

5. Bake in the pre-set oven for 30–40 minutes.

6. Take the pie out of the oven, brush with lightly whipped egg white and sprinkle with a little castor sugar. Return the pie to the oven and bake for a further 5 minutes or until glazed.

7. Serve hot or cold with cream.

Upside Down Apple Flan

1 oz (25 g) unsalted butter
castor sugar for dredging
4 large or 5 medium cooking apples
1 lb (450 g) sweet shortcrust pastry
icing sugar for decoration

1. Set oven at 350°F (180°C) or Mark 4.

2. Grease the base of a 7 inch (18 cm) sponge tin with butter. Line it with a fitting circle of greaseproof paper and butter the paper well. Dredge the buttered paper with a liberal layer of sieved castor sugar.

3. Peel and core the apples and slice into very thin rounds. Working from the centre of the tin outwards, overlap the apple rings about ¼ inch (1 cm) between each overlap until the tin is filled to within ½ inch (2 cm) of the top. Press down firmly.

4. Roll out shortcrust pastry to about ½ inch (2 cm) thick and cut a round from it by lightly resting the clean based sponge tin on it and cutting around neatly with a sharp knife. Using palette knives or a fish slice to lift it, transfer the pastry to cover the apple slices and press down lightly.

5. Bake in the pre-set oven until the top of the pastry is golden brown.

6. Refrigerate until cold. Invert over a serving dish and carefully remove the greaseproof paper. Dust with sifted icing sugar.

Upside Down Apple Flan.

Desserts and puddings

Crumb Crust Fruit Flan.

Crumb Crust Fruit Flan

8 oz (225 g) butter or margarine
1 lb (450 g) digestive biscuits
3 egg yolk quantity confectioners' custard
soft fruit as desired
redcurrant glaze

1. Place biscuits in a polythene bag and break into crumbs with a rolling pin.

2. Melt the butter or margarine in a saucepan and stir in the crumbs until the fat is absorbed.

3. Press the mixture evenly into the base and sides of a 9 inch (23 cm) flan ring standing on a lightly greased baking sheet. When cool and firm, carefully remove flan ring and place on serving dish.

4. Put the confectioners' custard in the base of the flan.

5. Cover with raspberries or other soft fruit arranging the fruit either in circles or triangle sections.

6. Brush the top with redcurrant glaze.

Lemon Meringue Pie

6 oz (175 g) sweet shortcrust pastry

For filling
1 tbsp (15 ml) cornflour
½ pt (300 ml) milk
1 tbsp (15 ml) sugar
2 egg yolks
grated rind and juice of 1 lemon

For meringue
2 egg whites
4 oz (100 g) castor sugar

1. Set oven at 375°F (190°C) or Mark 5.

2. Line a 7 inch (18 cm) diameter flan ring with pastry and bake blind.

3. Reduce the oven temperature to 325°F (160°C) or Mark 3.

4. Mix the cornflour with a little of the milk in a bowl. Heat the remaining milk and pour onto the cornflour paste, stirring well. Return the mixture to the pan and bring to the boil, stirring continuously. Boil for 3–4 minutes, still stirring, until smooth and thickened.

5. Add the sugar and allow to cool.

6. Beat in the egg yolks and the grated lemon rind and juice. Pour the lemon mixture into the baked pastry case.

7. Bake in the pre-set oven for about 10 minutes or until lightly set.

8. Reduce the oven temperature to 275°F (130°C) or Mark 1.

9. Pile the meringue on top of the lemon filling, covering completely.

10. Sprinkle with castor sugar and place in the pre-set oven for 10–15 minutes. The meringue should be crisp on the outside and soft inside. Serve hot.

Fruit Slice

1 rectangular case of puff pastry
½ pt (300 ml) milk and 3 egg quantity of confectioners' custard
a mixture of all or some of the following fruits: peeled, halved, or sliced and stoned, peaches, apricots, pears, black and red cherries, raspberries, strawberries and plums.
angelica and glacé cherries for decoration

1. Cover the base of the pastry case with the confectioners' custard.

2. Pile the fruits on top arranging them in a colourful way and taking them above the top of the pastry case.

3. Warm the apricot glaze and pour between the spaces of the fruit until it comes to just below the rim of the pastry. Brush the top surfaces of the fruit with this glaze.

4. Decorate with angelica and cherries if desired.

Chantilly Cream

¼ pt (150 ml) double cream
2 tsp (10 ml) castor sugar
½ tsp (2.50 ml) vanilla essence
1 egg white

1. Whisk the chilled cream until just thick – don't overwhip or it will become too firm to use properly. Stir in the sugar and vanilla essence.

2. In another bowl, stiffly whip the egg white and lightly fold into the whipped cream mixture. Use immediately according to recipe.

Fruit Slice.

Desserts and puddings

Apricot Flan

1 cooked flan case made of sweet shortcrust
*   pastry 9 inch (23 cm) in diameter*
3 egg yolk quantity confectioners' custard
1 lb (450 g) fresh apricots or 1 large can
*   apricot halves*
redcurrant glaze
chantilly cream
sugar syrup
vanilla pod

1. Half fill the cooked flan case with the confectioners' custard.

2. Poach apricots if fresh ones are being used. Slice fruit in half and remove stones. Place the halved fruits in a single layer over the base of a wide shallow pan. Cover with stock sugar syrup, add a vanilla pod, and poach very gently over a low heat. Remove vanilla pod and wipe and store. Remove apricots carefully so that they retain a dome shape.

3. Put apricot cups as closely together as possible over the custard.

4. Brush the apricots with redcurrant glaze making sure that the glaze fills the empty spaces between the fruit. Leave until cold.

5. Pipe cream around the edge of the flan using a decorative pipe.

Confectioners' Custard

½ pt (300 ml) milk
1 vanilla pod
1 oz (25 g) plain flour
3 egg yolks
4 oz (100 g) castor sugar

1. Gently heat the milk with the vanilla pod in a pan over a very low heat, until tiny bubbles just start to rise to the surface. Do not allow to boil. Immediately take the pan off the heat, remove the vanilla pod, and reserve for future use.

2. Sift the flour. Whisk together the egg yolks, flour and sugar. Stir in the vanilla flavoured milk. Pour the mixture into a bain marie or into a basin standing in a pan of hot water over a gentle heat. Using a wooden spoon stir custard until it becomes thick and creamy and evenly coats the back of the spoon. Remove from the heat at once and use hot or cold according to recipe.

Almond Paste

4 oz (100 g) ground almonds
8 oz (225 g) sifted icing sugar
1 lightly whipped egg white
½ tsp (2.50 ml) each orange flower
*   water and rose water*
cornflour for dusting

1. Knead together the ground almonds and icing sugar. Make a well in the centre and pour in half the egg white and the flavoured waters. Knead until a smooth paste is formed.

2. Turn paste onto work surface, dusting with cornflour, and knead until it resembles a soft but not sticky dough. Only add more egg white if the paste is still crumbly. Wrap in foil and store in refrigerator until needed and then use according to recipe.

Apricot Flan.

Crêpes Suzette

Crêpes Suzette

butter for frying
2 oz (50 g) castor sugar
2 oz (50 g) butter
the juice of 2 mandarins, tangerines or
small oranges and the grated rind of 1
lemon
1 tbsp (15 ml) brandy
2 tbsp (30 ml) Cointreau

For rich pancake batter
4 oz (125 g) plain flour
salt
2 eggs
½ oz (15 g) butter
½ pt (300 ml) milk

1. Mix the batter in the same way as for basic pancake batter, adding the butter at the same time as the eggs.

2. Heat a little butter in a 7 inch (18 cm) thick based frying pan, pour off the excess and cook the pancakes in the same way as ordinary pancakes. When all 8 are made keep them warm between 2 plates in a warm oven until serving.

3. Wipe around the pan, put in the sugar and heat until the sugar has melted and turned golden brown.

4. Remove the pan from the heat, add the butter, orange juice, lemon rind and Cointreau. Mix well together and replace over a low heat.

5. Fold each pancake in half and then in half again to form a quarter circle.

6. Place all the pancakes in the pan and when they are reheated and soaked in the sauce, pour the brandy over them and ignite it.

7. Serve at once by transferring the pancakes to a large flat oval dish, pour over them the sauce and dust the whole with sifted icing sugar.

Orange and Lemon Curd Pudding

8 oz (225 g) quantity suet crust pastry
skinless orange segments of 4 oranges
6 tbsp (90 ml) lemon curd
icing sugar for dusting

1. Half fill a steamer or large saucepan with water and put it on to boil.

2. Cut one quarter from the prepared suet pastry and leave to one side for the lid. Roll out the remainder until about ¼ inch (0.1 cm) thick and 2 inches (5 cm) wider than the top of the basin. Grease the pudding basin and line it with the pastry.

3. Fill the basin with alternative layers of the orange segments and lemon curd. Turn the pastry overhanging the rim of the basin in over the filling. Roll out the pastry for the lid, damp the edges of the pastry in the basin and cover with the lid pressing the edges together well to seal.

4. Fold a pleat in a square of foil or buttered greaseproof paper – the pleat allows the pudding to rise during cooking. Place the paper or foil over the pudding and twist it under the rim of the basin to secure it.

5. Steam for 2½ hours taking care not to let the steamer boil dry. Add boiling water when the water level gets low.

6. Turn pudding out onto a dish and dust with sifted icing sugar.

Lemon Curd

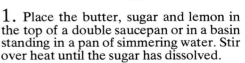

8 oz (225 g) butter
juice and finely grated rinds of
8 lemons
2 lb (1 kg) castor sugar
8 beaten and strained eggs

1. Place the butter, sugar and lemon in the top of a double saucepan or in a basin standing in a pan of simmering water. Stir over heat until the sugar has dissolved.

2. Add the eggs and continue stirring over heat until the mixture turns thick and creamy.

3. Strain into small pots, cover, and store in a cool place for up to 1 month.

Desserts and puddings

Coconut and Maple Syrup Pudding.

Suet Crust Pastry

8 oz (225 g) self raising flour
½ tsp (2 ml) salt
4 oz (100 g) finely shredded suet
¼ pt (150 ml) water

1. Sift the flour and salt into a bowl; add the finely shredded suet and stir well.

2. Add cold water gradually to form a light elastic dough and knead lightly on a floured board until smooth.

Coconut and Maple Syrup Pudding

8 oz (225 g) quantity suet crust pastry
½ pt (300 ml) maple syrup
4 oz (100 g) coconut

1. Roll out three quarters of the pastry to a circle approx 2 inches (5 cm) bigger than the top of the basin and line a greased 1½ pt (900 ml) pudding basin with it.

2. Roll out the remaining quarter of the pastry and cut 3 circles, one larger one to fit as a lid, and 2 smaller circles.

3. Mix the maple syrup and coconut together to a paste. Place a third of this in the lined basin and cover with one of the small circles of pastry.

4. Add another third filling, then the second small circle, rest of filling and seal the lid on the top by dampening the edges with water and pressing well together.

5. Cover and steam for 2½ hours as for orange and lemon curd pudding.

Golden Syrup Pudding

4 oz (100 g) butter
4 oz (100 g) castor sugar
6 oz (175 g) self raising flour
2 beaten eggs
milk to mix if necessary
2 tbsp (30 ml) golden syrup

1. Half fill a steamer or large saucepan with water and put it on to boil.

2. Cream the butter and sugar together until pale and fluffy. Sift the flour, add the beaten eggs a little at a time alternatively with a spoonful of the flour. Beat well.

3. Fold in the rest of the flour. Add a little milk if necessary to make a soft dropping consistency.

4. Grease a 1½ pint (900 ml) pudding basin. Place the golden syrup in the bottom and the pudding mixture on top.

5. Cover with greased greaseproof paper or foil in which a pleat has been made to allow for rising. Tie firmly around the rim of the basin with string.

6. Steam for 1½ hours. Keep the water in the steamer boiling rapidly and have a kettle of boiling water nearby to top it up regularly or it may boil dry.

7. Turn out onto chosen dish and serve hot with extra golden syrup if desired.

Steamed Chocolate Pudding

4 oz (100 g) butter
4 oz (100 g) castor sugar
4½ oz (115 g) self raising flour
1½ oz (40 g) sweetened drinking chocolate
*   powder*
2 beaten eggs
approx 4 tbsp (60 ml) milk

1. Half fill a steamer or large saucepan with water and put it on to boil.

2. Cream the butter and sugar together thoroughly. Sieve the flour and chocolate powder together and add to the creamed mixture a little at a time alternately with each egg.

3. Add the milk to give a soft dropping consistency, put the mixture in a greased

1½ pint basin and cover lightly with a circle of buttered paper. Cover the top of the basin with foil and steam for 1½ hours. Care must be taken not to let the steamer boil dry. Add boiling water from a kettle when the water level gets low.

4. Invert over serving dish and dredge with sifted icing sugar.

5. Serve hot with hot chocolate sauce and cream if desired.

Hot Chocolate Sauce

5 oz (150 g) cooking chocolate
2 tbsp (30 ml) brown sugar
2 tbsp (30 ml) water

2 oz (50 g) butter
1 tsp (5 ml) rum

1. Put the chocolate, sugar and water in the top of a double saucepan over gently boiling water. Stir until all the ingredients are smoothly blended together.

2. Add the butter gradually, beating well all the time, then add the rum.

3. Serve immediately or to keep it hot cover the pan with a tight fitting lid to prevent a skin forming on the surface and keep the pan on the heat watching that it does not boil dry.

4. Any remaining sauce may be beaten until smooth and reheated.

Steamed Chocolate Pudding with Hot Chocolate Sauce.

Sponge Buns.

Cakes and bread

Sponge Buns

4 oz (100 g) softened butter or margarine
4 oz (100 g) castor sugar
8 oz (225 g) self raising flour
2 eggs
1 tbsp (15 ml) milk
2½ oz (60 g) fruit (sultanas, currants,
  seedless raisins, chopped glacé cherries),
  desiccated coconut, or flavouring (finely
  chopped orange or lemon rind, cocoa or
  coffee powder)

1. Set oven at 375°F (190°C) or Mark 5.

2. Cream together the fat and sugar until light and pale coloured. Fold in 2 oz (50 g) flour and 1 egg, then beat well. Do the same with another 2 oz (50 g) flour and remaining egg. Then beat in remaining flour a little at a time until a stiff mixture is formed. Stir in the milk and the fruit, coconut or flavouring.

3. Fill mixture into greased bun tins and bake just above the centre of the pre-set oven for 15 minutes. Cool on a wire rack.

Raspberry Buns

8 oz (225 g) self raising flour
salt
4 oz (100 g) butter or margarine
4 oz (100 g) castor sugar
1 lightly beaten egg
1 tbsp (15 ml) milk
2 oz (50 g) raspberry jam

1. Set oven at 425°F (220°C) or Mark 7.

2. Sift the flour and a pinch of salt into a bowl, then rub in the fat until the mixture resembles fine crumbs. Stir in the sugar. Make a well in the centre, then stir in the egg, followed by the milk, and blend to form a smooth dough.

3. Turn the dough onto a floured work surface and knead for a few seconds. Then press out a little with your hand and cut dough into 12 pieces. Shape each piece into a round bun and place on a greased and floured baking sheet.

4. Using the handle of wooden spoon, make a small hole in the top of each bun and spoon in a little of the jam. Put the buns into the pre-set oven and bake for about 10 minutes or until well risen.

Cakes and bread

Featherweight Jam Sponge

2 eggs and 1 egg yolk
2½ oz (62 g) icing sugar
2 oz (50 g) self raising flour
raspberry, strawberry or blackcurrant jam
*   for filling*
icing sugar for sprinkling

1. Set oven at 375°F (190°C) or Mark 5.

2. Beat the eggs, egg yolk and sugar together in a mixing bowl until thick and creamy. Sift the flour and fold into the egg mixture, using a metal spoon.

3. Grease and flour an 8 inch (20 cm) diameter deep cake tin, then line with greased greaseproof paper cut to fit. Turn into the prepared cake tin and bake in the pre-set oven for 30 minutes or until pale gold and the top of the cake springs back when gently pressed with a finger.

4. Cool on a wire rack, then turn out of the tin and cut in half. Sandwich with chosen jam and sprinkle the top generously with icing sugar.

Coffee Gâteau

8 oz (225 g) softened butter or margarine
8 oz (225 g) castor sugar
4 eggs
7 oz (200 g) self raising flour
1 oz (25 g) cornflour
2 tbsp (30 ml) coffee syrup
6 oz (175 g) butter quantity coffee butter
*   cream*

1. Set oven at 350°F (180°C) or Mark 4.

2. Cream the fat and sugar in a mixing bowl until pale coloured and fluffy. Using a metal spoon fold in a quarter of the flour, then carefully beat in 1 egg, a little at a time to avoid curdling the cake batter. Continue folding in portions of flour, followed by an egg each time, until all are incorporated. Beat in the coffee syrup.

3. Well grease the sides of a 12 inch (30 cm) diameter, 1 inch (3 cm) deep cake tin and line with greased and floured greaseproof paper cut to fit.

4. Pour the cake batter into the prepared tin. Bake the cake in the pre-set oven for 30 minutes or until it is golden, well risen, firm to the touch and just pulls away from the sides of the tin. Take out and cool on a wire rack.

5. With the bottom side up (this always has the smoothest and best looking surface) completely cover the sponge with a good half of the coffee butter cream, chill in the refrigerator, then smooth the top with a knife. Fill remaining butter cream into a piping bag fitted with a plain writing nozzle and pipe a trellis pattern on top of the cake. Change the nozzle to a small rosette nozzle and pipe rosettes all round the sides of the cake. Pipe a single small rosette at each point on the trellis where the lines cross each other.

Featherweight Jam Sponge.

Sand Cake

8 oz (225 g) unsalted softened butter
finely grated rind of 1 small lemon
  (optional)
3 oz (75 g) self raising flour
3 oz (75 g) potato flour
5 oz (150 g) sifted icing sugar plus a little
  extra for sprinkling
6 separated eggs

1. Set oven at 350°F (180°C) or Mark 4.

2. Cream the butter in a mixing bowl, with the lemon rind if using, until pale and fluffy. Sift the flours together and then gradually beat in the icing sugar and about a quarter of the flours. Next beat in 2 egg yolks until well combined. Beat in another quarter of the flours and 2 more egg yolks, and repeat this process until all the flour and egg yolks are incorporated and you have a smooth batter. Stiffly whip the egg whites and fold into the batter. Then beat until combined and no streaks of egg white remain.

3. Grease and flour a rectangular cake tin measuring 9 by 5 by 3 inches (22×12×8 cm). Turn cake mixture into the prepared tin and smooth the surface, flattening the centre slightly, so it remains flat during baking. Bake in the pre-set oven for about 40 minutes. Take out and cool cake in the tin until only just warm. Turn out and sprinkle thickly with icing sugar.

Orange or Lemon Gâteau

8 oz (225 g) softened butter or margarine
finely grated rind of ½ orange or lemon
8 oz (225 g) castor sugar
4 eggs
8 oz (225 g) self raising flour and cornflour,
  mixed
crystallized orange or lemon slices for
  decoration
juice of 1 orange or lemon

For vanilla frosting
5 oz (150 g) sifted icing sugar
1½ tbsp (22 ml) vegetable oil
1–1½ tbsp (15–22 ml) milk
2–3 drops vanilla essence

1. Set oven at 350°F (180°C) or Mark 4.

2. Put the softened fat in a mixing bowl

Madeira Cake.

together with the orange or lemon rind. Add the sugar and cream with the fat until pale coloured and fluffy. Using a metal spoon fold in a quarter of the flour, then carefully beat in 1 egg, a little at a time to avoid curdling the cake batter. Continue folding in portions of flour, followed by an egg each time, until all are incorporated. Beat in the orange or lemon juice.

3. Well grease 8 inch (20 cm) diameter sandwich tins and line with greased and floured greaseproof paper cut to fit. Pour cake batter into the prepared tins.

4. Bake the cake in the pre-set oven for 20 minutes or until golden, well risen, firm to the touch and they just pull away from the sides of the tins. Take out and cool on a wire rack.

5. Make vanilla frosting by beating together in a bowl the icing sugar, oil, milk and vanilla essence until very smooth. Sandwich the sponge rounds with vanilla frosting and decorate the top of the gâteau with crystallized orange or lemon slices.

Madeira Cake

7 separated eggs
2¼ oz (62 g) castor sugar
7 oz (200 g) self raising flour
icing sugar for sprinkling

1. Set oven at 350°F (180°C) or Mark 4.

2. Stiffly whip the egg whites in a large bowl until they hold a peak. In another mixing bowl beat the egg yolks until they are doubled in volume and foamy. Add the castor sugar and beat the eggs again. Sift the flour and beat into the sugar mixture. Using a metal spoon, fold in the egg whites, adding them a third at a time.

3. Make a domed cap of foil to fit over cake tin. Grease and flour a loaf tin measuring 9 by 5 by 3 inches (22×12×8 cm). Turn the cake batter into the prepared tin and three quarters fill. Not all of the batter is required so either bake a second smaller cake in a greased and floured 8 inch (20 cm) deep cake tin or fill into greased and floured bun tins for miniature Madeira cakes.

4. Bake the cake in the pre-set oven for about 15 minutes. Then take out and cover tin with foil. Return cake to oven and bake for 35 minutes longer or until risen and golden. (Reduce overall baking time by 5 minutes for smaller cake, and by 15 minutes for Madeira buns.) Cool on a wire rack, then sprinkle with icing sugar.

Cakes and bread

Angel Cake.

Angel Cake

5 egg whites
1 tsp (5 ml) cream of tartar
5 oz (150 g) castor sugar
salt
2 oz (50 g) self raising flour
2 oz (50 g) cornflour

To decorate
4 oz (100 g) flaked almonds
icing sugar for sprinkling

1. Set oven at 325°F (160°C) or Mark 3.

2. Stiffly whip the egg whites in a large bowl until they stand in a firm peak; there should be no liquid egg white at all.

Sprinkle over the cream of tartar, then gently draw them to the sides of the bowl to make a well in the centre.

3. Pour the sugar and a pinch of salt into the well, then fold in carefully with a metal spoon or spatula to retain as much beaten in air as possible. When the sugar is completely combined, make a well again. Sift the flour and the cornflour together and repeat the folding in process with the flours.

4. When combined turn at once into an ungreased 6 inch (15 cm) loose bottomed cake tin. Cut through the mixture a few times with a knife to break up any air bubbles present, then cover the top thickly with flaked almonds.

5. Bake in the pre-set oven for 45 minutes or until light and fluffy. Do not be tempted to open the oven during the cooking period because the mixture is very delicate and cannot survive sudden changes of temperature or knocks caused by opening and shutting the oven door or moving the tin. Cool in the tin until cold, then turn out onto a wire rack. Sprinkle with icing sugar.

Glacé Icing

Basic Recipe ☆

8 oz (225 g) icing sugar
2 tbsp (30 ml) cold water or
   flavoured liquid such as fresh
   orange or lemon juice or other
   fruit juice, or black coffee

1. Sift the icing sugar into a mixing bowl. Gradually add the water or other preferred liquid and mix until the icing is smooth but fairly stiff. If too much liquid is added, the icing will become too runny and more sieved icing sugar will have to be added until it returns to the required stiffness.

2. If not using the icing immediately, cover the bowl with foil or a damp cloth, or stir in a little lemon juice if not already used to prevent the icing hardening.

Variation:
Use a few drops of edible food colouring to give pink, blue, mauve etc coloured icing. Add colourings sparingly to avoid the result being too garish or dark.

Special Iced Cake

8 oz (225 g) softened butter or margarine
8 oz (225 g) castor sugar
4 eggs
8 oz (225 g) self raising flour
2 tbsp (30 ml) milk
6 oz (175 g) butter quantity brandy
    flavoured butter cream
glacé icing
edible food colouring

1. Cream the fat and sugar in a mixing bowl until pale coloured and fluffy. Using a metal spoon fold in a quarter of the flour, then carefully beat in 1 egg, a little at a time, to avoid curdling the cake batter. Continue folding in portions of flour, followed by an egg each time, until all are incorporated.

2. Grease the sides of a 12 inch (30 cm) diameter 1 inch (3 cm) deep cake tin and line with greased and floured greaseproof paper cut to fit.

3. Set oven at 350°F (180°C) or Mark 4.

4. Pour the cake batter into the prepared tin. Bake in the pre-set oven for 30 minutes or until it is golden, well risen, firm to the touch and just pulls away from the sides of the tin. Take out and cool on a wire rack.

5. With the bottom side up to give the smoothest possible surface for icing, cover with flavoured butter cream, and work it down the sides. Put the sponge into the refrigerator to chill until the butter cream is hard. Take out and smooth off the surface for icing by drawing a palette knife dipped in hot water over the butter cream; shake off the drops of water each time before applying the knife. Return the sponge to the refrigerator and chill again until the butter cream is hard.

6. Meanwhile tint the glacé icing to desired shade, then spread over butter cream covered sponge cake. Decorate the iced cake according to personal preference with crystallized fruit, sugar roses, finely chopped nuts etc.

Butter Cream

Basic Recipe ☆

6 oz (175 g) softened, unsalted
    butter
12 oz (350 g) icing sugar
½ tsp (2.50 ml) vanilla essence
3–4 tbsp (45–60 ml) milk or
    warm water

Cream the butter until it is soft and fluffy and pale coloured, then gradually beat in the icing sugar, together with the vanilla essence and enough milk or water to blend to a smooth mixture. Use according to recipe.

Variations:
Orange, lime or lemon butter cream: omit vanilla essence and add a little grated orange, lime or lemon rind plus about ½ tbsp (7.50 ml) juice. Beat well to prevent mixture from curdling.
Coffee butter cream: omit vanilla essence and add 1–2 tbsp (15–30 ml) instant coffee powder, according to taste.
Chocolate butter cream: omit vanilla essence. Add 1–1½ tbsp (15–22 ml) cocoa dissolved in a little hot water; cool before beating into butter mixture, or melt 1 oz (25 g) chocolate until just liquid and blend into icing sugar.

Special Iced Cake.

PIPING A TRELLIS

1. Using a piping bag filled with a small writing nozzle, practise drawing a series of straight lines in icing. Try it out on a sheet of cardboard first before decorating the cake.

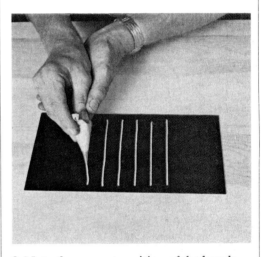

2. Note the correct position of the hands. The second hand steadies the first.

3. Pipe another series of lines across the first set. Try to keep the hands clear of the work surface so that the second line of piping does not pull the first line out of shape and spoil the result.

Cakes and bread

Meringue Pavé

8 oz (225 g) browned flaked almonds
icing sugar for sprinkling

For Swiss meringue
10 egg whites
1 lb (450 g) castor sugar

For coffee butter cream
6 oz (175 g) softened unsalted butter
12 oz (350 g) sifted icing sugar
3–4 tbsp (45–60 ml) coffee syrup

1. Set oven at 275°F (140°C) or Mark 1.

2. Make the meringue in 2 batches (halve the ingredients given above). Stiffly whip the egg whites in a mixing bowl until they stand in a peak. Sprinkle over 2 oz (50 g) of the sugar and whip again for about 3 minutes. Sprinkle over the remaining sugar and fold in lightly with a spatula.

3. Line 2 baking sheets with a piece of well greased greaseproof paper cut to fit. Drop spoonfuls of meringue onto the prepared baking sheets, spacing them fairly wide apart, and bake in the pre-set oven for about 55 minutes or until pale brown and crisp. Take out and cool on a rack.

4. Make the coffee butter cream. In a mixing bowl cream the butter until pale and soft, then gradually beat in the icing sugar, and enough coffee syrup to blend to a smooth mixture.

5. Crumble the cold meringues into a mixing bowl and blend in just enough of the butter cream to form a smooth ball of paste, working the mixture in your hands. Divide the paste in half, then place each one on a piece of greased greaseproof paper and roll out into 2 equal narrow strips. Cover one strip with butter cream. Top with the remaining strip, using 2 palette knives to lift it, then cover the top and sides with butter cream. Sprinkle thickly with browned almonds, then icing sugar. Pipe rosettes of coffee butter cream around the base.

Cream Horns

1 lb (450 g) puff pastry
1 beaten egg
¼ pt (150 ml) cold water
2–3 tbsp (30–45 ml) raspberry or other chosen jam
3 tbsp (45 ml) confectioners' custard
¼ pt (150 ml) whipped double cream
few finely chopped pistachio nuts (optional)

1. Set oven at 400°F (200°C) or Mark 6.

2. Lightly flour a work surface and roll out the pastry very thinly to a square large enough to give a trimmed square measuring 24 inches (60 cm). Cut this into 1¼ inch (3 mm) strips.

3. Grease and flour the outside of metal cream horn moulds. Take one strip of pastry per mould and carefully wind it around the mould, starting from the point and overlapping the pastry as you wind. Moisten the overlapping edges with a little cold water to help them stick together. Trim excess pastry from the top.

4. Place moulds, flat side down, on a floured baking sheet. Brush with beaten egg and bake just above the centre shelf in the pre-set oven for about 15 minutes or until the pastry is golden. Take out and transfer to a wire rack; holding a cloth in both hands, immediately begin to ease the pastry off the moulds. This is best done before the pastry cools.

5. Mix together the jam, confectioners' custard and about 3 tbsp (45 ml) whipped cream. Spoon this into each horn, then fill remaining cream into a piping bag fitted with a star nozzle and pipe a large swirl of cream over the end of each pastry horn. Sprinkle with a little of the chopped pistachio nuts if liked.

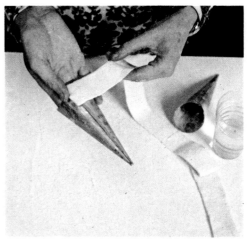

1. The traditional method of winding the pastry round cream horn moulds is to start at the top, leaving some surplus pastry over the edge, and wind downwards overlapping generously.

5. When you reach the top of the mould, trim away the surplus pastry making a sloping edge, Stick the top under edge to the upper edge with a little water, and dip the pointed end in cold water and pinch firmly together. This seals the pastry and holds the shape.

 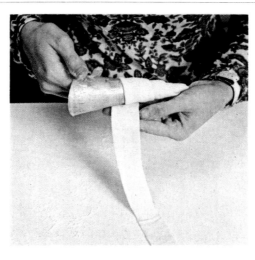 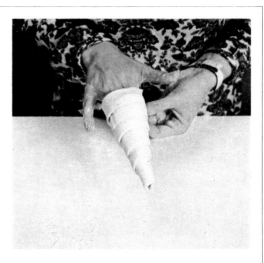

2. However, you may find it easier to start at the bottom and wind towards the top. Make sure that each overlapping strip is at least a third over the previous one.

3. Continue winding round the horn mould, taking care not to stretch the pastry as this will spoil the finished shape.

4. Wind the pastry right to the top of the horn mould, leaving some surplus. Make sure the winding ends at the shallow back part of the mould.

Cream Horns.

Variations:
Cream horns can also be filled simply with plain whipped cream, lightly flavoured with vanilla. Add fresh raspberries or strawberries, if in season, for a special treat.
  For another alternative filling using whipped cream, add sugar and a dash of rum instead of vanilla, and stir in a little grated chocolate before filling the cream horns.

Swiss Roll

2½ oz (62 g) self raising flour
4 oz (100 g) castor sugar
3 eggs
icing sugar for sprinkling

For filling
red jam or butter cream

1. Set oven at 425°F (220°C) or Mark 7.

2. Line a swiss roll tin measuring 10 by 14 by ¾ inches (25 cm by 35 cm by 19 mm) with greaseproof paper, cut to fit. Brush the paper lightly with oil. Prepare a work surface of several layers of newspaper topped with a sheet of greaseproof paper. All papers should be about 3 inches (8 cm) larger than the swiss roll tin. Sift a little flour over the greaseproof paper.

3. Sift the sugar onto a piece of foil and heat in the pre-set oven for about 6 minutes. Sift the flour. Whisk the eggs with the hot sugar until pale and foamy. Fold in the flour quickly but gently so the air bubbles are not lost.

4. Pour the batter into the prepared tin, spreading it evenly, and bake in the pre-set oven, just above centre, for 8 minutes or until golden. Take out of the oven and flip the sponge over and carefully place on the prepared greaseproof paper. Leave to cool.

5. Trim the sides and spread with jam. To roll up, grip the ends of paper nearest you at either side, lift up and start to roll the sponge away from you. Put one hand behind the papers and push firmly on the sponge as you roll. Ease the paper away from the sponge, keeping it taut and at an angle above the sponge. Keep rolling until the swiss roll is completed. Brush off any surplus flour and sprinkle with icing sugar.

1. Make greaseproof paper fit your swiss roll tin by drawing round the tin onto the paper, cut through and place the pencilled side downwards.

2. Lay paper on the tin and brush all over – including the sides – with oil.

6. Stop whisking, then shake the sifted flour over the surface of the egg and sugar mixture.

7. Using a spatula, gently fold and cut the flour into the mixture until completely blended. Take care not to lose any of the air bubbles which you have just been whisking up.

9. Trim the sides of the cooled sponge with a sharp knife. This gives a neat finish to the end result.

10. Pick up the papers nearest you and hold them in the way shown above. Press the edge firmly onto the jam.

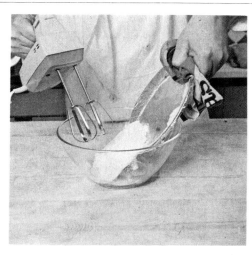

3. Prepare a work surface with newspaper and greaseproof paper, then sift a little flour onto the greaseproof paper.

4. Heat the sifted sugar in the oven for 6 minutes. Break the eggs into a large bowl and, when the sugar is really hot, quickly tip it onto the eggs and start whisking immediately.

5. Continue whisking until the mixture looks like this. It should almost have doubled its bulk and be pale and foamy.

8. Turn the mixture into the prepared tin and spread with the spatula right over the surface, taking care to reach right into the corners of the tin.

11. Roll up quickly, using one hand to hold the papers taut and the other to push from behind.

Swiss Roll filled with butter cream instead of the usual jam. Fillings of whipped cream or confectioners' custard also make a pleasant change.

Cakes and bread

Chocolate Layer Cake

2 eggs plus 1 egg yolk
2¼ oz (62 g) icing sugar
2 oz (50 g) self raising flour
2 tbsp (30 ml) drinking chocolate powder
2 tbsp (30 ml) coffee syrup
coffee butter cream for filling

For chocolate icing and decoration
4 oz (100 g) castor sugar
1¾ fl oz (40 ml) water
6 oz (175 g) plain dessert chocolate, broken
  into pieces
1–2 drops of olive oil

1. Set oven at 350°F (180°C) or Mark 4.

2. In a mixing bowl beat together the eggs, egg yolk and sugar until thick and creamy. Sprinkle over the flour together with the drinking chocolate, then fold in lightly. Stir in the coffee syrup.

3. Line a greased and floured shallow roasting tin with greased greaseproof paper cut to fit.

4. Turn the mixture into the prepared tin and bake just below the centre of the pre-set oven for about 30 minutes or until risen and the sponge springs back when pressed lightly with a fingertip. Turn out onto a wire rack to cool, then trim the sloping edges.

5. With a sharp knife cut the sponge in 3 equal pieces lengthways. Cover one piece with coffee butter cream, place the second piece of sponge on top, then cover with more butter cream and top with the third piece of sponge.

6. Make the chocolate icing by dissolving 4 oz (100 g) castor sugar in the water in a pan over a moderate heat. Bring to the boil, reduce heat at once and simmer until the sugar syrup is a light yellow colour.

7. Take the pan from the heat and cool until the syrup is tepid. In a heavy based pan heat the chocolate until just liquid. Stir the sugar syrup into the chocolate, add the olive oil and continue stirring until the icing is of a spreading consistency. Spread the icing over the top and sides of the cake to cover them completely and leave to set.

8. When icing is cold and firm, melt the remaining chocolate in a pan over a low heat until liquid, fill into a piping bag fitted with ¼ inch (6 mm) plain nozzle and pipe thin lines of chocolate at random all over the top and sides. Leave to set.

Viennese Torte

1 packet round Vienna wafer biscuits
13 coffee beans for decoration

For coffee butter cream
2¼ oz (62 g) softened, unsalted butter
5 oz (150 g) sifted icing sugar
1–2 tsp (5–10 ml) coffee liqueur
2–3 drops of coffee syrup

For coffee glacé icing
8 oz (225 g) sifted icing sugar
2 tbsp (30 ml) warmed coffee syrup

1. Make the coffee butter cream by creaming the butter in a mixing bowl until soft and light, then beat in the icing sugar and the coffee liqueur. Gradually stir in enough coffee syrup to flavour it delicately and still retain a fairly firm mixture. Spread butter cream over all the wafers except for one. Carefully sandwich them together, topping with the remaining plain wafer.

2. Make the coffee glacé icing. Sift the icing sugar into a bowl and gradually add coffee syrup. Mix until smooth and of a thick spreading consistency. Smooth glacé icing over the top and sides of the wafer cake, using a palette knife dipped in hot water.

3. Before the icing sets, mark off 12 portions with a sharp knife and place a coffee bean at the edge of each one; place remaining coffee bean in the centre.

Chocolate Layer Cake.

Cream Slices

8 oz (225 g) puff pastry
½ pt (300 ml) confectioners' custard
strawberry or raspberry jam
¼ pt (150 ml) whipped double cream
glacé icing
3 oz (75 g) melted plain dessert chocolate

1. Set oven at 425°F (220°C) or Mark 7.

2. Roll out the pastry to a thickness of no more than ¼ inch (6 mm). Using a rectangular metal flan frame measuring 14×4½ inches (35×12 cm), cut out, inside the frame, a wide strip of pastry. Reroll remaining pastry and repeat this process until you have 4 equal pastry rectangles.

3. Lightly flour a baking sheet; place one pastry rectangle on prepared baking sheet, fit over flan frame and bake above the centre shelf in the pre-set oven for about 10 minutes or until the pastry is golden and well risen. Take out and cool, then carefully split in half lengthways. Repeat this process with remaining 3 rectangles to give 8 pieces in all.

4. Choose 7 of the neatest rectangles (the eighth piece isn't required for this recipe, so use up in another way), reserving the thickest and smoothest for the top piece.

5. Layer the first strip with confectioners' custard, the second with jam, the third with whipped cream, then repeat this layering with next 3 strips.

6. Top with the reserved strip of pastry, cover with glacé icing and before it sets pipe on melted chocolate, using a piping bag fitted with a fine writing nozzle, in 2 parallel lines. Feather the chocolate by drawing through it with a skewer or needle, if you like. Leave to firm before cutting into slices for serving.

1. Cut panels of pastry with a metal rectangular frame. Transfer each panel to a lightly floured baking sheet, leaving the frame in position whilst baking. This helps to keep the shape of the pastry.

2. After baking, slice each panel horizontally in half so that you have 8 panels out of the original 4.

3. When you have assembled the layers of pastry, and filled and iced them, decorate with melted chocolate. Pipe 2 lines of chocolate along the length and, using a skewer, draw out branches.

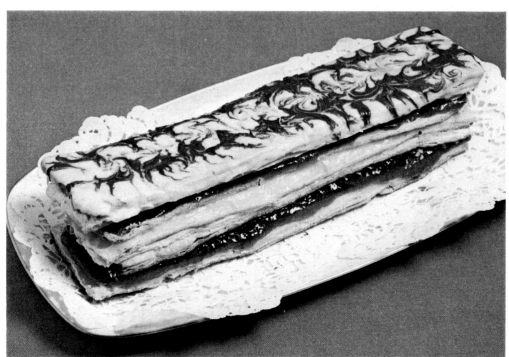

Cream Slice.

Cakes and bread

Rich Sponge Cake

4 egg yolks
3½ oz (87 g) castor sugar
3½ oz (87 g) self raising flour
icing sugar to finish

1. Set oven at 350°F (180°C) or Mark 4.

2. In a mixing bowl beat the egg yolks well until creamy. Beat in the sugar until the mixture is thick and frothy. Sift the flour and lightly fold in.

3. Line a 9 inch (22 cm) diameter sandwich tin with greased and floured greaseproof paper cut to fit.

4. Turn the cake batter into the prepared tin and bake just above the centre of the pre-set oven for 20 minutes or until brown and firm to the touch. Turn out and cool on a wire rack. Sprinkle thickly with icing sugar.

Cheesecake

3½ oz (87 g) unsalted butter or margarine
4 oz (100 g) crushed digestive biscuits
12 oz (350 g) curd cheese
1 egg
juice and finely grated rind of ½ lemon
2 tbsp (30 ml) vanilla flavoured icing sugar

For choux pastry topping
2 oz (50 g) unsalted butter
4¾ fl oz (130 ml) cold water
2½ oz (62 g) self raising flour
2 eggs

1. Set oven at 350°F (180°C) or Mark 4.

2. Line a rectangular metal flan case measuring 4½ by 11 inches (12×30 cm) with well greased and floured greaseproof paper so that it stands at least one inch (2.50 cm) above the rim.

3. In a pan over a moderate heat melt the fat and stir in the biscuit crumbs until they bind together. Press the biscuit mixture into the prepared case.

4. In a mixing bowl work the curd cheese until soft, then beat in the egg, lemon juice and rind and the flavoured icing sugar. When well blended turn into the biscuit lined case and smooth the top.

Rich Sponge Cake.

5. Make the choux pastry. In a heavy based pan over a moderate heat melt the butter in the water until dissolved and the mixture comes to the boil. Add the flavour at once and as the mixture bubbles up turn off the heat immediately. Using a wooden spoon beat until the mixture forms a smooth paste and comes away cleanly from the sides of the pan. Beat in 1 egg, until the mixture becomes smooth again, then beat in the remaining egg. Place a plate over the pan and leave at room temperature until the choux paste is completely cold.

6. When cold fill choux into a piping bag fitted with ¼ inch (6 mm) plain nozzle and pipe a trellis pattern over the top. Bake cheesecake in the pre-set oven for 20 minutes, take out and cool. Then refrigerate for about 6 hours before serving. To serve, carefully remove metal case and peel away the paper.

Variation:
Instead of covering the top with a trellis of choux pastry leave cheesecake plain, then after baking spread over ¼ pt (50 ml) soured cream, top with rosettes of stiffly whipped cream and sprinkle with either icing sugar or browned almonds.

Coffee Syrup

Basic Recipe

1 pt (600 ml) black coffee, preferably made from ground coffee beans for the best flavour

Despite its name, no sugar is added to the coffee syrup because there will be sufficient natural sweetness in the other ingredients according to the recipe.

1. Bring coffee to the boil in a pan over a medium heat. Reduce by boiling to about 2 fl oz (50 ml) to concentrate its flavour.

2. Remove the pan from the heat, leave to cool, then pour into clean, dry containers or jars to store and use according to recipe.

Mocha Cake

3 eggs plus 1 egg yolk
5 oz (150 g) castor sugar
2¼ oz (56 g) self raising flour
4 oz (100 g) plain dessert chocolate, broken into pieces and melted until just liquid

For coffee almond paste
4 oz (100 g) ground almonds
8 oz (225 g) sifted icing sugar
1 lightly whipped egg white
1 tsp (5 ml) coffee syrup
cornflour for dusting

To decorate
apricot glaze
chocolate flakes
drinking chocolate powder for sprinkling

1. Set oven at 350°F (180°C) or Mark 4.

2. In a mixing bowl stood over a pan of hot water whisk together the eggs, egg yolk and sugar until thick, creamy and almost doubled in volume. Remove the bowl from the heat and continue whisking until just tepid. Sprinkle over the flour, then fold in lightly with a metal spoon, until blended. Stir in the melted chocolate.

3. Well grease and flour the sides of an 8 inch (20 cm) diameter sandwich tin and line with greased and floured greaseproof paper cut to fit. Turn the mixture into the prepared tin and bake in the pre-set oven for about 25 minutes or until risen and the cake just pulls away from the sides of the tin. Take out and turn onto a wire rack to cool; remove paper from the base.

4. Meanwhile make the almond paste. In a mixing bowl work together the ground almonds and the icing sugar with your hand. Make a well in the centre and pour in half the egg white and the coffee syrup. Work again until a smooth paste is formed. Turn onto a work surface dusted with cornflour and knead to a soft dough. Only add remaining egg white or part of it if the paste stays stiff and crumbly. Roll out to a round large enough to cover the top and sides of the chocolate cake.

5. To decorate: brush the cake with warmed apricot glaze, then cover with the almond paste. Tie a satin ribbon around the sides of the cake. Pile chocolate flakes on top and sprinkle with drinking chocolate powder.

APPLYING GLACE ICING FOR A SMOOTH FINISH

1. Stand the cake to be iced on a wire rack or cake board or any other flat surface. Pour all the icing into the middle of the cake, scraping every bit from the bowl.

2. Dip the palette knife in the hot water, shaking off all the drips, and run the flat of the blade quickly through the glacé icing, working it from the centre to the sides and down to give an even layer overall.

3. Keep dipping the knife blade in and out of the hot water so that it runs freely, and smooth off any remaining ridges around the edges of the cake. Smooth the icing on the sides and leave to set until hard. Place chosen decorations for top of the cake on just before the icing sets completely.

Wedding Cake

3 lb (1.35 kg) softened butter
3 lb (1.35 kg) soft brown sugar
3 lb (1.35 kg) self raising flour
2 tbsp (30 ml) grated nutmeg
2 tbsp (30 ml) cinnamon
2 tbsp (30 ml) ground cloves
2 tbsp (30 ml) ginger
1¼ lb (675 g) roughly chopped glacé cherries
1½ lb (675 g) chopped mixed peel
1½ lb (675 g) chopped seedless raisins
4¼ lb (2 kg) currants
4¼ lb (2 kg) sultanas
12 oz (350 g) ground almonds
6 oz (175 g) chopped walnuts
18 eggs
12 fl oz (350 ml) brandy
1 bottle (750 ml) port
4 tbsp (60 ml) orange flower water
finely grated rind and juice of 6 oranges
finely grated rind and juice of 6 lemons
6 tbsp (90 ml) golden syrup
6 tbsp (90 ml) black treacle

To decorate
apricot jam glaze
almond paste
royal icing

These quantities are too large to mix in one batch, so divide ingredients into 2 or 3 and make up shallow batches. Quantities given above are enough for 3 round tiers, measuring 9 by 4 inches (22×10 cm), 11 by 4 inches (28×10 cm) and 13 by 4½ inches (32×11 cm) respectively.

1. Set oven at 325°F (160°C) or Mark 3.

2. Cream the butter in a mixing bowl until light and soft, then gradually beat in the brown sugar. In another bowl mix together the flour, spices, glacé cherries, mixed peel, dried fruits and nuts. In a third bowl beat the eggs, then beat in the brandy and port, orange flower water, fruit juices and rinds.

3. In a pan over a low heat gently warm the syrup and treacle until blended, then stir into the egg mixture. Beat the flour mixture into the creamed butter and sugar, gradually blending in the egg and syrup mixture from time to time until a smooth mixture is formed.

4. Line the well greased cake tins (sizes as above) with greaseproof paper cut to fit. Turn into the prepared cake tins having same depth of mixture in the 9 and 11 inch tins and a little greater depth in the largest tin. Bake just below the centre of the pre-set oven for 1 hour for the 9 inch (22 cm) cake, 1½ hours for the 11 inch (28 cm) cake, and 2 hours for the 13 inch (32 cm) cake; then reduce the oven temperature to 300°F (150°C) or Mark 2 and bake for a further 3–4 hours, according to the size of the cake, until dark brown (but not burnt) and a heated thin skewer inserted in the centre comes away clean. Take out of the oven and cool on a wire rack. This mixture can be kept overnight, in the pan, in the refrigerator, when it is not possible to cook all cakes on the same day.

5. To complete the wedding cake, first brush the top and sides of each cake with warmed apricot glaze, then cover with almond paste. To ice the cakes, stand the largest cake on a silver cake board about 16 inches (40 cm) in diameter; thickly coat the top and sides with royal icing and smooth off; leave to harden before proceeding with the decoration. Stand the other 2 cakes on cake boards or an icing table if you have one and coat with royal icing as for the base cake. Leave to harden before proceeding with the decoration as given below. When the icing is hard, put the 3 tiers together, the smallest cake being the top tier, and decorate the top according to choice.

1. On a large piece of paper trace 3 11-pointed stars, their diameters equalling those of the cakes to be decorated ie. 13 inch (32 cm) for the 13 inch (32 cm) cake. Place the paper star on top of the cake and, using a fine needle, prick round the star shape to leave a star design on the icing.

3. Fill in a side outline of linked half circles, using the same nozzle. Each half circle meets directly below each star point, and these half circles should arc to a depth of 1 inch (2.50 cm) on the 13 inch (32 cm) cake, ¾ inch (19 mm) on the 11 inch (28 cm) cake, and ½ inch (12 mm) on the 9 inch (22 cm) cake.

5. Change the nozzle for a finer one. Then pipe directly on top of the first series of arcs that formed the basis of the trellis pattern to give a raised effect and make the lines stand out.

2. Fill a quantity of royal icing into a piping bag fitted with a plain nozzle and pipe a thin line along the pin pricks to form the frame of the star design.

4. The next step is to fill the triangular spaces between the points of the star with a simple trellis pattern. Using the same nozzle, pipe a series of fine arcs across each space, and complete the trellis effect.

6. Fill royal icing into a piping bag fitted with a rosette nozzle and pipe tiny rosettes along the outline of the star, so concealing the beginnings of the trellis pattern. Repeat on the 2 smaller cakes and when completely hard, assemble the tiers.

Wedding Cake.

APPLYING ALMOND PASTE

1. Brush the top of the cake generously with sieved apricot jam.

2. Roll out the almond paste and place the cake, jam side down, in the middle.

3. Cut off the almond paste round the cake, using a sharp knife.

4. The neat almond paste top will adhere to the jammy cake.

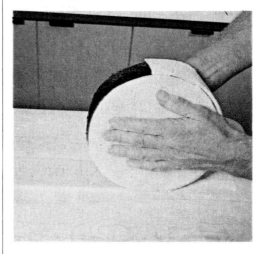

5. Gather up the trimmings and roll out the paste again in a strip which is slightly longer than the circumference of the cake and exactly the depth. Brush the cake sides with jam and roll the cake over the paste to coat the sides.

Gâteau St Honoré

For sweet shortcrust pastry
1 lb 2 oz (500 g) plain flour
salt
11 oz (300 g) butter
2 oz (50 g) sifted icing sugar
1 lightly beaten egg
¼ pt (150 ml) cold water

For sweet choux paste
1 oz (25 g) unsalted butter
¼ pt (150 ml) milk
1 sugar lump
3 oz (75 g) plain flour
2½ eggs

To finish
3 oz (75 g) castor sugar
3 tbsp (45 ml) water
½ pt (300 ml) confectioners' custard
½ pt (300 ml) chantilly cream

1. Set oven at 350°F (180°C) or Mark 4.

2. Make the shortcrust pastry. Sift the flour and a pinch of salt onto your work surface, make a well in the centre and into this put the butter, sugar and egg. Using 2 knives, gradually blend the flour into the other ingredients, adding a little water from time to time, until a soft but not sticky dough is formed. Wrap in greased greaseproof paper and chill in the refrigerator for 30 minutes before rolling out to 8 inch (20 cm) diameter, ½ inch (12 mm) thick, round. Put on a greased and floured baking sheet and bake in the preset oven for 20–25 minutes or until golden. Take out and cool.

3. Increase the oven temperature to 400°F (200°C) or Mark 6. Make the sweet choux pastry. In a heavy based pan over a low heat melt the butter in the milk and heat until the milk starts to bubble. At once add the sugar and stir until it is dissolved. Increase the heat and bring the mixture to the boil, then stir in the flour at once and let the mixture bubble up quickly. Take off the heat immediately and beat in the eggs until a smooth paste is formed and it comes away cleanly from the sides of the pan. Set aside to cool.

4. When cold, fill the choux paste into a piping bag fitted with a medium or small plain round nozzle and pipe about 16–18 choux buns onto greased and floured baking sheets, spacing them wide apart. Bake

Gâteau St Honoré.

in the pre-set oven for 10–15 minutes or until puffed and golden. Take out and cool on a wire rack. Split in half when cold and fill with a little confectioners' custard. To finish the cake, place pastry base on a serving dish. In a heavy based pan over a low heat dissolve the sugar in the water, then bring to the boil and boil until the syrup starts to go straw coloured at the edges. Remove from the heat at once.

5. Dip the choux buns in the syrup, using a pair of kitchen tongs, and arrange in 2 circles, one on top of the other, around the pastry base. Use the syrup to anchor them in position. Spoon confectioners' custard into the centre of the cake, then cover with about two thirds of the chantilly cream. Fill the remaining chantilly cream into a

piping bag fitted with a rosette nozzle and pipe rosettes on top and over the cake.

Royal Icing

Basic Recipe

*1½ lb (675 g) sifted icing sugar
juice of ½ lemon
several egg whites
edible food colouring if required*

1. In a mixing bowl work the icing sugar with the lemon juice and 1 egg white; continue adding egg white until the mixture is smooth, free from any air bubbles and of a thick spreading consistency. Too much egg white will make the icing runny, in which case add more icing sugar; too little egg white will make the icing stiff and

very difficult to work.

2. To colour royal icing, spoon a little of the mixture on to the work surface; work in a few drops of chosen colour so icing is vividly coloured, then blend this into the main quantity of icing; this will tone down the brightness and the icing will gradually assume a pastel shade.

Cakes and bread

Fruit Loaf Cake

1 lb (450 g) mixed dried fruits or sultanas
8 oz (225 g) soft brown sugar
½ pt (300 ml) cold strained tea
1 lb (450 g) plain flour
salt
1 lightly beaten egg
plain glacé icing to finish

1. Set oven at 375°F (190°C) or Mark 5.

2. In a mixing bowl stir together the dried fruits or sultanas and the sugar. Stir in the tea. Sift the flour with a pinch of salt. Add to the mixture with the egg.

3. Combine together until the mixture forms a soft dough, then turn into a greased and floured, 9 by 5 by 3 inches (22×12×8 cm) loaf tin.

4. Bake in the pre-set oven for 1 hour, then take out and cool slightly on a wire rack before removing from the tin. If liked, cover loaf with a thin topping of plain glacé icing.

Cherry Cake

6 oz (175 g) softened unsalted butter
finely grated rind of 1 small lemon
8 oz (225 g) castor sugar
1 lb (450 g) self raising flour
4 eggs
12 oz (350 g) glacé cherries

1. Set oven at 325°F (160°C) or Mark 3.

2. In a mixing bowl cream the butter with the lemon rind until very soft. Sift the flour, stir in 1 oz (25 g), 1 egg, beat well. Continue adding the flour a little at a time, with an egg each time, and beating well. Then beat in the remaining flour until a smooth, creamy mixture is formed.

3. Put the glacé cherries in a sieve with a little flour and shake over a bowl. Fold them into the cake mixture.

4. Line the bottom and sides of a loose-bottomed, deep 8 inch (20 cm) cake tin with a piece of greased and floured greaseproof paper cut to fit. Turn the mixture into the tin. Bake in the pre-set oven for about 1½ hours. Take out and cool in the tin for a while before turning out onto a wire rack to cool completely.

Apricot Glaze

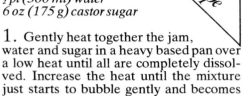

8 oz (225 g) apricot jam
½ pt (300 ml) water
6 oz (175 g) castor sugar

1. Gently heat together the jam, water and sugar in a heavy based pan over a low heat until all are completely dissolved. Increase the heat until the mixture just starts to bubble gently and becomes fairly thick but still of a pouring consistency.

2. Work through a sieve, and use the glaze while still warm. Store in clean, dry jars if not using immediately.

Moist Tea Bread

2 eggs
6 oz (175 g) castor sugar
10 oz (275 g) self raising flour
1 oz (25 g) butter or margarine
4 oz (100 g) chopped candied peel
2 oz (50 g) currants
1 tsp (5 ml) ground mixed spice
2 tsp (10 ml) baking powder
milk to mix

For topping
4–6 oz (100–175 g) sugar lumps, or apricot glaze, 8 oz (225 g) crystallized fruits and 4 oz (100 g) chopped walnuts

1. Set oven at 325°F (160°C) or Mark 3.

2. In a mixing bowl beat the eggs and sugar together until well blended. Sift the flour into another bowl. Rub the butter or margarine into the flour until the mixture resembles fine breadcrumbs, then stir in the rest of the ingredients except the milk.

3. Beat portions of the flour mixture into the egg mixture, together with just enough milk to form a soft dropping consistency. Turn into greased and floured 6–7 inch (15–18 cm) diameter deep cake tin and bake for about 1 hour or until a skewer comes away clean. Take out of the oven, turn out of the tin, upside down, on a wire rack to cool.

4. When it is cold either cover it with a topping of crushed sugar lumps and caramelize under a hot grill or brush the top with warmed apricot glaze and cover with fruit and nuts.

Kugelhopf

½ oz (12 g) fresh yeast
9 oz (250 g) castor sugar
2 fl oz (50 ml) lukewarm water
1 lb 11 oz (750 g) self raising flour
1 tsp (5 ml) salt
1 tsp (5 ml) vanilla powder
4 oz (100 g) seedless raisins
3 oz (75 g) blanched, flaked almonds
finely grated rind of 1 lemon
2 beaten eggs
2¼ oz (62 g) melted butter or margarine
10 fl oz (300 ml) warm milk
icing sugar for sprinkling

1. Blend together the yeast and 2 tbsp (30 ml) castor sugar until completely dissolved and liquid. Stir in the lukewarm water and set aside yeast mixture to prove in a warm place for 30 minutes. Grease a kugelhopf tin.

2. Warm a mixing bowl and sift the flour and salt into it; stir in the remaining castor sugar, vanilla powder, raisins, almonds and lemon rind. Make a well in the centre of the mixture, tip in the yeast liquid and blend.

3. Stir in the eggs a little at a time, then add the melted butter or margarine. Blend in enough of the warm milk to form a smooth dough.

4. Lightly sprinkle with flour, cover with a warm cloth and stand the bowl in a warm place so the dough can prove for about 2 hours or until doubled in size.

5. Place the risen dough on a floured work surface. Using your fist, knock down the dough several times, then place in the prepared tin. Cover again with a warm cloth, put in a warm place and leave to rise for about 1 hour. Set the oven at 350°F (180°C) or Mark 4.

6. When risen put the cake into the pre-set oven and bake for about 1 hour or until a rich brown. If the top browns too quickly cover with a piece of greased greaseproof paper. When baked take out of the oven and cool on a wire rack.

7. Leave for 24 hours before cutting and sprinkle with icing sugar before serving.

MAKING BREAD

1. Warm a crock or a deep bowl and put half the flour into it. Beat the yeast and sugar together and pour this mixture over the flour.

2. Add milk and water. Mix to a batter.

3. Cover the crock with a clean cloth and leave to prove.

4. Add the remaining flour and mix.

5. Knead the dough thoroughly; pull the dough towards you.

6. Press the dough down and forwards with the palms of the hands.

7. Press dough into baking tin.

8. Leave in a warm place to prove, make cuts on the surface with scissors.

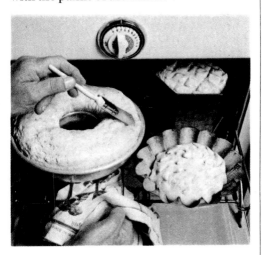

9. After baking for 5 minutes, quickly brush beaten egg over the bread and return it to the oven.

Cakes and bread

White Bread

1½ lb (700 g) strong plain flour
2 tsp (10 ml) salt
½ oz (15 g) lard rubbed in
  either ½ oz (15 g) fresh yeast dissolved in
  ¾ pt (400 ml) warm water,
  or dissolve 1 tsp (5 ml) sugar in ¾ pt
  (400 ml) warm water at 110°F (43°C)
  and sprinkle on 2 tsp (10 ml) dried yeast
  and leave for 10 minutes until frothy

1. Add the yeast liquid to the dry mix and work to a firm dough that leaves the bowl clean.

2. Turn the dough onto a lightly floured surface and knead by folding the dough towards you, then pushing down and away from you with the palm of your hand. Give the dough a quarter turn and repeat the kneading process. Knead until the dough feels firm and elastic and no longer sticky – about 10 minutes. If you have a mixer follow the manufacturer's instructions for using the dough hook. Place yeast liquid and dry ingredients in the bowl and turn onto lowest speed and mix for 1 minute. Increase speed and mix for a further 2 minutes to knead dough.

3. Shape the dough into a round ball and place in a lightly oiled polythene bag, lightly tied.

4. Leave it to rise to suit your convenience: 45–60 minutes in a warm place, 2 hours at average room temperature, 12 hours in a cold room, 24 hours in a refrigerator. The colder the dough is kept and the slower it rises the better your finished bread will be.

5. When it has doubled in size, springs back when lightly pressed with a floured finger and is back to room temperature, knock it back by flattening each piece with the knuckles to knock out the air bubbles. Knead again to a firm dough.

6. Shape into a desired shape and place on a lightly greased and floured baking sheet or half fill a greased and floured tin. The quantity given makes 2 loaves.

7. Set oven at 450°F (230°C) or Mark 8.

8. Leave to prove inside an oiled polythene bag for about 1 hour at room temperature until the dough rises just above the tops of the tin. Remove the polythene bag. Brush tops with egg wash if a shiny crust is desired.

9. Bake in the centre of the pre-set oven for 30–40 minutes when the loaves should sound hollow when tapped on the base.

Sally Lunn

7½ fl oz (210 ml) milk
1 oz (25 g) butter
12 oz (350 g) plain flour
¼ tsp (2 ml) salt
1 egg
¾ oz (42 g) fresh yeast
1 tsp (5 ml) sugar

For glaze
1 tbsp (15 ml) sugar
1 tbsp (15 ml) milk

1. Place the milk and butter in a pan and heat gently until the butter melts. Cool until just warm.

2. Warm the flour slightly, then sift into a bowl with the salt. Beat the egg and add to the cooled mixture.

3. Cream the yeast and sugar, and add to the milk.

4. Make a well in the flour and strain the liquid into it. Mix to make a dough. Turn onto a floured board and knead lightly.

5. Grease and warm 2 5 inch (12 cm) diameter cake tins. Divide the dough into the tins. Cover with a cloth and leave to rise for about 30 minutes or until the dough has doubled in size.

6. Set oven at 425°F (220°C) or Mark 7.

7. Bake in the pre-set oven for 20–25 minutes. Dissolve the sugar in the milk and brush the dough with this mixture. Return to the oven for a few minutes to dry the glaze. Turn out of the tins and leave on a rack to cool.

8. Slice into rounds, toast each side and spread generously with butter. Reshape the Sally Lunn and slice vertically for serving.

White Bread baked in a variety of tins.

Milk Bread

For batter
5 oz (150 g) strong plain flour
1 tsp (5 ml) sugar
½ oz (15 g) fresh yeast or 2 tsp (10 ml) dried
  yeast
8 fl oz (225 ml) warm milk.

For dough
11 oz (300 g) strong plain flour
1 tsp (5 ml) salt
2 oz (50 g) margarine
1 beaten egg

1. Blend the batter ingredients together in a large bowl. Leave in a warm place for 20 minutes until it becomes very frothy.

2. Mix together the flour and salt from the dough ingredients and rub in the margarine. Add this and the egg to the batter and mix well to form a soft dough that leaves the sides of the bowl clean.

3. Turn onto a floured surface and knead until smooth – about 10 minutes.

4. Place in a lightly oiled polythene bag, loosely tied and allow to rise until double it size and the dough springs back when pressed gently with a floured finger. Quick rise – 45–60 minutes in a warm place. Slower rise – 2 hours at average room temperature. Overnight – up to 12 hours in a cold room, larder or refrigerator.

5. Using dough at room temperature mould into rolls, plaits, crowns, baps, batons or tins as desired and place on a greased, floured baking sheet.

6. Cover with a sheet of oiled polythene and leave for 1–1½ hours at room temperature to prove.

7. Set oven at 450°F (230°C) or Mark 8.

8. Remove the polythene. Brush the top of bread with a little egg wash – beaten egg to which a little sugar and water have been added.

9. Bake in the pre-set oven for 30–40 minutes until the crust is golden brown and it sounds hollow when tapped on the base.

MAKING A PLAITED LOAF

1. Roll out the dough to a rectangle and mark off the top end in 5 equal divisions and cut with a knife.

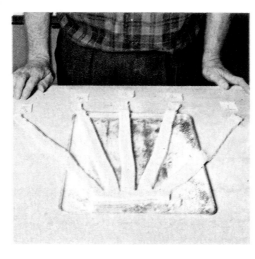

2. Label each strand 1–5, left to right.

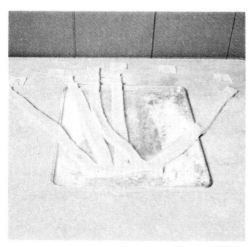

3. Cross strand 2 over strand 3.

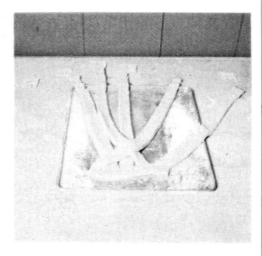

4. Cross strand 5 over strand 2.

5. Cross strand 1 over strand 3. Repeat this sequence until all dough is used.

6. When the plait is complete, dip the ends with cold water, pinch together and tuck them underneath.

Rye Bread

1½ lb (700 g) rye flour
1 lb (450 g) strong plain white flour
1 tbsp (15 ml) salt
1 oz (25 g) butter or lard
1 tsp (5 ml) sugar
¾ oz (20 g) fresh yeast
¾ pt (450 ml) milk and water mixed

1. Mix the flours and salt together and rub in the fat.

2. Add the sugar and yeast to ½ pt (300 ml) of the liquid and stir thoroughly.

3. Add the yeast liquid to the flour and mix to a firm dough adding gradually the remainder of the liquid.

4. Knead until smooth, place in a lightly oiled polythene bag and leave to rise in a warm place until double in size, about 1½ hours.

5. Knock back by flattening it with the knuckles to knock out the air.

6. Set oven at 450°F (230°C) or Mark 8.

7. Divide the dough in 2 and shape into desired shape or half fill a loaf tin. It is most usual to make rye bread in oval shapes – round and fat in the middle tapering at each end.

8. Place on a greased and floured baking sheet to prove for about 15 minutes.

9. Bake in the pre-set oven for 40–50 minutes, until crust is a deep brown colour and the loaf sounds hollow when tapped on the base.

Wholemeal Bread

3 lb (1.4 kg) wholemeal flour
2 tbsp (30 ml) sugar
2 tbsp (30 ml) salt
1 oz (25 g) lard rubbed into flour
2 oz (50 g) fresh yeast or 1 oz (25 g) dried
  yeast
1½ pt (900 ml) water

1. Mix the flour, salt and sugar together in a bowl.

2. Blend the fresh yeast with the water, add to the flour and mix to a soft dough

until the bowl is left clean. If using dried yeast, dissolve 1 tsp (5 ml) of the sugar in $\frac{1}{2}$ pt (300 ml) of the water in the recipe. Have the water warm, then sprinkle the dried yeast on top. Leave for about 10 minutes until frothy. Add this to the flour, salt, remaining sugar and water.

3. Knead thoroughly until it is no longer sticky – about 5–10 minutes.

4. Shape the dough into a round ball and place in a lightly oiled polythene bag, lightly tied.

5. Leave it to rise to suit your convenience: 45–60 minutes in a warm place, 2 hours at average room temperature, 12 hours in a cold room, 24 hours in a refrigerator. The colder the dough is kept and the slower it rises the better your finished bread will be.

6. When it has doubled in size, springs back when lightly pressed with a floured finger and is back to room temperature, knock it back by flattening each piece with the knuckles to knock out the air bubbles. Knead again to a firm dough.

7. Shape into a desired shape and place on a lightly greased and floured baking sheet or half fill a greased and floured tin.

8. Set oven at 450°F (230°C) or Mark 8.

9. Leave to prove inside an oiled polythene bag for about 1 hour at room temperature until the dough rises just above the tops of the tin. Remove the polythene. Brush tops with salt and water to get a good crust.

10. Bake in the centre of the pre-set oven for 30–40 minutes when the loaves should sound hollow when tapped on the base.

Variation:
Follow the recipe for wholemeal bread using 6 oz (175 g) cracked wheat in place of 6 oz (175 g) of the flour. When shaping the bread after proving, scatter a little cracked wheat on the board and this will be picked up on the dough. Finally scatter cracked wheat over the surface of the loaf or rolls just before they go in the oven.

Brioches

8 oz (225 g) plain flour
½ oz (15 g) fresh yeast
2–3 tbsp (30–45 ml) warm water
1 tbsp (15 ml) castor sugar
1 tsp (5 ml) salt
2 eggs
2–4 tbsp (30–60 ml) milk
4 oz (100 g) butter
extra flour for sprinkling

For brushing
1 beaten egg
1 tbsp (15 ml) milk
salt

1. Sift the flour. Dissolve the yeast in the water and mix with a quarter of the flour to make a small ball of dough.

2. Mark a cross on top of the dough ball and place it in a large bowl of warm water. Leave until the dough has doubled in size and has risen to the surface.

3. Make a well in the remaining flour. Place sugar, salt and eggs in it and mix to a loose dough, using milk as necessary.

4. Cream the butter until soft and work it into the dough.

5. Drain the ball of yeast dough, then cut and fold it into the mixture. Knead the dough. Place in a greased bowl, sprinkle with a little flour, cover with a cloth and leave to rise for about 2 hours at room temperature.

6. When the dough is doubled in size, knock down and knead it. Sprinkle with more flour, cover and leave overnight in the refrigerator.

7. Grease 8 individual brioche tins and divide the dough to fit the tins with a small ball of dough on the top. Leave to rise in a warm place for 20 minutes.

8. Set oven at 425°F (220°C) or Mark 7.

9. Mix the beaten egg with the milk and a pinch of salt, and brush the brioches with this mixture. Bake in the pre-set oven for 15–20 minutes.

Wholemeal Plaited Loaf and Wholemeal Bread.

Croissants

For butter dough
12 oz (350 g) butter
1½ oz (35 g) plain flour

For yeast dough
1½ oz (35 g) fresh yeast
1 oz (25 g) castor sugar
1 egg
8 fl oz (225 ml) water
15 oz (425 g) plain flour

1. Work the flour into the butter and chill in the refrigerator.

2. Mix the yeast with the sugar. Add the egg and beat well. Stir in water.

3. Sift the flour onto a clean work surface. Make a well in the centre. Pour in the yeast mixture. Using 2 knives gradually work in the flour to make a smooth dough.

4. Slap the ball of dough from hand to hand until there is a slight rising and falling movement in the dough. This is necessary to activate the yeast.

5. Roll out the dough and place the chilled slab of butter dough in the centre. Fold into a parcel. Turn and roll out with a jerky uneven movement so that the surface is corrugated but unbroken.

6. Fold the dough in 3, turn 90°, then roll out again. Repeat this folding, turning and rolling out procedure twice then chill the dough for at least an hour.

7. Set oven at 400°F (200°C) or Mark 6.

8. Roll out the rested dough and cut triangles 6 by 6 by 6½ inches (15×15×16.5 cm). Wet the tips and stretch the base slightly before rolling up from the base. Shape into crescents.

9. Place on a baking sheet, brush with beaten egg and bake in the pre-set oven for 20–25 minutes or until golden brown.

Variations:
Croissants can also be sprinkled with almond flakes, dusted with icing sugar or brushed with apricot glaze before baking.

1. Cut the butter into the flour.

2. Make the butter dough into a slab and refrigerate.

6. Slap the ball of dough from one hand to the other. This reactivates the yeast.

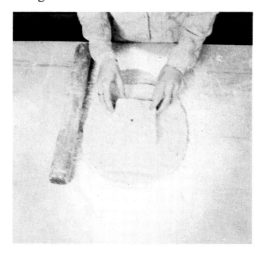

7. Roll out the dough and place the butter dough in the centre.

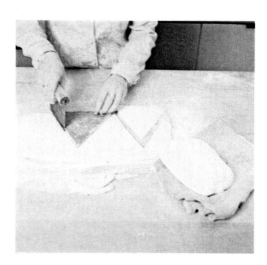

11. Roll out thinly and cut out triangles.

12. Wet the angles with cold water and pull the base to stretch it.

3. Work yeast and sugar together.

4. Make a well in the centre of the flour and pour in the yeast.

5. Work together with 2 knives to form a smooth dough.

8. Fold dough into a parcel.

9. Roll out, pressing unevenly, to give the above effect. Fold into a parcel.

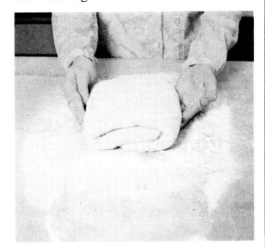

10. Turn 90 degrees. Reroll, fold and turn twice more. Refrigerate for an hour or more before using.

13. Roll up from base to top.

14. Make into a curve and flatten ends.

Croissants.

Index

Index

Index

proost Turnhout (Belgium)